The Right
Way to Invest
in Mutual
Funds

Other books in the
Money® America's Financial Advisor series:

How to Retire Young and Rich

401(k) Take Charge of Your Life

Paying for Your Child's College Education

The Right Way to Invest in Mutual Funds

Walter Updegrave

Money
BOOK CLUB

New York

Copyright © 1996 by MONEY magazine
All rights reserved.

Warner Books, Inc., 1271 Avenue of the Americas, New York, NY 10020
Visit our Web site at
http://pathfinder.com/twep

 A Time Warner Company

Printed in the United States of America

Book design by Giorgetta Bell McRee

This hardcover edition was especially created for Money Book Club
in 1996 by arrangement with Warner Books, Inc.

CONTENTS

INTRODUCTION

I've never much liked—or understood the value of—book introductions. When I pick up a book about, say, investing in mutual funds, I want to start reading about the main event— funds—not some preliminary observations about life and the financial markets. So I'll keep this real short.

Over the past 10 years I've written extensively about mutual funds for **MONEY** magazine and read much of what others have written. What has always amazed me is the way that people have tried to make fund investing more complicated than it needs to be. After reading some books and articles on funds, you get the impression that you're supposed to be scanning the financial markets every second for a signal to jump out of one type of fund and into another or watching the yield curve every time the chairman of the Federal Reserve Board clears his throat so you can decide whether to extend or shorten maturities in bond funds. ("The last time he *ahem*med like that, he cut the discount rate half a point!") I call this papier-mâché advice: it looks solid as a rock on the written page, but when you examine it closely, you realize it's a facade. You can't actually follow it. To do so would require all your time and effort and not a small bit of luck, too. And you certainly wouldn't have time left over for incidentals like holding down a job or spending time with your family.

My approach is different. I don't believe planning and carrying out a successful strategy of investing in funds has to be all-consuming. And I especially don't think anyone has to feel guilty or inadequate for not following a type A investing approach. Quite the opposite. I feel you'll do better by rejecting intricate strategies and favoring a simpler, more reasoned approach. What's more, I completely reject the notion that there is only one elite, very small group of top-performing funds—and that unless you own them, you are a failure as an investor. Fact is, there are plenty of good funds to go around.

On the other hand, investing isn't a free ride. To be successful, you do have to take some time to become an informed investor. And you should also plan on doing a bit of research to find superior funds. But once you've put together a group of solid funds with different investment objectives and investing styles, the heavy lifting is over. It's mostly maintenance after that, monitoring your funds and making occasional adjustments.

For the most part, therefore, this book represents my attempt to give you the information you need to build your investing strategy and find the funds that can help you pull it off. Naturally I hope you'll consider the advice I offer (but not follow it blindly) and, in so doing, make zillions of dollars in funds. If that happens, I hope you'll credit my sage counsel for your success. If that doesn't happen, I'm sure you'll be savvy enough to realize that my advice was fine—you just didn't follow it correctly.

Finally, I would like to thank my colleagues at **MONEY** magazine for helping me in numerous ways with this book; the people at Morningstar for doing an extraordinary amount of number crunching for me; my agent, Rich Pine, and my editor, Rick Wolff; my wife, Mary, for letting me use her as a sounding board for various parts of the manuscript; and, finally, my son, Henry, for generously shutting down *Harry and the Haunted House* so I could squeeze in some writing time on the Mac.

The Right
Way to Invest
in Mutual
Funds

CHAPTER 1

The Mutual Fund Revolution

Funds Have Improved the Way We Save and Invest

Every once in a while an innovation comes along that profoundly changes our lives for the better. The lightbulb. The automobile. Häagen-Dazs ice cream. In the realm of personal finance, mutual funds clearly stand out as such an advance. By making investing so accessible that novices with just a few hundred dollars (in some cases even less) can invest with confidence by phone or through the mail, funds have effectively democratized America's financial markets. They've given Americans of modest means the investing advantages that had once been available only to big institutions or the wealthy—namely, the ability to earn high rates of return by investing in a diversified portfolio of securities such as stocks and bonds that are chosen and monitored by some of the best professional money managers in the nation.

As a result of their sheer convenience and accessibility, mutu-

1

al funds have dramatically changed the way Americans save and invest their money, and in the process become the investment of choice for individual investors. As recently as 1980, for example, people looking to tuck away cash for their retirement, a child's college education, or a down payment for a new home nearly always went to their local bank or S&L and opened a savings account or bought a certificate of deposit. Mutual funds were available back then, but only one in 16 U.S. households—a mere 6%—owned them. During the past 15 years, however, the number of Americans who invest in funds has grown tremendously. Today nearly one of every three households owns one or more funds. That translates to some 40 million fund investors. In another sign of the coming of age of funds, by early 1996 the total value of mutual funds' assets (over $3 trillion) had surpassed the amount of savings on deposit at U.S. commercial banks and savings institutions. In short, mutual funds are helping us make the transition from a nation of savers (people concerned primarily with safety of principal) to a nation of investors (people willing to take prudent risks to earn higher long-term returns on their money).

Of course, convenience isn't the only reason people have been flocking to funds. Mutual funds have also delivered some pretty spectacular returns, especially when you compare them to the traditional places people have tucked away their money, such as savings accounts and CDs. To get an idea of just how much more you can make your money grow by investing in mutual funds, take a look at the following graph.

The Mutual Fund Advantage

The dotted line in this graph shows that if you had invested $10,000 in a bank CD on January 1, 1986, and reinvested your $10,000 plus interest every six months in a new CD, your orig-

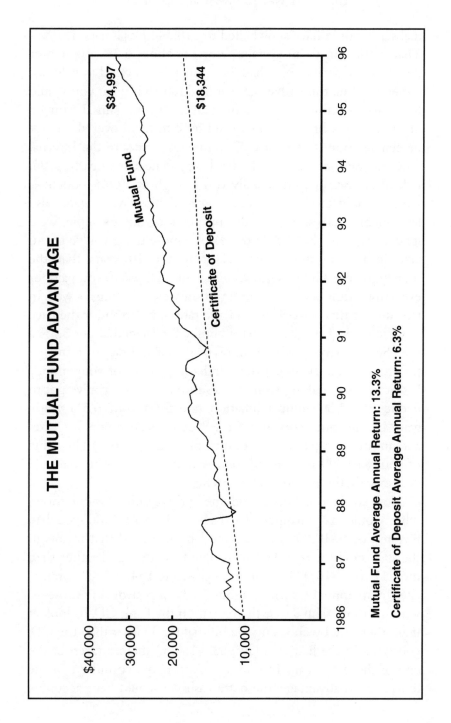

THE MUTUAL FUND ADVANTAGE

Mutual Fund

$34,997

Certificate of Deposit

$18,344

$40,000

30,000

20,000

10,000

1986 87 88 89 90 91 92 93 94 95 96

Mutual Fund Average Annual Return: 13.3%

Certificate of Deposit Average Annual Return: 6.3%

inal stash would have snowballed to $18,344 by January 1, 1996. That works out to an average return of about 6.3% a year over that 10-year period. Not bad, but not quite as good as it looks, either. For one thing, that 6.3% annual return is what you would have earned before paying income taxes on your gains. If you are in the 28% tax bracket, you would have to hand over about 1.8 percentage points of your 6.3% return each year to the Internal Revenue Service. (Under the tax laws in effect as of early 1996, federal tax rates could actually run as high as 39.6%—ouch!— which would erode your return even further. Most states also levy income taxes, but for the purposes of this example, we'll ignore the states' bite.) And there's one more thing you've got to take into account—inflation. During the 10 years that the money in your CD was growing in value, the prices you paid for everything from a car to school tuition were climbing as well. In fact, during that 10-year period, the rate of inflation (or the pace at which prices in general have climbed) averaged about 3.5% a year. So to arrive at what is known as your *real* rate of return— that is, the pace at which the purchasing power of your money has grown after taking rising prices into account—you've got to deduct the 3.5% annual inflation rate from your 6.3% yearly gain. By the time you subtract 1.8 percentage points for taxes and another 3.5 percentage points for inflation, voilà! The value of your $10,000 investment increased at only a 1% annual rate. Not exactly the inside track to riches.

Now take a look at the solid line in the graph. This one shows what would have happened if back in January 1986, you had invested that $10,000 in the typical mutual fund that invests in the U.S. stock market. Had you opted for the fund rather than the CD, your $10,000 would have grown to $34,997. That translates to an annual return of about 13.3% a year during those 10 years, or more than *double* the return on the bank CD. To look at it another way, by choosing the mutual fund rather than the CD, you would have had an additional $16,653 (before taxes) at the end of those 10 years. In one sense you could consider that the mutual fund advantage: the extra cash you could have accumulated by investing in a fund instead of a CD. Of course, as with the CD, you would have to pay taxes on the profits you earned in your mutual fund. Assuming a 28% tax rate, the IRS would have skimmed off approximately 3.7 percentage points a year from your 13.3% return. (I say "approximately" since the exact amount of tax you would owe in a given year can vary depending on how much of the fund's gain is distributed to shareholders that year.) And you would also have to subtract another 3.5 percentage points from the fund's return to account for inflation. But after deducting 3.7 percentage points for taxes and another 3.5 percentage points for inflation, you wind up with a 6.1% annual return after taxes and after inflation—or *six* times the 1% you would have earned on the CD. So any way you look at it— before taxes, after, adjusting for rising prices, leaving inflation out of it entirely—you would have done far better in the fund than in the CD.

To be fair to the CD, it should be pointed out that not once during those 10 years did its value ever decline. Like the Energizer Bunny, it kept going and going and going. . . . The mutual fund, on the other hand, did run into occasional short-term power outages. When the stock market crashed in October 1987, for example, the average stock mutual fund lost roughly 22% of its value. And in 1990, another lousy year for the stock market, the typical stock mutual fund dropped 3.1%. Anyone who panicked or simply got discouraged and sold out during one of those periods wouldn't have reaped that tantalizing 13.3% return. But that is one of the true pluses of mutual funds. If you stay calm and hold on through the temporary setbacks, you can power your way to impressive long-term gains that will help you reach your financial goal, whether it's saving for a down payment for a home, building a nest egg for retirement, saving for your kids' college tuition, or accumulating a stash you could live on in the event you tell your boss to take his job and shove it.

What Kinds of Returns Should You Expect?

The double-digit gains that many mutual funds have generated through the 1980s and 1990s have certainly been rewarding to investors who've been along for the ride. And it would be terrific if some financial seer could promise that funds would continue to cruise to similar gains over the next 10 years or longer. But the real world doesn't give such guarantees, and neither does Wall Street. The fact of the matter is that rates of return can vary considerably over different periods of time for a number of reasons. First, the gains you earn depend on the type of fund you invest in. The 13.3% returns in our earlier example were generated by **stock funds**—that is, mutual funds that invest entirely or mostly in stocks.

There is another type of mutual fund called **bond funds,** which, as their name implies, invest in bonds. Their returns weren't included in our chart. But if you had put your $10,000 into the typical government bond fund back in January 1986, you would have earned about 8% before taxes and inflation during the period we reviewed, which would have pushed the value of that original $10,000 investment to nearly $22,000 by the end of the period. The returns would have been different still if we had chosen any one of a number of other different types of mutual funds—money-market funds, growth funds, or balanced funds, to name a few—that will be discussed later in this book. But you get the idea: different types of funds produce different levels of returns, so no one can say what is a typical or usual return for mutual funds overall.

What's more, predicting returns is difficult because the prices of securities such as stocks and bonds can vary tremendously without warning, not just from day to day, week to week, and month to month, but even from year to year or longer. For example, 1995 was a terrific year for stocks, whose value zoomed ahead a sizzling 37.5%. But you need go back only to the previous year, 1994, to find a time during which the stock market eked out a mere 1.3% gain. Go back even further and you can find periods such as 1981, when stocks fell 5.1%, and ones like 1974, when stock prices plummeted a stomach-wrenching 26.4% for the year. You'll find similar ups and downs for bonds, although the fluctuations in their returns are usually much tamer than is the case for their stock counterparts. In 1994, for example, bonds in general posted a 2.9% loss. Just three years prior to that, however, in 1991 bonds returned a healthy 16%. So even though TV financial shows and personal finance magazines are bursting with putative experts making all sorts of predictions about what investments will generate the highest returns over the next year, no one really has a good handle on how the financial markets are likely to fare from one year to the next.

Lest you be tempted to use the 13.3% 10-year stock fund gain in our chart as a predictor of what returns will be over the next 10 years, consider this: High returns in one decade are sometimes followed by lackluster gains in subsequent periods. Stocks gained 19% a year on average during the 1950s, for example, after relatively modest 9% annual returns during the 1940s. What's more, the 1950s bull market was followed by relatively flat returns in the 1960s (8% annually) and even more modest gains in the 1970s (6% a year). The roaring bull market of the 1980s saw stock returns zoom upward again to a nearly 18% annual gain for the decade. In the first six years of the 1990s, stock returns have averaged about 13%.

Year to year and decade-to-decade fluctuations tend to iron themselves out over much longer periods, however. Over the 60 years to 1996, for example, large-company stocks, such as those in widely used barometers of stock market activity like the Standard & Poor's 500 index, have returned between 10% and 11% annually. Government bonds, meanwhile, have posted returns of 5% to 6% a year over spans of several decades. Inflation has averaged about 3% long term. So stocks clearly have protected the purchasing power of investors' money better than bonds, outpacing inflation over the long run by seven percent-

7

age points or more annually vs. just two to three percentage points for bonds.

Taking all this into account, it's clear that the roaring eighties' near-18% returns in stocks were an aberration on the high side, while the 1970s' 5.9% gains represent a below average period. As a general benchmark for investors in stock funds, therefore, annual gains of roughly 10% seem to be a reasonable target for the next decade or so. As for bond funds, it's doubtful we'll see the 12% or better returns of the 1980s again any time soon, although many experts believe bond investors should probably do a bit better than bonds' historic 5% or so annual gains. A return of 7% or so over the next decade or so seems reasonable for bond funds.

TRACKING FUND PERFORMANCE

Throughout this book I refer to two widely used barometers of fund performance—**total return** and **yield.**

Total return: This is the best measure of a fund's performance, since it tells you how much a fund has actually gained or lost over a specific period. Total return reflects all the dividends and capital gains a fund has paid to shareholders over a given period, as well as any increase or decrease in the price of the fund's shares. When I say that a fund "gained" or "returned" a certain amount, I am referring to its total return. Unless otherwise noted, all the returns in this book are before income taxes.

Yield: A fund's yield tells you how much dividend or interest income the fund is generating yearly as a percentage of the fund's latest share price. The best gauge to use for yield is the so-called 30-day or SEC yield. This figure, which is calculated according to a standardized Securities and Exchange Commission formula, eliminates much of the chicanery some fund companies resort to in order to pump up their yields. Yield is a useful way of looking at the income-producing ability of money-market, bond, and certain types of stock funds. But to get a comprehensive picture of performance, you should also look at the fund's total return.

Remember, though, that these are only forecasts, not ironclad guarantees. Some investing experts, such as John Bogle, chairman of the Vanguard Group mutual fund company, think that 10% might be a bit on the high side for stocks over the next decade or so. Bogle believes that because stock returns have been so robust in recent years, they're likely to be dragged down below the 10% average to 8% or so. What's more, returns will vary substantially once you get into more specific categories of funds. For example, if you invest in funds that buy the shares of very small companies, you should expect to do something closer to 12% annually over the long term, largely because these are riskier investments than other stock funds, which prompts investors to demand better returns. Also keep in mind that even if these forecasts are accurate, they are long-term *averages.* You will not get these returns every year. Even in a stellar decade such as the 1980s, there was one year when stocks lost money (1981: a 5.1% loss) and two years in which returns were mediocre (in 1984 and 1987 stocks were up just 6.3% and 5.3%, respectively).

So before you invest in stock or bond funds, prepare yourself for some fluctuations in their returns. The ride isn't always smooth month to month or year to year. For example, if you look at the 60 calendar years from 1936 through 1995, you'll see that stocks lost money in 15 of those years. The longer you hang in, however, the more you improve your chances of making money. In the 51 overlapping 10-year periods from 1936 through 1995, stocks never posted a loss, although there were two periods following the 1929 stock market crash in which stocks ended up in the red even over 10-year spans.

Stocks' record of keeping you ahead of inflation over the long term is also pretty awesome. Except for the occasional stretches when inflation soared, such as in the 1970s, stocks' 10-year gains have nearly always outpaced the rate of inflation. In short, if you stay invested in funds for long periods of time, chances are good that you'll make real money—that is, inflation-beating returns. On the other hand, if you jump into funds when returns look good and sell in a panic when the market heads south, you're setting yourself up for substandard gains—or losses. Professional investors call this phenomenon of bailing out of the market when prices are hitting a bottom and getting back in as they're nearing a top "getting whipsawed." Such behavior virtually guarantees lousy performance because you're essentially buying high and selling low, exactly the opposite of what you must do to earn a profit. The best way to avoid getting whipsawed: Ignore temporary setbacks in stock and bond prices and focus instead on piling up long-term gains.

What This Book Will (and Won't) Do for You

If you aren't already investing in funds but would like to begin, this book will help you get started and show you how best to use funds to achieve your financial goals. If you already own funds, this book can show you ways to improve your performance. The underlying premise of this book is that you don't have to be a financial genius to be a successful investor. Investing isn't brain surgery, after all, although some financial counselors try to make it seem complicated so that you will rely on them for advice. (Not surprisingly, they get a fee or earn a commission for providing that advice or selling you funds or other investments.) Nor do you have to devote your life to poring over reams of financial data or stay up nights worrying whether the Federal Reserve Board is going to cut or jack up interest rates. Rather, you must be willing to apply some common sense and discipline to develop and carry out an investing strategy that's appropriate for your goals and then spend a bit of time—as little as a few hours each month—making sure that your strategy and the investments you've chosen are still on track. You will have to provide the common sense and the discipline. The book can help with the rest by explaining in plain English how funds work and how you should work them into your overall financial strategy. Here are some specifics about what this book will and won't help you do.

It *will* help you:

• **sort through the mind-numbing multiplication of funds:** One result of the increasing popularity of funds is that everyone from fund sponsors to brokerage firms to banks to insurance companies has churned out an ever-increasing number of portfolios to capture the flood of money that investors have been pouring into funds. (Nearly $125 billion of new money flowed into stock and bond funds in 1995 alone.) In 1980 investors had about 446 stock and bond mutual funds from which to choose. By 1990 that number had grown to just over 2,000, and by 1996 the ranks of stock and bond funds had swelled to a staggering 7,000 or so choices—that's 2,800 more funds than there are stocks listed on the New York Stock Exchange and American Stock Exchange combined. While some of these new funds represent a chance for fund investors to profit from innovative investment strategies, a large portion are simply rehashes of existing funds and have been brought out because the fund sponsor thinks they can be sold to investors. This book will help you cut through the confusion this thicket of funds can create and home in on those choices that benefit you rather than the fund company.

• **find the right funds to do the job:** If you needed a car to cart your three kids and a changing cast of friends to school, music lessons, sporting events, etc., you wouldn't buy a two-seater Mazda Miata. And if you were looking for a nifty roadster to drive down the highway with the wind in your hair, you wouldn't buy a four-door Buick Roadmaster Estate Wagon. You would buy the right car for the job. The same principle applies to mutual funds. Some funds aim to throw off a steady stream of income while keeping the value of your initial investment relatively steady. Others are designed to help you accumulate big gains over a long period of time but may subject your capital to temporary losses along the way. This book will show you that one type isn't inherently better than the other and that what matters most is choosing the type that suits your needs and helps you achieve your goals.

• **learn to take prudent risks:** Many investors spend their time avoiding the wrong risks. They are so fearful of losing their money in a stock market crash that they avoid stock funds altogether, limiting themselves to savings accounts and CDs where they feel their money is safe. What they don't realize is that they are subjecting themselves to another risk that may be even more dangerous: the chance that the returns they earn won't be high enough to get them the money they'll need to retire in comfort or send their kids to college. One of the premises of this book is that when you are investing for long-term goals, you should be invested mostly in stock funds. Indeed, over a long period of time stock funds are a less risky investment than, say, bond or money-market funds. Why? Because stock funds are the most likely to power your investment portfolio to inflation-beating double-digit gains that will actually increase the purchasing power of your money. If, conversely, you confine your money to the perceived safety of bond funds—or, worse yet, money-market funds or CDs—you run a much higher risk that your investment stash will barely keep pace with inflation or even lose ground.

This focus on stock funds for the long term doesn't mean, however, that you should ignore how funds behave over the short term. After all, you may feel too queasy owning a fund that soars to stratospheric gains only to be followed by stomach-wrenching losses. And even if you can handle such volatility, huge fluctuations in return can be a problem if you need to get to your cash during one of the trough periods. But short-term drops aren't such a big deal when you're investing over a period of five years or more, since stock funds can come roaring back from setbacks and charge on to big gains by the time you're ready to pull out your money. It's impossible to eliminate all risk when investing in funds (or anything else, for that matter). This book will help you understand what risks you face, so you can decide how much of these risks you feel comfortable taking on.

• **get the most value for your investment:** While most investors, understandably enough, focus on a fund's rate of return, there's another side to the investing equation: the fees that a fund charges the people who invest in it. All funds incur ongoing expenses that include the payment to the fund's portfolio manager for choosing and monitoring the securities in the fund, the cost of accounting for shareholder accounts, and other administrative costs. Some funds also levy charges known as **loads,** or sales commissions that are paid not to the fund managers, but to the brokers, financial planners, and others who sell the fund to investors. This book will explain the impact such fees and expenses can have on the rate of return you actually get on your money and will also demonstrate how to compare funds' fees and expenses to assure you are not overpaying for performance.

• **think in terms of building a portfolio of funds:** Many people collect mutual funds as if they were walking along a beach picking up seashells—they grab whatever appeals to them at the moment without regard to whether it fits into an overall strategy or financial plan. Bad move. You can earn higher returns and subject your money to less risk by spreading your investment stash among a group of funds that invest in a variety of securities and employ different investing styles. This process of spreading your money among different types of funds or other investments—which goes by the grand-sounding name asset allocation—is so crucial that I devote an entire chapter (Chapter 10) to explaining different ways to build a diverse portfolio that can thrive in a variety of market conditions.

• **adopt an investing approach that works for you:** Everyone who invests should have a strategy for reaching his or her goals. But that doesn't mean everyone should have the same strategy. Indeed, the approach you take should be consistent with the time and effort you want to devote to investing in funds. If, for example, you truly enjoy poring over reams of performance statistics and you have the time to indulge this fascination, you can put together a finely tuned portfolio of five to 10 funds with a wide range of investing styles and monitor its progress regularly.

But if you don't have the time or inclination to do so, there's no sense in embarking on a complicated and time-consuming strategy of building a 10-fund portfolio just because some book or financial expert tells you that's the right way to do it. Rather than launch a plan you won't keep up with, you would be far better off choosing just a few funds—or, for that matter, one fund that buys all different types of securities—and monitoring performance maybe once every three months or so. If you prefer the hands-off approach, make sure you read Chapter 11, in which I discuss such options as index and life-cycle funds, two underrated but nonetheless acceptable choices for time-pressed fund investors.

One of the interesting quirks of the investing world is that being a fanatic—that is, putting in tons of time, reacting to the market's every move, and monitoring your portfolio's returns like the pulse of a patient in intensive care—doesn't guarantee superior returns. Indeed, when it comes to investing, less is often more. Someone who puts a reasonable strategy in place and doesn't tinker endlessly with it stands a decent chance of earning better returns than someone who's always overhauling his or her investments. Whatever your style—less is more or eternally vigilant—you will find advice and information in this book to help you carry out your strategy successfully.

Equally important, however, are the strategies you will not find in this book. Anyone who's leafed through personal finance magazines or perused the mutual fund coverage in the financial section of the local newspaper has been regaled with lists of the top 10 performing funds or stories on how to pick the funds that will land at the top of the fund heap during the coming year. Such coverage may make interesting reading (okay, that's a stretch). But few investing experts believe that putting money into last year's superstars or engaging in a futile effort to predict next years' winners will help you become a more informed and successful investor. So, in the spirit of truth in advertising, let's make it clear right now that this book will *not:*

• **offer any secret sure-fire formulas for investing success:** Yes, it would be wonderful if all you had to do was follow the Five Simple Steps to Investing Riches. Unfortunately there is no guaranteed route to investing riches—and anyone who suggests otherwise probably makes his or her money by selling such a program, not by investing with it. There are, however, a few investing strategies or methods that, by providing the discipline to invest regularly, can help you build wealth with mutual funds. These will be discussed in Chapter 11.

• **tell you how to find the "best" funds:** Most people feel enough pressure trying to choose a few funds from among the nearly 7,000 out there without the suggestion that they've missed the boat because they don't own a handful of what some quasi expert has dubbed "the best funds." But what does "best" actually mean? Best for what goal? Over what time period? Were they the best last year, too—and the year before that and before that? The notion that there is a mere handful of top 10 or 20 or 40 funds that all investors should pick from is utter nonsense. What's more, the fund that soars to huge gains one year often flames out the next. That's because outsize returns over a short period are often more the result of luck or a quirk in the markets rather than a reflection of the fund manager's skill. The basic premise of this book is that if you invest in funds that over long periods of time (say, three to 10 years) outperform most of their competitors, you will do just fine. So don't spend more than a nanosecond worrying about it if the funds you own don't show up on any mutual fund Hit Parade list.

• **help you outguess the market:** One common delusion that affects many investors is the belief that they can see ahead of time that stock prices are about to fall and, just before that happens, can unload their funds to sidestep losses. Of course, these savvy investors then imagine themselves investing again just in time to ride the rebounding market to new gains. The operative word here is "delusion." The consensus among investment experts is that market timing—the practice of attempting to jump in and out of the market at opportune times to grab gains and avoid losses—is nearly impossible to pull off, regardless of whether you're a sophisticated professional armed with a battery of high-powered computers or an individual investor who goes by instinct.

One reason market timing is so difficult is that you've got to make two timely calls: first deciding when to get out of the market, then figuring out when to get back in. Exit too soon and get back in too late and you miss some juicy returns. Missing big returns is pretty easy, by the way, because they often come in quick spurts. If you need convincing about that, consider this: Remember those fantastic 17.5% annual average gains investors earned during the 1980s bull market? Well, if you missed just the 40 best days of the stock market during that decade—that's right, gains that came from just 40 of the 2,528 days that stocks were traded during that decade—you would have earned only 3.9% annually instead of 17.5%. In other words, you'd have been better off in that low-yielding CD in our original example. So rather than waste your time and effort playing a guessing game you're likely to lose, stick with a group of funds that you put together as described in Chapter 10 and investing in them regularly as suggested in Chapter 11.

Just Do It

Okay, now that you know the ground rules, you can delve into the heart of this book. Before you do that, though, there's one more thought I'd like to leave you with—namely, don't procrastinate putting to work the advice you'll find here. It's easy to come up with reasons to put off investing. Maybe you're worried that stock prices are too high and are about to fall. Perhaps you're concerned that they've fallen lately and you're not sure when they'll rebound. Maybe you're simply paralyzed at the thought of having to choose from among the thousands of different funds vying for your attention, each proclaiming to be *the* best one to buy. Well, whatever your excuse, just remember that the ideal time to invest is whenever you have the money. And procrastination can be costly. For example, someone who begins putting away $2,000 a year at age 25 would accumulate a nest egg worth just over $470,000 by age 60, assuming a relatively modest 9% annual return. If that same person holds off until age 30 and begins setting aside $2,000 a year to age 60, he or she would wind up with just over $297,000, or $173,000 less than the early bird. Moral: The sooner you launch a plan of regular investing, the greater chance you have of reaching your goals. So let's get started.

CHAPTER 2

The Advantages of Investing in Funds

What Exactly Is a Mutual Fund?

You've probably heard and read so much about mutual funds in recent years that even if you don't own any, you may already have an idea of what they are and how they work. But just to clear up any possible misconceptions and to make sure we're all starting on the same page, let's quickly go over a few basics. By the way, even if you're already investing in funds, I wouldn't be too quick to blow off this section or, worse yet, this chapter. Why? Because even seasoned investors can sometimes benefit from a review of fund basics. Consider this: With the help of the Vanguard fund company, **MONEY** magazine gave a relatively easy 20-question quiz on mutual fund investing to nearly 1,500 fund investors in November 1995. How did the investors do? To put it kindly, let's say their performance showed lots of room for improvement. The average score on the test was 49 out of 100, which means on average investors answered only 10 of 20 questions correctly. Even people who described themselves as veteran investors scored only 62 out of 100, which even by today's liberal grading standards still rates a big F, the old flunkeroo. So unless you're a real fund savant, chances are you can profit from a bit of background on funds and how they work.

A mutual fund is essentially a company that pools money from investors like you and then hires an investment adviser (usually known as the **portfolio manager** or **fund manager**) to buy stocks, bonds, money-market instruments, or a combination of all three of these securities with that pool of money. When you invest in a fund, you purchase shares that represent part ownership of the securities in the fund. These shares also entitle you to a share of the income and profits (or, yes, it happens, losses) that those securities generate.

The price you pay for a fund's shares is determined by its **net asset value, or NAV,** which is the total value of the securities the fund owns divided by the number of shares outstanding. So if a mutual fund has a portfolio of stocks and bonds that are worth $10 million and a million shares of the fund are outstanding, each share would have a net asset value of $10. A fund's net asset value changes every day, depending on how much the prices of the securities in the fund's portfolio fluctuate. A fund is required by law to calculate its net asset value daily—which funds do after the stock market closes at 4 P.M. eastern time—so you will know on a regular basis how much the shares you own are worth and how much you'll have to pay if you want to buy more. The fund is also required to redeem or buy back your shares at the current net asset value on any day the financial markets are open. You will usually find a fund's NAV for the previous day listed in the financial section of most newspapers. As long as the fund does not charge you a sales commission, the net asset value is the price you would pay for additional shares of the fund, as well as the amount per share you would get if you cashed in your holdings. Thus, if you invested $1,000 in a fund with an NAV of $10, you would own 100 shares. You usually do not have to pay a sales charge or commission when you buy funds directly from a mutual fund company. (Some companies, however, such as the nation's largest fund group, Boston-based Fidelity Investments, do levy a small sales charge for some of their funds even if you buy the fund directly from them.)

You typically *will* have to pay a sales commission, however, if you buy a mutual fund from a stockbroker, financial planner, insurance agent, or other adviser. The reason, quite simply, is that financial advisers have to get paid somehow, and the overwhelming majority do so by collecting commissions on the investment products, such as funds or stocks or bonds, that they sell. Although the sales commission on funds can run as high as 8.5% (or $85 for each $1,000 you invest), these days the commission or load on a fund more likely comes in at 3.0% to 5.75% (or $30.00 to $57.50 per $1,000 invested). If a fund does carry a sales charge, then the amount you invest will be reduced by the sales load, thereby lowering the number of shares you get. When you buy a load fund, instead of buying shares at the NAV, you pay a higher price that is known as the **offering price** per share. For example, a fund that has a $10 NAV and imposes a 5% sales charge would have an offering price of $10.53, which means your $1,000 investment would buy you only 95 shares. While you would pay $10.53 for each share, each share would still be worth only the $10 net asset value. The 53¢ difference between the NAV and the offering price per share represents the 5% sales commission on your $1,000 investment, or $50 (95 shares x 53¢).

Rather than collect the commission up front, some funds levy what are known as **back-end sales charges,** which generally start at about 5% and then decline by one percentage point a year until they disappear. If you invest in these so-called **back-end-load funds,** you don't pay a sales charge when you invest. So the price you pay for shares equals the fund's net asset value. But you would pay, say, a 4% commission if you cashed out your shares after owning them only one year, or 3% after owning them two years, and so on. That percentage would typically be levied against what you originally paid for the shares or their current market value, whichever is less.

Unfortunately the whole area of fund sales fees and other

expenses has become extraordinarily convoluted in recent years (unnecessarily so, in my opinion). We won't delve into more detail about fund sales charges here, but since fund loads and other expenses eat into the returns you earn, you will definitely want to check out Chapter 8, which will alert you to both overt and covert fund fees and give advice on how to boost your returns by keeping down your investing costs.

A Dozen Good Reasons to Invest in Funds

This basic structure of pooling together the money of many investors gives funds some distinct investing advantages, as well as a few drawbacks. First, let's take a look at the 12 most important pluses funds offer. I'm sure that there are more than a dozen reasons to buy funds, but if you're not convinced by these 12, it's doubtful any others are going to sway you.

1. Competitive returns on your investment. As we saw with the mutual fund versus CD example in the first chapter, funds can clearly provide you with the kinds of gains you need to meet your financial goals. If you're willing to take some reasonable risks and put the bulk of your money in stock mutual funds, you should be able to rack up double-digit returns over long periods of, say, a decade or more. If you're more interested in generating income from your investment stash to meet day-to-day living expenses, then bond funds as well as funds that invest in a combination of stocks and bonds offer yields that can beat those available on such alternatives as CDs and bank savings accounts. You can even shelter some of that income from taxes, if you like, by investing in bond funds that hold municipal bonds whose interest payments are untaxed by Uncle Sam (and in some cases by state and local governments as well). Is it possible you could earn a higher return on your money by, say, choosing your own stocks and buying them through a broker? Sure, it's possible—if you know which stocks to buy, and if you don't mind keeping track of them, and if the trading costs you incur don't eat up your returns, and if you don't wind up dealing with a broker who's more interested in lining his or her pockets than yours. By investing in mutual funds (especially no-loads, which don't charge sales commissions), you can effectively eliminate most, if not all, of these ifs.

2. Professional money management. Giving individual investors access to some of the top investment talent in the world is perhaps the biggest benefit mutual funds have to offer. Every fund has a portfolio manager—or in some cases a team of managers—and researchers who work full-time doing all the things individual investors should do but often don't have the time, skill, or inclination to do: track the securities markets, monitor the investments the fund owns, and decide which additional stocks or bonds to buy and which to jettison.

As part of their job, fund managers and analysts will typically analyze the financial statements of companies and bond issuers, meet with executives of firms whose shares the fund is considering buying, talk with securities analysts who cover specific industries and companies, and attend industry meetings such as trade shows or seminars where the latest developments in an industry are often unveiled.

On average, managers have about four years tenure at their present fund; it's not unusual, however, to find the same manager running the same fund for five to 10 years, and a handful of managers have remained at the helm of their fund for 20 years or more. There are no specific educational requirements for managers, although they typically (though not always) hold a master's in business administration or other graduate degree from a well-regarded business school.

A growing number of managers also hold the chartered financial analyst designation, a professional certification earned by demonstrating proficiency in a variety of investment disciplines, including securities law and regulation, financial accounting, quantitative analysis, and portfolio management. Aside from a few legends such as Peter Lynch, the former manager who led Fidelity's Magellan fund to spectacular 28% average annual gains through the 1970s and 1980s, and John Templeton, a pioneer of international investing who also ran the Templeton mutual fund company, which recently merged with the Franklin fund family, most managers don't achieve celebrity status with the wider public.

Among fund aficionados, however, a number of managers— Mutual Shares' Michael Price, Gabelli Asset's Mario Gabelli, and New York Venture's Shelby Davis, to name a few—have cultivated reputations as savvy investors based on their outstanding long-term track records. There's no reason to shun a fund, however, just because you haven't heard of the manager or you don't see his or her name bandied about in newspaper or magazine articles. More important than the PR that a manager gets is how well the fund has done when compared with similar funds during the manager's tenure.

3. You don't need big bucks to get in the game. Ordinarily a professional money manager wouldn't be interested in investing your money unless you had at least $100,000 to sock away. And many of the best private money managers require a minimum initial investment of $1 million or more. By pooling their cash with that of other investors, however, fund investors can tap into the services of top portfolio managers even if they don't have the financial wherewithal of a Rockefeller or Microsoft's Bill Gates.

In fact, you don't need much of a stake at all to get started in funds. You can get into more than 4,000 funds with an investment of $1,000 or less. If a grand is too high—or you would like to test the fund waters with a small chunk of cash—then there are nearly 1,200 funds that will let you in for $500 or less and another 200 or so where the entry level is a mere $100. And there are nearly 50 funds that have no minimum requirement— they'll take whatever you're willing to invest. If you're investing money for an individual retirement account or another retirement savings plan, some funds lower their minimum, often to

$500 or less. Once you've gotten over that initial hurdle, funds typically allow you to make additional investments for $250 or less. The ability to add small amounts on a regular basis is an important advantage for the vast majority of investors, since that's the way most of us invest. We put away a little each week or month or every few months, when we have money left over after paying living expenses. While being able to get into a fund for a relatively small sum is a definite benefit, I would avoid putting too much emphasis on the minimum initial investment when choosing a fund. After all, your primary concern should be finding a fund that fits your needs and offers superior performance (and unfortunately, funds with low minimums often levy sales commissions which eat into your return).

Of course, if you have only a small amount of money, then you have little choice but to find funds that welcome cash-challenged investors. One solution: Consider funds that waive their normal initial minimum for investors who agree to invest via an automatic investing plan—that is, to make regular investments of $50 or $100 a month, typically by direct deposit from a checking account. Automatic or systematic investing plans also help you build wealth over the long term by making you a more disciplined investor who's less likely to get spooked when the market takes one of its periodic dives. For more on the benefits of regular investing, see the discussion of dollar-cost averaging in Chapter 11. And for a list of funds that have automatic investing plans that don't require deep pockets, see Table 1 (page 264) in the appendix.

4. A variety of ways to buy. If you want to invest in individual stocks or bonds, you have little choice but to do so through a full-service or discount broker. (Yes, you can buy shares of stock directly from some companies, but there may be restrictions on how much you can buy and how often or at least how quickly you can trade the stock.) You have lots of flexibility, however, when it comes to buying funds. If you prefer choosing your own funds, you can buy funds from sponsors who sell shares directly to investors. By so doing, you can avoid paying a sales commission completely (in which case you're getting a no-load fund) or reduce the amount of sales charge you pay (a low-load fund).

If you feel you need some advice in sorting through the thousands of funds available, then you can buy funds through a broker or a financial planner. In that case, however, you will almost assuredly wind up in a fund that charges an up-front or back-end sales commission, or load. What's more, if you deal with a broker whose firm happens to have its own line of mutual funds, as most national and even some regional brokerages do, don't be surprised if the fund that the broker recommends as the perfect one for you happens to be one from his firm's stable.

In the past few years most banks have also jumped into the fund arena by offering either their own funds or the portfolios of large fund sponsors. So chances are you can pick up a fund at your local bank. Although some banks do offer no-loads, the majority levy some type of sales charge on the funds they sell, especially when they are selling not their own funds, but those of another fund company. Finally, an increasing number of national and regional discount brokerage firms, such as Schwab and Jack White & Co., have introduced no-transaction-fee programs through which they sell no-load funds of several different sponsors without sales commissions. These programs will also sell load funds that are not part of their program, although you will have to pay a transaction fee that usually starts at around $27, plus the fund's regular sales commission. (Some discount brokers, however, will waive the transaction fee on funds with loads of 3% or more.) By using one of these no-transaction-fee programs to mix and match funds from several different fund sponsors, you can essentially create your own extended fund family. To learn more about each of these different fund purveyors and to figure out which one best suits your needs, check out Chapter 12.

5. Reasonable costs and fees. Apart from the sales commissions some funds levy, all funds also charge investors for the costs of operating the fund. (These ongoing operating costs are deducted automatically from the money you have invested in the fund; you're not charged separately for them. The returns that you see reported in magazines and newspapers are net of all the fund's operating expenses. Sales commissions, however, are typically *not* factored into reported returns.) The fact that a fund would have regular expenses—and that the shareholders would have to pay them—isn't surprising considering that the terrific management talent I referred to earlier isn't free. Nor are the other services that many funds offer: 24-hour access by phone to your account transactions and balances, check-writing privileges on many accounts, the statements funds send to confirm your purchase of shares, the periodic statements that show you the number of shares you own and total the current value of your holdings, semiannual and annual reports updating you on the progress of your fund. Funds also incur trading costs when they buy and sell securities.

Although these benefits and services aren't free, they are, with some exceptions, pretty reasonably priced—and certainly a much better deal than what you'd have to pay if you tried to buy individual securities on your own and duplicate all the additional services funds offer. Depending on the type of fund, the fund's investment adviser, or money manager, typically takes 0.5% to 1.0% of the fund's assets each year as an advisory fee for choosing and monitoring the fund's securities. Then there are annual fees of 0.3% or so for administrative tasks such as keeping track of shareholders' purchases, redemptions, and balances and providing custodial services—the securities and cash for each fund are generally held in trust for the fund by a bank or other custodian. Some funds that are sold by brokers, financial planners, or other salespeople may also add marketing and distribution charges known as 12b-1 fees (the name comes from the Securities and Exchange Commission rule that allows these charges), which nick the fund for another 0.25% to 1.0% of assets each year.

Fortunately, you don't have to keep track of each and every one of these fees to know how much you're paying in ongoing expenses for your fund. All these charges are totaled and reflected in a figure known as the fund's expense ratio, which is expressed as a percentage of the fund's assets and disclosed in the fund's prospectus, the legal document a fund is required to give you before you first purchase shares. The expense ratio for stock funds, on average, is about 1.5%, which means for every $100 you have invested, you pay about $1.50 or so a year in expenses. Bond funds' expenses average about 1% annually ($1 for every $100 invested), while the average annual expense ratio for money-market funds is much lower, about 0.5% to 0.7% (or $.50 to $.70 for every $100 invested). These are averages, though, and there can be quite a bit of variation from fund to fund. Many stock funds have expense ratios well below 1% annually, and some can climb to 2% or higher. In Chapter 8 we'll explore fund fees in more detail, but for now remember this: Every cent you pay in fund expenses reduces your net return. So in general, the more you home in on funds that hold down expenses, the higher the return you will see on your money.

6. Reduced risk through diversification. Diversification is nothing more than the simple principle of spreading your eggs among many baskets, although in the case of mutual funds, the manager is spreading your money among many stocks or bonds. The typical stock mutual fund usually holds shares of 100 or so different companies, while bond funds generally diversify their holdings among 70 or so different issues. When you buy shares of a fund, you effectively own a piece of all those securities.

By investing in such a large number of different shares, a fund virtually eliminates the risk that a plunge in the price of a single stock or bond will decimate the value of your holdings. The other securities in the portfolio provide a safety net of sorts that prevents one big loser from wiping you out. Of course, diversification also limits the upside you can earn, since huge gains by a big winner will be watered down somewhat by those securities in the portfolio that didn't generate eye-popping returns.

Certain types of funds make big bets by loading up on a relative handful of stocks or buy stocks only in a specific industry.

These are called **nondiversified** funds or **sector** funds. And, indeed, these funds can often soar to spectacular returns. Before you invest in such funds, just remember that those gains can evaporate pretty quickly if a few of those stocks get hammered or if a recession or other problem sends the industry or sector that's flying high today into a tailspin tomorrow.

7. Wide range of investment styles. Whatever your financial goals, chances are you can find a fund or group of funds that will help you meet them. Want to invest money for 20 years or more down the road so you'll have a comfortable retirement? Fine. You'll probably want to check out growth funds that can deliver double-digit gains that will keep your money growing faster than the rate of inflation. Need to tap your investment for day-to-day living expenses? No problem. You have plenty of bond funds to choose from that will send you a monthly dividend check. You just want a place to stash some cash that you know you'll need shortly—say, within a year or so? A money-market fund can give you returns that will beat what you'll find at your local bank or S&L (assuming you still have a local S&L after the 1980s thrift debacle), while offering a high degree of assurance that every penny you originally invested and all your earnings will be there when you need your money.

The ability to tap into a variety of funds with different investment objectives and styles is important to investors for a few reasons. First, it gives fund investors the flexibility to use funds to meet not just one, but a variety of financial needs. Chances are that at any given time you're trying to reach several financial goals, such as building an emergency fund, saving for retirement, tucking away cash for your children's education, or building the seed capital for a new business. Funds can help you achieve all these aims. What's more, the best way to achieve these and most other financial goals is to invest not just in a single fund or single type of fund, but to build a portfolio of several different types of funds. For example, you may wish to take advantage of the superior long-term gains of funds that specialize in small stocks, but you're wary of subjecting yourself to the temporary setbacks of 20% or so that such funds sustain from time to time. Solution: Combine small-stock funds with other types of funds—for example, those that invest in bonds or international shares or stocks of large, less volatile companies, or funds that buy shares of dividend-paying stocks that hold up well when the market turns sour. This way, when your small-stock fund is getting hammered, chances are that other parts of your portfolio will continue to cruise to gains. By mixing and matching various types of funds, you can build a portfolio of funds that provides you with the highest level of gains for whatever level of risk you feel you can comfortably handle.

8. Ready access to your money. Another advantage of funds is that you can get to your cash easily whenever you need it by redeeming shares, or selling them back to the fund. The price you get is the net asset value per share—the total value of all the securities in the fund divided by the number of shares outstanding—on the day that you redeem. In other words, you get the per-share worth of your fund's portfolio.

Most funds will let you redeem shares by telephone (in which case the fund sends you a check for the amount of the withdrawal) or by allowing you to have the fund wire the cash to your bank. In the case of some bond and most money-market funds, you can redeem shares simply by writing a check. A relatively small number of funds require that you write a letter to the fund to redeem shares. Before you invest in any fund, make sure its redemption policies will give you adequate access to your cash. A fund's sales representative can tell you what options are available for getting to your money, and the fund's prospectus (covered in more detail in the next chapter) also has a section that spells out the various ways you can cash in shares.

There is also a relatively small group of funds known as **closed-end funds,** which trade on a stock exchange much like regular stocks. Closed-end funds generally do not buy their shares back from shareholders. Rather, owners of closed-end funds who wish to redeem shares must sell them to other investors through a stockbroker. In this book we'll restrict ourselves to regular funds (also known as open-end, funds), since they offer more choices, are somewhat less complicated, and are better suited to most investors.

9. Ease of monitoring. When you own any investment, you want to know how it's doing. Fortunately, keeping track of a fund's progress, or lack of it, is a breeze. In fact, unless your lifestyle is patterned after that of cloistered nuns or Trappist monks, you'd be hard-pressed to avoid reading and hearing about funds. The financial section of virtually any decent newspaper provides information on hundreds, if not thousands, of mutual funds daily, or at least in its Sunday business section. Many business and personal finance publications, such as **MONEY** magazine, also provide detailed data on fund returns and offer advice about investment strategies. And with the advent of cable TV, the tube is crawling with putative personal finance experts spouting what passes for wisdom about mutual funds.

So you should have no trouble tracking your fund's progress (or lack of it). Keep in mind, though, that just because you can *get* this information so readily doesn't mean you should feel obligated to tally gains and losses every day or every week or even every month. In fact, I would argue the opposite: you're better off not following your fund's returns on a daily, weekly, or even monthly basis since it may result in data overload that can cloud rather than clarify your decision making. For most investors, taking stock of their fund holdings every three months or so to see how their funds are doing compared with similar ones is more than enough monitoring. Of course, if your notion of achieving nirvana is sitting down every day to pore over mutual fund tables, then don't let me cramp your spiritual development. But for your financial well-being, I'd suggest that you not buy or sell funds on the basis of short-term performance.

10. Simplified record keeping. Unless you've got the organizational prowess of a CPA, buying and managing a portfolio of individual stocks or bonds can be a bit of a bookkeeping headache. You've got to keep track of statements and receipts for each issue you buy, not to mention holding on to records of the dividends you received and when they were paid. Most mutual funds, however, provide consolidated statements that gather into one place the various investments you made in the fund, the amount of shares you received each time, what you paid per share, and the current value of your account. If the fund passes along income (say, interest from bonds it holds or dividends from stocks) or a **capital gain** (that is, profits from stocks or bonds that the fund sold for a higher price than it paid), the statement shows the dollar value of the distribution, when it was made, and whether you took it in cash or used it to buy additional shares of the fund.

If you own several funds that are part of a single fund family (like Fidelity Investments, which sells 167 different portfolios directly to individual investors, or Vanguard, which has a lineup of 80 or so funds, or one of the other large fund sponsors that offer a smorgasbord of portfolios) or if you buy funds through one of the no-transaction-fee discount broker programs, then information about all the funds of the family you own will be consolidated periodically onto a single statement. By providing this record-keeping service, fund companies make it much easier for you to keep track of how your fund is doing and how your account balances are faring. They also make it easy for you to gather the records you will need when you're ready to sit down and prepare your annual tax return.

11. Gains can be reinvested automatically—or you can live off the income. Funds chalk up their alluring returns in several ways—and allow investors either to take those gains in cash or to plow them back into the fund by buying additional shares that, in turn, can generate yet more profits.

Here's how that process works: Funds earn income when stocks pay dividends or when bonds or other interest-bearing securities that a fund owns make interest payments. Government and corporate bonds, for example, usually pay interest semiannually. Funds can also make money trading stocks. When a fund sells shares of stock in its portfolio for a higher price than it originally paid, that profit is called a **realized capital gain**. (If the fund has held the stock for more than a year, the profit is considered a long-term capital gain. Otherwise it is a short-term capital gain, which in the case of funds is considered the same as dividend income.)

Conversely, **unrealized capital gains** are paper profits that a fund has built up in shares that have appreciated in value but have not been sold. By law, funds are required to pass along to their shareholders virtually all realized capital gains as well as interest and dividends. Typically, funds pay out their capital gains once a year in a single capital-gains distribution—usually at the end of the year—although a handful of funds may distribute capital gains more frequently. (Unrealized capital gains aren't paid out at all, since they represent only paper profits in stocks that the fund hasn't sold. These unrealized gains are reflected in a fund's return, however, because the higher stock prices boost the fund's net asset value.) Interest and dividends, on the other hand, are paid out in more frequent so-called **income distributions**. For example, bond funds usually make monthly income distributions to shareholders, while funds that own dividend-paying stocks may pass along those dividends via quarterly or semiannual income payments.

When you fill out an application to invest in a fund, you can choose to have either or both types of distributions paid to you in cash, which is an option you might take if you plan to live off the income and capital gains generated by your fund. On the other hand, if your goal is to build your wealth as much as possible, you're better off instructing the fund to reinvest your income and capital-gains distributions in additional shares. If you take the reinvestment option, the fund will automatically buy new shares for you when it makes a distribution. By the way, if you later decide you want to take distributions in cash rather than have them reinvested—or vice versa—you can make the switch simply by notifying a representative of the fund.

12. Security from bankruptcy and fraud. Given the thousands of banks and S&Ls that failed in the '80s and early '90s and the various investment scams that seem to make the headlines with increasing regularity, it's understandable that investors handing over a good part of their life's savings might worry whether their fund could go bust or if an unscrupulous money manager could abscond with a fund's assets.

Relax. Although no investment is absolutely, positively free of such risks, for all practical purposes it is nearly impossible for a mutual fund to go bankrupt—and there are a variety of regulatory safeguards that protect fund investors from fraud. On the bankruptcy issue, you should know that most funds deal in assets, such as stocks and bonds, that are widely traded and highly liquid—that is, easy to sell even at short notice. Indeed, mutual funds are required by law to price the securities in their portfolios each day.

Thus, while many banks and S&Ls that failed had carried real estate and other investments on their books at highly inflated prices, chances are incredibly slim that the value of a fund's assets would be overstated anywhere close to that magnitude. Yes, there have been cases recently where doubts have been raised about the ways funds were valuing the securities in their portfolios. In 1994, for example, there was some question as to the accuracy of the prices some bond and money-market funds placed on highly complex and difficult-to-value **derivatives** (securities whose value is based on some underlying asset, commodity, or index). And, indeed, some of the portfolios ultimately marked down the value of those investments.

Similarly, some stock funds that buy stock in tiny companies whose shares are traded infrequently may have trouble accurately pricing those shares and could assign higher values than the shares would fetch when they're sold.

In both cases, however, we are talking about a relatively small number of funds that experienced problems, and the variance in prices wasn't enough to make the funds go bust. In fact, in the five decades since the Investment Company Act of 1940 was passed to regulate the activities of mutual funds, not a single fund has gone bankrupt, although some funds with lousy performance records have been merged with larger or more successful funds.

And in 1994 and 1995 sponsors of several dozen money-market funds had to put money into their funds to shore up their net asset values because of problems with derivatives or other securities. But in all these cases the potential losses to investors were on the order of a penny to a few pennies per dollar. In 1994 one money-market fund that catered to institutional investors—Community Bankers U.S. Government Money Market—closed up shop because some of its investments went sour. After the fund's assets were sold, the fund's investors got 96 cents for each dollar they had invested. As a result, this fund became the first money-market fund to "break the buck," or let its net asset value slip below the one-dollar-per-share level money-market funds try to maintain.

While there is always the possibility you may not get back everything you put into a mutual fund because the value of the securities held by the fund can go down as well as up, it's also true that the fund's shareholders will own those securities, whatever their value. So the chance that you won't get anything back is microscopic. For that to happen, the value of every single security in the fund would have to shrink to zero, which is about as likely as seven-footer Orlando Magic center Shaquille O'Neal riding to a Kentucky Derby win this year.

As for fraud and similar shenanigans, fund investors have several layers of protection. First, the portfolio manager doesn't have direct access to the fund's assets. Those are held by the fund's custodian, usually a bank or other financial institution. Even in the extremely unlikely event that a fund employee did manage to pilfer fund assets, the insurance that the Investment Company Act requires all mutual funds to buy would cover the loss. The Securities and Exchange Commission (SEC) also protects investors' interests. Among other things, the SEC periodically audits and inspects funds to make sure they are abiding by federal securities laws and that the fund is carrying out its stated investment strategy and has adequate procedures in place to account correctly for the fund assets. The SEC has the power to censure and fine funds that run afoul of securities laws. What's more, state securities regulators and even state attorneys general can step in to protect consumers' interests, if necessary.

The fund industry itself also realizes that if it expects people to keep plowing money into funds, it must maintain investors' trust. So, overall, the industry has a pretty decent record of maintaining high ethical standards and toughening up those standards when necessary. For example, after the Denver-based Invesco Group fired star manager John Kaweske in January 1994 for failing to report stock trades in his personal account, the fund industry's main trade association, the Investment Company Institute (ICI), issued a stringent set of trading guidlelines for fund personnel that would help prevent a manager from putting his or her interests above those of the fund's shareholders. The ICI has since reported that 70% to 88% of fund complexes have adopted the guidelines, which include bans on managers profiting on short-term trades and buying initial public offerings of stock for themselves. The SEC also launched an industrywide investigation into the personal trading practices of fund managers, after which the agency concluded there were no widespread problems. The commission subsequently filed a civil suit accusing Kaweske of violating antifraud provisions of federal securities laws. The suit was settled in November 1995 when, without admitting or denying the allegations in the complaint, Kaweske agreed to pay a $115,000 penalty to the U.S. Treasury. In a related proceeding, the SEC also barred Kaweske from working in the securities business for five years.

In September 1995 the SEC ordered another fund manager, Roger Honour, to pay a civil penalty of $275,000 for personal trading in securities he was also buying or selling for the mutual funds he ran as well as for other clients. The commission also required Honour to pay to the U.S. Treasury $115,615—his profit from these personal trades—plus interest. In the wake of such incidents, the SEC has proposed that each mutual fund be required to note in its prospectus that the fund's code of ethics concerning personal trading is filed with the SEC and available to the public.

Of course, no amount of regulation can stem all illicit activity. After all, there are more than 8,000 stock, bond, and money-market funds, and the SEC can't have an inspector by each fund employee's side every day. As it stands now, the SEC has about 250 fund inspectors, which it attempts to focus on fund groups that the commission believes—based on investor complaints or problems uncovered in past inspections—might be managing or selling funds in ways that could harm investors. Even fund companies that the SEC has no reason to suspect of shenanigans of any type would likely be inspected at least once every five years.

Despite the SEC's presence, however, savvy investors should always exercise common sense and temper their trust with a healthy dollop of skepticism. So don't be afraid to question any unusual aberrations in your fund's performance. If the value of your fund suddenly drops 5% to 10%, for example, while the value of similar funds remains stable or increases, that's worth a call to the fund's telephone rep for an explanation. If the explanation doesn't sound plausible or you have other reasons to be concerned, you might consider contacting the SEC's Office of Investor Education and Assistance at 202-942-7040 and even perhaps your state securities regulator. (You can get the name and phone number of the regulator in your state by calling the North American Securities Administrators Association at 202-737-0900.) If you feel the fund was misrepresented in the way it was advertised or by the person who sold it to you, you should contact not just the SEC and your state securities regulator, but the National Association of Securities Dealers (800-289-9999), an industry organization that oversees mutual fund marketing as well as the sales practices of brokers and others who sell securities. Overall, however, mutual funds are among the most tightly regulated investments, and, in terms of protection from mismanagement and fraud, definitely one of the safest.

But Funds Aren't the Investing Equivalent of Utopia

At this point you must be figuring that, washing windows and making coffee aside, there's nothing these amazing mutual funds can't do. Not exactly. Funds do have some shortcomings and drawbacks. There are even some instances in which you may not want to use funds at all. Here are a few examples of funds' limitations, followed by some suggestions about when you might be better off not buying a fund.

• **Funds won't protect you from marketwide declines.** Many investors mistakenly believe that because a stock or bond mutual fund has a diverse portfolio of securities, the fund won't get dragged down when the market heads south. Wrong. By spreading your money among many securities, diversification prevents a blowup in a single security or a small handful of securities from decimating the value of your portfolio. But if stock or bond prices overall are falling, then the value of your fund, which, after all, is made up of many stocks or bonds or a combination of both, will also drop. (Money-market funds are a different story, since they hold neither stocks nor bonds, but ultra-short-term interest-paying securities whose value rarely fluctuates very much.)

For example, when stock prices took a 13.8% nosedive between August and November 1990, the average stock fund actually fell a bit more than the market: 16.3%. Now, that average includes many types of funds. In fact, some categories of funds dropped more than 16.3%, and some fell less. For example, funds that specialize in the stocks of small companies lost 22.5% of their value during this period. That's because small-company shares tend to bounce around more—both up and down—than the stock market overall, which is dominated by shares of large, more stable companies. On the other hand, so-called **equity-**

income funds, which own a combination of shares of large companies that pay dividends as well as some bonds, fell just 11.2% during that period. These funds held up better because the dividends tend to cushion a stock's fall, plus the interest payments on the bonds in these funds' portfolios also provide a bit of a safety net. In short, all types of stock funds dropped along with the overall market, but how hard they fell depended on the types of securities they were holding.

Similarly, if you own a bond fund that holds a diversified portfolio of 50 to 100 bonds, you don't have to worry that a default by one of the issuers will wipe out the fund's value. There are plenty of other issues to soften the impact of the default. But if interest rates rise, prices in the bond market will drop, as will the value of your bond fund. The exact amount of decline your fund will suffer will depend primarily on two factors: how far rates shoot up and the maturity of the bonds in your fund. (A bond's maturity is simply the number of years remaining until the issuer repays the bond's principal. In Chapter 6 we'll discuss in more detail the risks that interest rates and default pose to bond fund investors.) By the way, the fact that a fund will drop during a marketwide decline in stock or bond prices shouldn't scare you off funds. Such ups and downs are a normal part of the course of stock and bond prices, and as long as you don't panic and sell after prices have dropped, you can ride the market back up again. For example, stock fund investors who simply rode out the drop in the market back in 1990 earned an average of 18% a year over the following five years.

• **Fund managers can stray from their investment strategies.** If you choose your own stocks, you have complete control over what winds up in your portfolio. If you want to focus exclusively on dividend-paying stocks, you'll be sure to buy only those. If you prefer growth stocks, you'll home in on shares of companies with fast-growing profits. You can also decide whether to invest primarily in shares of small, medium-size, or large companies—or a combination of all three. You're in control.

With a mutual fund, however, the manager is in control. And

you're depending largely on the manager to do exactly what the fund says it will do in its prospectus or what you'd expect it to be doing based on the type of fund it is. For example, if the fund is a small-company stock fund, you'd naturally expect it to invest in the shares of small companies. Pretty simple, right? Well, not always.

Sometimes fund managers might invest a bit more aggressively than the fund's name or category would suggest. For example, the manager of a **growth-and-income fund**—a relatively conservative type of fund that generally holds shares of large companies that pay dividends—might throw some growth or small-company shares into the portfolio. Why? Could be that the manager happens to see some great values in stocks the fund doesn't usually specialize in. Or it could be that the manager figures that by investing a tad more aggressively than other growth-and-income funds, the fund will post a higher return than its competitors—and entice more investors to put their money into the fund.

A study by Northfield Information Services, a Boston investment research firm, found that many funds that posted the highest returns in their categories achieved their superior performance by investing more aggressively than their peers. For example, many of the growth-and-income funds with the highest returns actually invested more like funds that specialize in much more volatile growth stocks. The lesson here is that while you want a fund that excels compared with similar funds, you should be wary of a fund that outdistances the competition regularly by a suspicious margin—say, more than one or two percentage points a year. If such a margin is achieved because the manager is just a terrific investor, great. You should hold on to the fund. But if it's because the manager is taking a lot more risk than the competition, well, then you want to see how that fund would stack up against funds that are buying the same types of securities.

• **Funds can give you an Excedrin tax headache.** For the most part, mutual funds make investors' lives easier.

Unfortunately the opposite can be true at tax time. For one thing, funds are required each year to pay out virtually all their dividends, interest payments, and capital gains. And you must pay taxes on those distributions, even if you didn't take them in cash. That's right, even if you choose to have all your dividends, interest, and capital gains reinvested in additional shares, you pay taxes even though you never actually got your hands on the money. It's only fair that you do pay tax on these distributions, since you did make a profit and chose to reinvest it (although it does strike some investors as inequitable).

What also seems a bit unfair is another peculiarity of funds—namely, you can owe taxes even if your fund lost money for the year. Consider this: Although the Massachusetts Investors Growth Stock fund lost 6.7% in 1994, it still paid out $1.08 per share to shareholders in taxable capital gains because the fund had sold some of its holdings for a profit during the year. The fund was hardly alone that year. In 1994, which was a lousy year for both stocks and bonds, more than 3,733 funds lost money. Many of those nonetheless still distributed income or capital gains or both to their shareholders, who had to pay taxes on those gains, unless the funds were held in a tax-sheltered account such as an IRA (individual retirement account).

But the fun really begins when you're ready to sell shares. If you're like most funds investors, you have your income and capital-gains distributions reinvested in additional shares. Each of those reinvestments—which are made at the fund's price per share at the time you get the distribution—is considered a separate purchase of the fund. So if you sell shares in a fund you've owned for a number of years, you must figure out the cost of the shares you've unloaded to calculate your gain or loss. Is the cost the price you paid for the shares you bought when you made your initial investment? Or the price of the shares you bought at different times with reinvested distributions? Or the price you paid for shares you acquired by making subsequent additional investments on your own? Or perhaps it's the average price you paid for all these shares? The answer you give will affect the gain or loss you wind up with, as well as the tax you pay, because each group of shares was bought at a different price and at a different time.

Profits on shares you've held more than a year would be considered long-term capital gains and, as of early 1996, would be taxed at a maximum rate of 28%. Gains on shares held a year or less, however, would be taxed at ordinary income rates, which means you could pay as much as 39.6%. As you might imagine, keeping track of all your shares and then calculating your gain can be about as appealing as a winter trip to Buffalo. Nonetheless, since the amount of tax you pay will depend largely on how you calculate your gain, it pays to know what options are available to you. For a look at those options and when you might choose one over the other, see page 266 in the appendix.

When You Don't Need a Fund

Why, you may ask, is a book on mutual funds telling you when you *shouldn't* invest in funds? The answer: While funds are a great choice for the vast majority of investors, my journalistic ethics (and the fact that sooner or later you're bound to hear this anyway) require me to tell you that there are times when you should consider other alternatives. Here are a few such instances:

• **You're adept at picking individual stocks.** If you believe you have a knack for picking good stocks (or that your knowledge of a certain industry gives you insight into a particular type of company), then you might consider buying shares of individual companies instead of or in addition to investing in funds. You shouldn't go this route unless you're willing to put in the time to research, choose, and monitor your investments. And you should probably be willing to invest $20,000 or more to set up a diversified portfolio of 10 or more stocks. If you're just buying a few stocks in addition to a broadly diversified portfolio of funds, you don't have to worry about owning a broad range of stocks. However many stocks you own, avoid the temptation—often fostered by a broker, who, of course, is getting paid every time you make a move—to buy and sell shares frequently. Even if you happen to display the prescience of an investing genius, transaction costs can quickly whittle away your profits, blunting the advantage of even the most savvy (or lucky) moves.

• **You plan to invest in Treasuries.** If you're going to live off interest payments from U.S. Treasury notes and bonds, you might be better off owning the bonds themselves. This way you'll boost the income you receive because you won't be paying fund expenses, which siphon off one-half to a full percentage point of the yield you would receive. Treasuries are backed by the full faith and credit of the U.S. government, so unless you believe the federal government is likely to be overthrown or renege on its obligations, there's no risk of default.

That means you don't really need the widely diversified portfolio that funds provide, so you need only buy a handful of bonds. You should, however, buy Treasuries that come due at different times—say, some that mature in two to five years and some that come due in 10 years or longer. If interest rates rise, then at least you'll be able to reinvest some of your principal at higher rates when the two-year Treasuries come due. If rates fall, you'll still enjoy the higher rates on the longer-term bonds you own.

Treasury bonds, which have maturities of 10 years or more, are sold in denominations of $1,000. **Treasury notes** have maturities of two to 10 years. Like Treasury bonds, notes with maturities of five years or more are sold in $1,000 amounts, while notes that come due in fewer than five years require a $5,000 minimum investment, although you can buy them in $1,000 increments once you meet the minimum. **Treasury bills,** conversely, come due within a year and have a $10,000 minimum purchase requirement, so most people are better off getting these via a money-market fund (see Chapter 4).

You can buy Treasuries without sales charges directly from the

Federal Reserve Bank in your area. For information, call the U.S. Treasury, Bureau of Public Debt, at 202-874-4000, extension 232. You could also choose to own individual tax-exempt municipal bonds rather than a muni bond fund. But muni bond issuers can run into trouble, as did Orange County, California, which filed for bankruptcy in December 1994. Even though defaults are relatively rare—less than 1% in any given year for top-rated muni bonds—anyone considering buying individual munis should stick to the highest-quality bonds, buy from a reputable brokerage firm, and invest in issues of several states to prevent problems with one issuer from zapping your holdings.

If you prefer to reinvest the interest from Treasuries or munis, however, owning individual bonds may be impractical. For example, $10,000 worth of Treasury notes yielding, say, 6%, would pay $300 in interest every six months—not enough to buy another bond. So you could simply invest in a fund that buys Treasury notes, or you could invest in what are known as **zero-coupon Treasuries**. Zeros make no interest payments. Instead you buy them at a discount of their face value—depending on the level of interest rates, you might pay $250 or so for a 15-year zero with a $1,000 face value—and your return is the difference between what you pay up front and the face value you get at maturity.

You must buy zeros through a broker, so you will pay a commission, but that shouldn't eat too much into your return if you shop around for a good price and if you hold the bond until it matures. Warning: The price you could get at any given time for a zero gyrates up and down much more than the price of a bond that makes regular interest payments. For most people, therefore, zeros usually work best for goals such as saving for future college tuition, since you can count on having a specific sum of money (the zero's face value) when the bond comes due.

•**You have incredibly unique financial needs.** Funds may also not be the right choice for you if you happen to have very complicated personal finances that require more investing flexibility than funds allow. For example, perhaps you have investment income from other sources, so you want to have more control over when you recognize gains or losses. Or maybe a rich relative left you a cache of securities or a trust fund loaded with stocks that you want to use as the core around which to tailor the rest of your portfolio. In that case you might not be able to get the precise mix of stocks or bonds or both you need through a fund.

Then again, maybe you like the concept of funds—investing with a professional who is managing a diverse portfolio of securities—but you need more hand-holding. If the market takes a dive, you want to be able to talk to the manager to find out how your portfolio is doing. People in any of these situations might prefer to hire their own individual money manager to create a portfolio of securities and oversee it. Problem is, to make it worthwhile for the manager and to prevent the manager's fee plus transaction fees from eroding your returns, you generally must have at least $100,000 to invest. And to get the services of the best managers, you need upward of $1 million.

So unless you fall into one of these three categories, chances are that funds are the right investment for you. In that case flip the page to Chapter 3 so you can get started investing in funds or, if you already are invested, pick up some tips to boost your returns.

CHAPTER 3

Getting Started

Deciding What You Need from Funds

The best way to begin your search for the right mutual funds is to look within yourself. No, I'm not trying to get metaphysical here. I just mean that before you can begin sorting intelligently through the thousands of mutual fund choices out there, you've got to figure out just what it is you want funds to do for you. If you ignore this first step of examining your financial goals and simply plunge ahead, looking for a top-performing fund, chances are you're going to end up investing in a fund whose performance disappoints you because it doesn't suit your needs.

Actually, you may end up investing in a string of funds that don't satisfy you, since investors who don't identify their goals and then systematically home in on those funds that are likely to help them achieve those goals often wind up jumping aimlessly from one fund to the next. You can avoid this unprofitable wandering by doing a little financial soul-searching. Here are three

47

questions you can ask yourself that will help you get a handle on what kinds of funds you should be concentrating on:

1. What do you need most—growth of capital, income, or safety of principal? It would be great if we could have all three of these things—an investment that spins out 20% annual returns, throws off reliable and generous dividends, and never goes down no matter what the market does. There's only one problem: such an investment doesn't exist.

Fact is that investing in mutual funds, like much else in life, comes down to making compromises. The higher the returns you seek, the more safety you'll have to sacrifice. The more safety you crave, the less you can expect in the way of stellar returns. To invest sensibly, therefore, you have to decide what trade-off of risk and return makes sense given the goals you've set to achieve.

If you are investing for a goal that is five or more years away—such as saving for retirement or putting away money for your children's college education—then you want your money to grow as much as possible. This means you should be focusing on capital growth, which in turn means you should be emphasizing stock funds to get the best shot at building the value of your capital. For example, growth stock funds—that is, ones that seek out companies that are able to increase profits at a rate of 10% to 15% or more each year—have posted returns of roughly 12% a year for the 10 years to April 1, 1996. At that pace the value of your money doubles every six years.

If you are depending on funds to help pay your ongoing living expenses, then you are an income investor—and you should look for funds that can generate a reliable stream of interest or dividend payments. You have two basic choices. The first is bond funds, which invest, as their name implies, in bonds and pass along interest payments to their shareholders in the form of monthly income dividend distributions that investors can take in cash (or reinvest in additional shares if they're not depending on the fund for living expenses).

The second choice for income investors is what are known as

total return funds, so-called because their returns are a total of the gains from capital growth and from interest and dividend payments. These funds—which include growth-and-income, equity-income, and balanced funds—typically invest in a combination of dividend-paying stocks and interest-paying bonds. Thus they too are able to pass along to shareholders income distributions that can be taken in cash, although total return funds typically pass along their income payments quarterly or semi-annually, not monthly as bond funds do. While both bond and total return funds churn out steadier gains than, say, growth funds, their reliability comes at a cost—lower returns than you could get with, say, growth funds. Balanced funds, for example, gained roughly 11% a year over the 10 years to April 1, 1996, while U.S. government bond funds, on average, returned just under 8% annually over the same period (and only 4.3% over the past three years).

If you are looking for a place to put money that you will need in a relatively short period of time—say, within three years or so—then you want to be sure the money will be there when you need it. So security of principal should be your overriding concern. Money-market funds, which invest in low-risk interest-paying investments, would be your best choice, since they offer rock-solid stability and a reasonable assurance that you will get your money back and more whenever you need it. In return for that security, however, you accept a much lower rate of return than you would get on either stock or bond funds. Over the 10 years to April 1, 1996, money funds have gained only 5.6% annually.

Of course, the returns shown here for stock, bond, and money-market funds are averages. Those returns can vary—substantially with respect to stock and bond funds—depending on which specific funds you choose. You'll get more detailed explanations in Chapters 4, 5, and 6 of the variety of choices you have within each of these types of funds. For now, though, it's important to understand that the mix of funds you own should be designed to help you achieve the goals you have set for yourself.

2. How much risk are you comfortable taking? Ask

most people whether they'd rather have stock funds' long-term double-digit gains or the lower returns of bond, total return, or money funds, and the answer is a no-brainer. Who wouldn't want higher returns? Trouble is, to get stocks' alluring gains, you must also be prepared to withstand periods where the value of your fund sinks 20% or more over a period of a month or longer.

If that type of setback is going to send you scurrying for the exits, then stock funds' attractive gains are meaningless because you won't be around long enough to reap them. In choosing funds, therefore, you've got to do some honest self-evaluation. If you chug Maalox every time the stock market takes a dive, then you don't want to put all your dough into funds that will subject you to double-digit losses, even if temporarily.

On the other hand, you don't want to be too much of a wimp. Why? Because if you cop out entirely and stick your cash only into conservative funds, you subject yourself to another risk: the danger that the returns you earn may be too low for you to accumulate the amount of money you need. So you must steer a course that gives you enough gut-level comfort but at the same time produces an acceptable level of return. For most people the solution is spreading their money among a variety of funds with varying degrees of volatility. By creating an appropriate mix of funds, as described in Chapter 10, you have the best shot at earning the returns you need without taking on outsize risks.

3. How long do you have before you must tap into your money? The longer you plan to hold your fund shares, the more aggressively you can afford to invest. For example, if you are salting away money you know you won't touch for a decade or more, then you should be investing primarily in stock funds. True, the value of these funds could drop significantly, but a 20% decline in stock prices that occurs, say, three years from now shouldn't really matter much to you. Your fund should have plenty of time to recover from that setback and generate double-digit gains by the time you're ready to start redeeming shares.

Conversely, if you are setting aside money that you plan to use within three years—to buy a new car, for example—then a stock fund would be a dicey choice. Who knows, maybe you would be lucky and hit a three-year period where stock prices surged, driving your fund to 15% yearly gains. Then again, maybe six months before you're ready to sell your shares and head to the car dealership, the stock market will tank and the value of your fund will drop 20%. The chances that your fund will recoup that loss in a mere six months are pretty slim. So if you really, really can't afford to take the chance that in three years there will be less of your money than you had planned on, you would be much better off putting your cash into a money fund and accepting a lower return.

Finding the Funds that Work for You

Once you've identified what you want from a fund and how much risk you're willing to take, you can start looking for funds that match your needs. Here are four of the best ways to begin that evaluation process:

1. Examine the fund's investment strategy. Before you invest in any fund, you should know how the manager intends to put your money to work. Will the manager buy stocks, bonds, a combination of the two? Does the fund home in mostly on the shares of large companies that are in such widely followed barometers of stock market performance as the Dow Jones Industrial Average (made up of the shares of 30 large, primarily industrial companies) or the Standard & Poor's 500 stock index (a benchmark that follows the shares of 500 large U.S. companies in several industries and accounts for about 80% of the market value of all stocks traded in the United States)? Or will the manager ferret out shares of very small companies that you may never have heard of?

Such questions are important because they give you clues as to how the fund might perform under certain conditions. For example, stock funds that leaven their mix with bonds or dividend-paying stocks typically hold up better than pure stock funds when the market heads south. And funds that emphasize the shares of small companies usually take a harder hit than those that specialize in large-company shares when the stock market slides.

Often, the fund categories devised by rating services such as Morningstar Mutual Funds and Value Line Mutual Fund Survey and Lipper Analytical Services give you an idea of what type of strategy a fund pursues. For example, a fund that's in the growth-and-income category most likely shoots for a combination of current income and capital growth, usually by investing in shares of medium- to large-size companies that pay dividends. But some funds in the growth-and-income category, such as the Oppenheimer Main Street Income and Growth fund, have taken a more aggressive stance by spicing their portfolios with shares of small companies.

Similarly, a fund's name may give you a good idea of what it does. For example, if a fund has the term "U.S. government securities" or "U.S. government income" in its name, it probably invests in securities issued by the U.S. government. But such a fund may not always be as safe and secure as it seems. For example, in 1994 many investors put money into the PaineWebber Short-Term U.S. Government Income fund because they figured it would invest in bonds issued by the U.S. government that would come due in two to four years, a fairly conservative investment. Investors were stunned, therefore, when some shares of the fund lost 6.2% of their value in the first eight months of 1994. Turns out the fund had been investing a substantial portion of its assets in arcane investments known as derivatives. These derivatives were indeed composed of securities backed by the U.S. government, but they were far more volatile than garden-variety Treasury bonds.

Derivatives aside, the fact is that you can't even assume that a fund that calls itself a U.S. government securities fund invests entirely in U.S. government securities, since under current regulations a fund that invests only 65% of its assets in government securities can still legally call itself a government securities fund. To find out a fund's actual investment strategy, therefore, you must look beyond its name and category label and peruse its prospectus, the document in which the fund describes how it invests and divulges details about the fees it charges. Fund prospectuses and how to read them will be discussed later in this chapter.

2. Evaluate past performance. Extrapolating a fund's past returns into the future can be dangerous. For example, funds that invest in the stocks of companies in emerging Latin American countries posted impressive gains of 80% or more in 1993. But investors who bought into such funds expecting an encore in 1994 were rocked with losses of 10% to 20%, as a devalued Mexican peso depressed stock prices throughout Latin America. Even a performance record as long as five years could be misleading. It could be based largely on one good call—a manager ducking out of stocks just before a market crash—or the fund could suffer after the manager who ran it during a period of spectacular gains jumps to another fund. That said, however, a fund's track record can yield clues about how the fund might react to a variety of market conditions in the future and how it might stack up against similar funds.

Thus, before investing in a fund, you should compare its returns over a variety of periods with those of similar funds. No fund is always going to be at the top of the performance charts for every period you examine. But over long periods of three, five, or even 10 years (if the fund and the manager have been around that long), you would at least want the fund to rank in the top half of its competitors. You should also check out how consistent those gains have been. Does the fund typically rank in the top half of its category year by year, or is it at the top one year and down in the cellar the next? Volatility isn't necessarily a problem—provided you know about it going into the fund and that the fund compensates shareholders for its rollicking ride with higher returns than those of its competitors.

3. Judge the riskiness of the fund. A common complaint from investors who buy a fund that later suffers a sizable loss is that they didn't understand the risk they were taking. For example, investors who buy U.S. government bond funds might believe that the value of their fund can't fall because the principal of the bonds in the fund is guaranteed by the federal government. Yes, Uncle Sam's backing does eliminate the possibility of losses resulting from defaults on the bonds. But government bonds, just like bonds issued by corporations and municipal bonds issued by states and cities, are also subject to interest rate risk. That is, when interest rates rise, the value of a bond falls. When you think of it, that relationship between interest rates and a bond's value makes perfect sense.

Let's say I own a bond that pays me 6% of its face value in interest each year. If interest rates later rise to 7%, why would anyone pay the same for my 6% bond as for a similar new bond yielding 7%? Clearly, someone would only pay less for a bond with a lower rate of interest. Exactly how much less depends largely on how many years remain until my bond repays its principal or face value—in other words, the length of time that someone would be locked in to the lower 6% interest payments.

The net result, though, is that when interest rates rise, the value of a bond fund, including government bond funds, typically falls. (The reverse happens when rates fall, of course, since the old bond's higher payments are more valuable compared with the lower payments on newly issued bonds.) Investors who aren't aware of this seesaw relationship between interest rates and bond prices are often shocked to find that the investment they considered absolutely safe has lost value. In stock funds, investors typically are more aware of the potential for losses. But even there investors may be surprised by the magnitude of the setbacks—or they may not understand what triggered them.

So how can you evaluate the level of risk you are assuming when you buy a fund? In 1995 the Securities and Exchange

Commission began looking into this question, hoping to find the barometers of risk that would help funds better disclose fund risks. As a result, a number of risk measures have gotten wide attention in personal finance publications. In this section I describe four such measures. The first is a simple, but still highly effective, way of gauging risk that virtually anyone can—and should—use. The other three, quite frankly, are probably more suited to number-crunching, calculator-wielding statistics junkies. So if the prospect of sifting through yet more quantitative measures leaves you cold (or scared stiff), just check out the first measure and then go on to the next section.

One caveat: All these measures are based on how the fund has performed in the past. Thus they are not rock-solid guarantees of what's to come. A fund representative should be able to provide you with some or all of these figures, or you can get them from fund research firms such as Morningstar and Value Line, which are profiled in Chapter 13.

• **Worst year, quarter, or down-market loss:** The concept here is simple. You find out the worst gain or loss the fund posted over the course of a year, three months, or a period when the market tanked, and then you decide if you could ride out such a period without jumping ship. For example, the Wasatch Aggressive Equity fund gained 21.3% annually on average for the five years through 1995. But had you been in that fund during the market downturn from August through October 1990, you would have seen the value of your shares skid 22.7%.

Clearly the fund recovered nicely in the years after that loss (which, by the way, wasn't out of line with the 22.2% average loss for all aggressive growth funds during that period). But if you would have been spooked enough to bail out of the fund before it had a chance to recover, then you might be better off in a less volatile fund. (The fund's subsequent recovery also shows that, over the long term, taking reasonable risks can really pay off.)

• **Beta:** This measure shows how a stock fund's value fluctuates relative to an index representing the overall stock market, usually the Standard & Poor's 500 index. (Beta can also be calculated for bond funds, but it isn't used as often by bond fund investors.) Beta is typically arrived at by comparing a fund's ability to beat the returns on Treasury bills versus the S&P 500's success in doing the same. By definition, the S&P's beta equals 1, so a fund with a beta of 1.1 would be expected to perform 10% better than the S&P 500 (minus the return on Treasury bills) in up markets and 10% worse when the market is declining. A fund with a beta of, say, 0.75 would be expected to underperform the S&P by 25% in bull markets but fall only three-quarters as much in bear markets. The higher (or lower) a fund's beta, the more (or less) you would expect it to rise (or fall) compared with stock prices overall in an up (or down) market.

• **Standard deviation:** This yardstick tells you how much a stock or bond fund's return bounces up and down around its average return. It can be derived by taking a fund's gains each month over a specific period (usually three or more years), translating those gains to annual returns (much the same as a bank gives an annual percentage rate for a six-month CD), and then seeing how much the individual monthly annualized returns deviate from the average return for all the months.

So a fund with a standard deviation of 8, for example, should usually yield an annualized return in any given month that is eight percentage points above or below its average return for the period. For reasons too technical and boring to go into here, you would actually expect the monthly return to be within eight percentage points of the average 68% of the time. Suffice it to say that the higher the standard deviation, the more volatile a fund's returns are likely to be. The standard deviation number itself also shows you how big the ups and downs in return are likely to be. Why bother with standard deviation if you've already looked up a fund's beta? Well, beta tells you only how a fund reacts in tandem with a market index. A fund could have a low beta yet still be very volatile, if some factor other than stock prices drives it.

One good example is a fund that owns gold stocks. Because these stocks move more in response to the price of gold than movements in the stock market, they often have betas that are half those of many stock funds but standard deviations that may be two times higher than those of other stock portfolios. By looking at a fund's standard deviation, you get an idea of how flighty its returns can be regardless of what is causing the volatility.

• **Average maturity and duration:** These two measures give you an idea of how sensitive a bond fund is to changes in interest rates—that is, how much the fund's value is likely to fall when interest rates rise or, conversely, how much it's likely to rise when rates fall. A bond's maturity is simply the number of years before the bond repays its principal or face value. A fund's average maturity is calculated by taking a weighted average of the maturities of all the bonds in the portfolio. In general, the longer the average maturity, the more volatile the fund is.

For example, a one-percentage-point jump in interest rates might knock off 5% or so of the value of an intermediate-term bond fund—that is, one with an average maturity of five to 10 years. The same increase in interest rates might result in more than an 8% loss for a long-term bond fund, or one that holds bonds maturing in 20 to 30 years. Unfortunately, although a fund's average maturity is an easy number to get, it's not always a completely accurate gauge of how a fund is likely to respond to interest rate movements. One reason is that several other factors, including early paybacks of principal and the fund's **coupon rate,** or the stated rate of interest when the bond was issued, also affect how a bond reacts to changing interest rates.

For a more precise idea of how changing rates will affect a bond fund's value, you should look at a fund's duration, a measure that takes into account not just the bonds' average maturity, but early redemptions and the interest payments thrown off by individual bonds. As with average maturity, the higher a fund's duration, the more its value will fluctuate when interest rates rise or fall. But the advantage to using duration is that the relationship is fairly precise. For example, a fund with a duration of 7 would lose 7% of its value if interest rates rose by one percentage point and gain a like amount if rates fell, while a duration of 9 would mean a loss or gain of 9% for a one-percentage-point rate change.

4. Look at what you're paying for the fund. Before sinking your cash into a fund, you also want to know what you will be paying in fees and expenses. Does the fund charge a sales commission, and if so, is it levied up front or only if you withdraw your money within a certain number of years? If you're buying the fund from a broker, financial planner, or other adviser-salesperson, chances are you will pay a commission, or load. That's fine if the advice you're getting is worth what you're shelling out in a commission (an assumption I would never take for granted). But if you don't mind doing your own legwork, you can sidestep that sales fee and have all your money working for you in a no-load fund.

You also want to evaluate the ongoing expenses you will pay. Just as you do with a fund's performance, you should compare the fund's expense ratio—that is, its annual expenses stated as a percentage of assets—with those of funds in the same category. So if the bond fund you're thinking of buying has an expense ratio of 1.5%, while the average expense ratio for bond funds is less than 1%, you might reasonably wonder why you want to give up a full half percentage point in yield year after year. If you check the fund's performance and find that, somehow, the manager outgains other bond funds despite the drag of higher expenses, then maybe you'll go ahead and invest in the fund anyway (although you'll also want to make sure the manager isn't getting those bigger gains simply by assuming more risk, a problem I'll describe in Chapter 8 when we go into detail about fund fees). But if the fund has high fees and a mediocre return to boot, find another fund. After all, the point to investing is to enrich yourself, not the fund company.

The Prospectus: The Fund Owners' Operating Manual

To say a prospectus makes for boring reading is to say that root canal causes slight discomfort. Crafted by a fund's lawyers to protect the fund from other lawyers, prospectuses are awash in language that is hopelessly dense, needlessly complicated, difficult to understand, and painful to read. No wonder a 1995 survey by the MainStay fund group found that only 28% of fund investors use the prospectus always or most of the time when choosing a fund and only 4.5% claimed the prospectus is written in language that's easy to understand (they must have been lawyers). That said, fund investors should still pore over at least key sections of this document because it gives you details about how a fund invests, what fees you will incur, and what risks you may encounter. This document is so important, in fact, that securities law prohibits a fund company from sending you sales material or an application for a fund without including the prospectus.

In 1995 the Securities and Exchange Commission (SEC) and eight major fund companies launched an experiment to make prospectuses more accessible to investors by making them shorter and having them written in plain English rather than a combination of sleep-inducing jargon and cover-your-posterior legalese. The result of their efforts is what is known as the **profile prospectus**. Basically, each profile prospectus has a standardized format that addresses 11 separate issues, including brief discussions of a fund's investment strategy, risks, fees, expenses, and what types of investors the fund is appropriate for. The key word here is "brief": profile prospectuses are easily contained within a single 8½-by-11-inch page. Conventional prospectuses can easily run to 20 or more pages.

What's more, profile prospectuses are written in, if not a breezy style, at least a straightforward one. The SEC will assess the results of this experiment and decide whether to make these simpler documents a permanent part of the fund scene. In the meantime, some fund companies, such as Vanguard, T. Rowe Price, and Fidelity, are also making their regular prospectuses more readable for nontechie types. For example, in its stock fund prospectuses, Fidelity and some other fund groups provide a table showing a fund's year-by-year returns versus those of competing funds. This not only helps you compare the fund's performance with that of its peers, but it shows you how steady or bumpy a ride the fund has provided its shareholders. But until understandable prose and clear presentation become the norm, investors will have to grapple with what's out there. To make that process less daunting, here's a rundown on the parts of the prospectus you absolutely ought to read and what you will find in those key sections.

• **Investment objectives and strategy:** Toward the front, most prospectuses outline the goals of the fund and then give investors some specifics on how they'll achieve those goals. For example, a bond fund might say that it seeks to maximize current income by investing principally in debt securities of domestic and foreign issuers, or a stock fund might say that it aims to provide long-term capital appreciation or a combination of dividend income and appreciation. Then, in a section often titled "Management Policies" or "Investment Policies" or "Strategies," the prospectus begins to explain, in its own convoluted, often unintelligible way, how it will achieve its goals. For example, a bond fund might say that it will invest at least 65% of its assets in bonds, and then go on to list the various types of bonds the fund can invest in—government and agency obligations, mortgage-backed securities, etc.

Funds tend to give themselves a lot of leeway in the prospectus. For instance, many bond funds that don't specifically have an international focus nonetheless say that they reserve the right to invest a certain portion of their assets in foreign bonds. This isn't necessarily the kind of information that should scare you off a fund, but it's something you would want to know. If you really want to own only U.S. Treasury securities, then you know to move on to another fund. After this overview, most prospectuses then go into excruciating detail about specific investments they may make or various investment strategies they may pursue.

Try to plow through it if you can, but believe me, you're not alone if you are stopped dead in your tracks by sentences like "The mortgage-related securities in which the Fund may invest include those with fixed, floating, and variable interest rates, those with interest rates that change based on multiples of changes in interest rates, and those with interest rates that change inversely to changes in interest rates, as well as stripped mortgage-backed securities which are derivative multiclass mortgage securities." Come again?

• **Risk factors:** This is the part of the prospectus that tells you what might go wrong with the various investments the fund makes. This is done partly to inform you of the risks and partly so the fund can later say "We told you so" if you're dissatisfied by the fund's performance. Typically it explains how the value of the fund might go down if stock prices slide or, in the case of funds that buy bonds, how defaults or rising interest rates would affect the fund's holdings. If the fund invests in foreign securities, the prospectus will alert you to the fact that currency exchange rates can fluctuate significantly, affecting the value of the fund. On occasion this section contains concise, useful, and readable information. For example, T. Rowe Price's bond funds prospectus contains a table that shows how the value of bonds of various maturities fluctuates if interest rates rise or fall one or two percentage points. In most cases, however, this section is a long, technical recitation of vaguely stated risks associated with various kinds of securities the fund invests or might invest in. Again, take a look, but don't despair if you find it too daunting or tedious to get through.

• **Fee table:** This is the one area of the prospectus that's pretty easy to understand. In one of its more investor-friendly moves in recent years, the SEC began requiring in 1988 that funds insert toward the front of the prospectus a table that lays out its sales and operating expenses. One section of the table lists, in percentage terms, the fund's sales charge, redemption fee, and exchange fee, if it charges any of these fees. Another part of the table lists, in percentage terms, the ongoing expenses that are deducted from the fund's assets. These include the investment management fee, other expenses (such as servicing and custodial costs), and any marketing fees the fund might charge. (A true no-load fund will show no sales or marketing fees.) Then, another section of the table gives a hypothetical example showing the actual dollar amount you would have paid in all fees and expenses after selling the fund after one, three, five, or 10 years, assuming a $1,000 original investment that earned 5% annually. By comparing the fee tables of two funds, you can quickly tell which is hitting you up for more money in fees and expenses.

What a Fund's Annual Report Can Tell You

Funds are required by law to send to shareholders annual reports that list each security owned by the fund. In 1993 the SEC also began requiring funds to update shareholders on the fund's performance over the past fiscal year, to discuss the factors that significantly affected that performance, and to include a graph that shows the fund's performance versus an appropriate market index. Funds can include this discussion and the graph in their prospectuses if they like, but most choose to put both in their annual reports. Funds must provide semiannual reports as well. These are somewhat shorter than the annuals, although they still contain a cursory discussion of performance plus a listing of the fund's holdings. At its best, an annual report amounts to an annual checkup of your fund's health, so you should definitely read it. Here are the three sections you will want to focus on:

1. Letter to shareholders. This letter, usually written by the fund manager or an executive of the fund company, should give you a straightforward assessment of the market conditions that prevailed over the past year and how the fund responded to them. If the fund has done well, it should explain why without turning the discussion into a cheerleading rally. (After all, it's not a major feat to make money when the stock market is rising.) The letter should also discuss how the fund has done relative to its competitors.

If the fund has fared poorly over the past year, you should get frank reasons as to why that's happened and what, if anything, is being done to improve performance. You shouldn't be overly concerned just because your fund has lost money in a given year or fallen behind its competitors. You should be concerned, however, if instead of owning up to the lackluster performance, explaining it, and giving a prognosis of future prospects, the manager or fund executive seems to dodge the issue or gives lame excuses that don't ring true.

2. Cumulative performance chart. Most funds include in their annual report a line graph that demonstrates how $10,000 invested in the fund would have grown over the 10 most recent fiscal years or since its inception—and shows how much money you would have accumulated had you invested instead in an appropriate market index. For a stock fund, such an index might be the Standard & Poor's 500; for a bond fund, it could be a common benchmark of bond market performance, such as the Lehman Brothers aggregate bond index. Some funds will also include a line that shows the performance of a fund category or a group of similar funds. Just a quick glance at this chart shows you how your fund performed vs. the market and competitors over a long period of time, and by looking at how often the line in the graph headed down rather than up, you can also gauge how vulnerable the fund is to setbacks.

3. Schedule of investments. This schedule lists by industry or sector (energy, financial, service companies, etc.) each security the fund owns and gives the market value of those shares. This listing, sometimes called the **statement of net assets,** also divulges what percentage of the fund's assets are invested in each industry or sector listed. Should you be poring over each of the securities on this list? Hardly. If you wanted to do that, you could invest in individual stocks. Besides, by the time you get the annual or semiannual report, several weeks have passed and the fund's holdings have probably already changed a bit.

Still, it doesn't hurt to take a glance at the list, if for no other reason than to make sure that there is no glaring discrepancy between what the fund owns and what you thought it owned— such as a large slug of foreign stocks when you thought it bought only domestic issues, or a big chunk of junk bonds (or high-yield bonds, as they're euphemistically called) when you thought you owned a government or investment-grade bond fund.

CHAPTER 4

Making the Most of Money-Market Funds

Safety and Bank-Beating Yields

You can think of money-market funds as mutual funds with training wheels. Money funds (as they're usually called) offer many of the same benefits as their stock and bond fund counterparts—namely, with a small initial investment you can buy into a diversified pool of securities overseen by a professional money manager. But they also come with the advantage of rock-solid stability of principal. Money funds are the only mutual funds whose value per share does not fluctuate from day to day. Rather, their price remains locked in at $1 per share, making them a great way for anxious novices to tiptoe into the mutual fund waters, as well as an ideal place for both tyros and seasoned investors to stash cash they might otherwise put in a bank savings account or CD.

Money funds' stability stems directly from two features. First, as a money fund earns interest on its holdings, it gives you additional shares worth $1 apiece. Result: The share price stays the same, but the value of your account rises as you accumulate more shares. Second, money funds invest almost exclusively in short-term debt securities—such as bank certificates of deposit, corporate IOUs known as **commercial paper,** and Treasury bills and other securities backed by the U.S. government—that have received the highest or nearly highest credit-quality ratings from independent ratings firms such as Standard & Poor's and Moody's Investors Service. Tax-exempt money funds invest in short-term debt securities that have been issued by states and local governments or entities that have the power to issue tax-free securities, such as a local bridge-and-tunnel or water-and-sewer authority.

The overwhelming majority of money funds buy securities of such high quality and spread their purchases among so many holdings (often a hundred or more) that your chances of losing money because of a default are pretty slim. (As explained later in this chapter, those odds are a bit higher for so-called single-state money funds, which stick to the securities of one state.) And since the securities money funds invest in have such short maturities—the SEC prohibits money funds from extending the average maturity of their portfolios beyond 90 days—the chances are also remote that an upward spike in interest rates would knock a money fund for a loss.

All of this means money funds should be able to keep their net asset values stable at $1 a share. Thus, even though money funds are not backed by federal deposit insurance like bank savings accounts and CDs, they offer a high degree of assurance that the value of your principal will never fall. Best of all, they give you better returns than you would earn from a bank. For example, the yield on money funds usually exceeds that offered on bank savings accounts and bank money-market deposit accounts (the banks' version of money funds) by anywhere from one to three percentage points a year.

JUST HOW SAFE ARE MONEY FUNDS?

The short answer: Extremely safe. Still, several episodes over the last few years have raised concerns about the security of money funds. In 1994 and 1995 an estimated 65 fund sponsors had to shore up their money funds' value after the funds suffered losses on so-called derivatives—complex securities whose value is derived from some other asset or index— or on tax-exempt securities whose value declined after Orange County, California, declared bankruptcy in December 1994. In only one case, however, did a fund's net asset value slip below $1. In September 1994 a small money fund that had only institutional shareholders—the $84 million Community Bankers U.S. Government Money Market fund—became the first money fund to break the buck after losing money in derivatives. The fund was liquidated, and investors—again, no individuals, only institutions—received 96 cents on the dollar.

Realizing that some securities simply aren't appropriate for money funds, the Securities and Exchange Commission now prohibits money funds from investing in certain types of derivatives. This and other restrictions make the likelihood of future losses small at best. Does that mean we'll never see other problems with money funds? Probably not. Indeed, some fund experts sensibly recommend against putting a significant amount of your money in single-state tax-exempt money funds because such funds can't cut risk by diversifying their holdings among several states. Nor can we be certain that if there are problems, the sponsor will always step up and bail out a fund. On the other hand, the troubles we're talking about have occurred infrequently—a relative handful of funds out of a total of more than 1,100—and the potential losses we're talking about are small, typically a few pennies on the dollar. So if you want to stay up nights obsessing about something, worry about the constantly expanding universe or why God allows bad things to happen to good people. But don't lose sleep worrying about the safety of money funds.

How Money Funds Should—and Shouldn't—Be Used

Given this combination of security of principal and yields that beat the bank, it's no wonder that by early 1996 investors had poured some $825 billion (or slightly more than a quarter of all the money in mutual funds) into more than 1,100 money funds. Fact is, nearly every investor ought to own a money fund—and use it for the right reasons. Here are a few of those appropriate uses, followed by some examples of ways money funds shouldn't be used.

You should use money funds as:

• **a turbocharged checking account:** Rather than keep your money in a checking account that pays no interest or a piddling amount, consider using a money fund as your primary or backup checking account. Most money funds allow you to write checks against your account balance, redeem shares by telephone, or even have cash wired to your bank account. True, some funds begin charging a per-check fee (typically $5 or so) if you write more than a certain number of checks each month (usually three or five). And many money funds won't let you write checks below a stated minimum amount—usually between $100 and $500. So if you plan on using your money fund as a checking account, make sure the one you choose allows checking privileges consistent with the number and size of checks you write.

• **a place to stash money you'll need soon:** If you are tucking away money you know you'll need within a few years— say, cash to repay a debt, to buy a car, or to put toward a down payment for a home—then a money fund is the ideal place for it. Your cash will earn a decent return, but you won't run the risk that the value of your savings will be decimated by a meltdown in stock or bond prices just when you're ready to tap into it.

- **a temporary parking space for cash you'll invest later:** Let's say you come into a big sum of cash—maybe you finally hit the lottery or (same thing) a rich relative remembered you in her will—but you're not sure how you want to invest it. While you're figuring that out, sink it into a secure money fund, where it will at least earn a reasonable return.

You should *not* use money funds as:

- **a "safe" stash for long-term savings:** Some investors mistakenly believe that money they will be counting on at some time in the future—such as retirement savings—must be kept in a safe place where it won't be subject to the dips and dives of the stock market. So they tuck it away in a money fund or a bank savings account or CD. Not a good idea. Sure, your money is safe from short-term fluctuations in the market. But you're opening yourself up to another even bigger risk—namely, the danger that inflation will erode the purchasing power of your savings.

To keep the value of your long-term savings ahead of inflation, you should invest most of it in stock funds. Of course, even investors who have the majority of their money invested in stock funds will also have a small portion in money funds, both to provide money for daily expenses and to temper the effects of setbacks in the stock or bond market. And if you find that your mix of stock, bond, and money funds still leaves your stomach churning every time you hear a TV report about dropping stock prices, you can always dial back the volatility of your overall holdings by moving some money out of stocks and increasing your money fund balance a bit.

- **a landing place for jumping in and out of the market:** Some financial advisers and mutual fund newsletter writers advocate switching all or most of your money out of stock funds and into money funds when the stock market looks as though it's ready to tumble and then doing the reverse when the market appears ready to rebound for big gains. The problem with such a market-timing strategy is that investors often miss gains by jumping out of the market too soon and waiting too long before getting back in, thereby missing the explosive surge in share prices typical of a rebounding market. Few investment advisers believe even seasoned professionals can successfully time moves in and out of the markets on a regular basis. My advice is don't even try.

You Don't Have to Agonize over Picking a Money Fund

One other big advantage of money funds is that you don't have to spend a lot of time and effort figuring out which one to invest in. Because most of them invest pretty much in the same types of securities, the differences in returns between funds usually aren't worth getting all worked up about. Let's say, for example, you have $10,000 in a money fund yielding 5.25% and you notice a newspaper ad for another fund that yields 5.75%. Should you bother to switch? The difference in return is a piddling $50 a year, *before* taxes. If your original stash is $5,000, then you're talking about only a $25 annual difference.

Unless you're investing substantially more than ten grand, it just doesn't seem worthwhile to spend your life scanning the newspaper ads for a money fund that beats its competitors by a quarter to a half percentage point a year. In other words, don't sweat the small stuff. Rather, take the effort you save from not agonizing over money funds and put it into building a diversified portfolio of funds with solid performance. That said, however, here are five easy-to-follow tips that will help you find a money fund that works for you:

1. Decide what type of money fund you want. You have three basic choices. First, there are **general-purpose money funds,** which typically hold short-term debt securities

such as commercial paper (the short-term IOUs many corporations issue to raise money), large-denomination bank CDs,
Treasury bills, and other U.S. government debt. All the interest
these funds pay is fully taxable at the federal and local level.
Since general-purpose money funds are very secure and usually pay the highest yields, they're the money fund of choice for
most investors.

Then there are **U.S. government-only funds.** As their
name suggests, these funds limit themselves to securities issued or
backed by the U.S. government, which makes them the safest of
an already safe category of funds. To get that extra (and in my
opinion largely unnecessary) margin of safety, you'll probably
have to accept a slightly lower yield than what you'd get on a
general-purpose fund. We're not talking a huge hit here, though,
maybe 0.15% to 0.25% less. So if you're a real risk-averse, belt-
and-suspenders investor, you don't have to give up much to sleep
soundly at night. Some government money funds, however, limit
themselves solely to Treasury bills. And because T-bills (as well as
other Treasury securities) are exempt from state and local tax in
most states, you may be able to grab the Gibraltar-like security
of a Treasury-only fund and still beat the yield of a general-
purpose fund. To compare a Treasury-only fund's yield with that
of a fully taxable general-purpose fund, calculate the taxable
equivalent yield of the Treasury fund by dividing its yield by one
minus your state tax rate.

Let's say you live in a state such as New York, which in 1995
levied a state income tax as high as 7.6%, and you had a choice
between a 100% T-bill fund paying 4.95% or a general-purpose
fund yielding 5.2%. In this case the T-bill fund would be the better choice because its 4.95% state-tax-free yield translates to a
5.4% taxable equivalent yield (4.95% ÷ 1 − .076). Of course, the
advantage isn't huge—0.2% represents just $20 a year extra on a
$10,000 investment. Remember too that the spread between the
yields on T-bill and regular money funds is shifting constantly, so
there's no guarantee the T-bill fund will always have the upper
hand. The best advice: If you really want the extra security, go

with the T-bill fund and don't worry about whether you're up or down a few measly bucks a year.

Finally, there are **tax-free money funds,** which invest in short-term securities issued by states and local governments. National-tax-free money funds invest in the securities of many states and pay interest that is exempt from federal taxes. Because the interest they pay is tax-exempt, the stated yields on tax-free money funds are well below those of general-purpose funds. In late 1995, for example, national-tax-free funds yielded 3.3% on average vs. 5.2% for general-purpose funds.

Depending on your federal tax bracket, however, the tax-free fund could still be the better yield. To someone in the top 39.6% federal tax bracket, for example, that 3.3% translates to the equivalent of a 5.5% taxable yield. (Same formula as above, except you divide the tax-exempt fund's yield by one minus your federal tax bracket, or 3.3% ÷ .604 in this case.) For people in the 36% bracket, the difference between the two funds is a wash: the tax-free fund's taxable equivalent yield is 5.2%, the same on average as for general-purpose funds. Anyone in the 31%, 28%, or 15% brackets would be better off in the general-purpose fund in this case (or, depending on your state and local tax bracket, a Treasury-only fund).

Remember, though, that the gap between taxable and tax-exempt funds is always changing. (Indeed, by early 1996 tax-free money fund yields had slipped to 2.8% on average, while taxable yields held steady at 5.2%, making the taxable funds a better deal even for people in the highest tax brackets.) So you may want periodically to see if you're better off in a tax-exempt, especially if you've moved up a tax bracket or two.

Another breed of tax-exempt money funds, called **single-state tax-free money funds,** limit themselves to the securities of just one state. As a result, the interest they pay is free of federal, state, and, in some cases, local taxes. By limiting themselves to issues of a single state, however, these funds violate a cardinal rule of prudent investing—namely, spreading risk by diversifying. This lack of diversity hurt several California-only tax-free money funds in 1994 when the Orange County, California, issues they held dropped in value after the county declared bankruptcy following an estimated $2 billion loss due to soured derivative investments in its investment fund. The sponsors of these money funds poured money into their funds to make up for the losses, so no fund shareholders lost a cent. Still, given the lack of diversity in these funds, I think conservative investors ought to avoid them altogether and even risk takers ought to put only a small portion of their cash into single-state tax-free funds.

2. Compare its yield to that of similar funds. Once you've decided what kind of money fund you want, you should make sure that the specific funds you're considering offer competitive yields. No need to make a federal project out of this. Just glance occasionally at the listings of money fund yields that appear in the Sunday business sections of many newspapers to insure that your fund's payout is within a quarter of a percentage point or so of the yield offered by similar funds.

3. Check out its fees. Virtually no money funds charge a sales commission to investors, but all pass on operating expenses to shareholders. Indeed, because all money funds largely mine the same vein of securities when they invest, differences in yields mostly come down to differences in expense levels. In other words, the funds with the lowest expenses will usually have the best yields and long-term returns. So if you really want to be diligent, check out the annual expense ratio of your money fund. That ratio shows, in percentage terms, how much the fund company siphons off to pay the expenses for running the fund. In general, money fund expense ratios range from 0.5% to 0.7%, and I'd be wary of paying much above that range.

One caveat: Sometimes half or more of money fund sponsors temporarily absorb a portion of their expenses or waive them entirely, according to IBC/Donoghue, Inc., a company that tracks money-market performance. This, of course, inflates the fund's yield—for a while. The fund sponsors aren't doing this because they're altruists. Rather, the idea is to lure people into the fund, start charging expenses later, and hope nobody notices—or that those who do will be too lazy or busy to move. Some investors make it a point to move their cash around so that it's always in a money fund that's cutting some slack on expenses. But unless you have huge amounts of cash and nothing better to do with your time than monitor money fund yields, I'd say the few extra bucks you gain aren't worth the effort.

4. Think big. All other things being equal, you should opt for a large money fund (say, $1 billion or more in assets) that is sold by a major fund sponsor such as Benham, Dreyfus, Fidelity, T. Rowe Price, or Vanguard. For one thing, larger funds can spread out their costs over a larger asset base, which can help keep expenses down. (Some big money funds, unfortunately, don't pass economies of scale onto shareholders. The $2.8 billion Alliance Money Reserves money fund, for example, had a whopping 1% annual expense ratio as of early 1996.) Size also counts another way: if a money fund buys securities that turn sour, a sponsor with big bucks and a high profile is more likely to have enough capital (and motivation to keep a clean image) to buy back the bad investments from the fund and keep investors whole. For a list of large money funds with reasonable fees and competitive returns, see pages 269–270 in the appendix.

5. When in doubt, opt for convenience. Since the difference in returns among most money funds is relatively small, don't be afraid to go with the fund that makes your life simpler. So if you invest primarily in the stock or bond funds of a certain fund family or you hold your mutual funds in a discount brokerage account, you should probably stick with the money-market fund offered by that fund group or broker. On the other hand, if you envision using your money fund as a souped-up checking account, make sure you get a fund that lets you write an unlimited number of checks and allows you to write checks for small sums. Life is too short to waste agonizing over money funds. Just pick one and move on.

CHAPTER 5

Aiming for Growth with Stock Funds

Why Most Investors Should Focus on Stock Funds

Stock funds are the workhorses of the mutual fund world. They are the ones you can depend on to power your portfolio to long-term double-digit gains that will keep the purchasing power of your investment stash ahead of inflation. For example, statistics dating all the way back to 1871—that's right, *1871,* not 1971—show that stocks have outperformed bonds just over 60% of the time over 12-month periods, nearly 75% of the time over five-year stretches, and more than 80% of the time over 10 years.

The message of stocks' superior performance is obviously getting through to fund investors. From 1985 through 1993 investors had more money stashed away in bond than in stock funds. But by early 1996 the situation had completely reversed, as investors boosted their stock fund holdings to just over $1.4 billion, or roughly 75% more than the $800 billion–plus they held in bond portfolios.

Stocks' performance edge is important to investors for two reasons. First, those superior returns increase your chances of achieving most financial goals. For example, let's say you'd like to accumulate a retirement fund of $300,000 over the next 20 years. With an average return of 10% annually, you could reasonably expect to reach that goal by investing just under $4,800 a year. But if you had to settle for, say, a 7% return, you wouldn't be able to reach your goal unless you came up with almost an extra $2,100 each and every year. (Technically you would have to put more away in each case because income taxes would reduce the buildup of your money, but you get the idea.)

Second, stocks' ability to generate returns that outrun inflation assures that the money you're putting away will actually grow in value, even after adjusting for the fact that most of the things you buy will be more expensive in the future. After all, what good is having more dollars if those greenbacks can't buy you as much as the stash you had when you started? So for keeping ahead of inflation and making your money grow, stock funds are clearly the superior choice for the overwhelming majority of fund investors. This means that people investing for the long term should have most of—in some cases nearly all—their money in stock funds. Even conservative investors, such as people nearing or already in retirement, should have at least a portion of their investment portfolio in stock funds to protect the purchasing power of their money.

Of course, just because stock funds have outperformed other types of funds in the past doesn't guarantee a repeat performance in the future. But I think, as do many investment advisers, that stocks are an odds-on favorite for coming out ahead over the long haul. Why? Because when you invest in a stock fund, you are actually buying a piece of all the companies in which the fund owns shares. Depending on the type of stock fund you choose, you may indirectly own stakes in firms ranging from large established firms like General Motors or large new firms like Microsoft to small, recently hatched, fast-growing companies that aren't household names today but may be the GMs and Microsofts of the future.

So you are essentially buying the growth potential of those businesses, which, while not quite limitless, is huge. Take Microsoft, for example. If you had been smart or lucky enough to invest $1,000 in Bill Gates's software company back in 1986, before anyone had ever heard of Windows 95, your one grand would have grown within nine years to more than $90,000. Bonds and money-market investments, on the other hand, merely offer the promise of paying interest and repaying your principal at the end of the bond's term. If you buy a bond when it's issued and hold it to maturity, your return is definitely limited: the best you can get is the rate of interest you were promised.

You would be making a colossal mistake, however, to assume that stocks will hand you a 10% or better return unfailingly year after year after year. That is an average that masks wide fluctuations in any given year. In 1995, for example, stocks went on a rampage, rolling up average gains of 37.5%. The year before that they gained just 1.3%. For stocks' higher returns, you also accept the possibility—make that the probability—of short-term setbacks or losses. More than 80 times this century stock prices have dropped 10% or more. Sometimes the losses can be wrenching. From its highest level in 1973 to its low point in 1974, for example, the Standard & Poor's 500 stock index fell a staggering 48%.

Nonetheless, investors who wait out these downturns rather than panic and sell are rewarded with attractive returns. For example, had you invested $10,000 in the typical stock mutual fund in September 1987, the stock market's crash the following month would have hammered down the value of your investment to less than $7,700. But if you hung in, you would have recouped your loss within roughly three years—and inside of eight years your 10 grand would have more than doubled to nearly $22,500, representing a 10.5% annual return—not bad for an investment made just prior to one of the scariest stock market meltdowns in recent history.

Recently stocks have performed closer to the 15%-a-year yardstick than the annual long-term average of 10% or so, which suggests that you shouldn't get too used to the fat returns of the last decade. That makes sense. Though no one knows what the future holds for stock returns (or the returns on any investment, for that matter), I think it would be unreasonable to expect—and pure folly to count on—returns continuing to exceed the historical averages indefinitely. On the other hand, you shouldn't hold off investing in stocks simply because returns appear likely to slip back somewhat from their recent abnormally high levels—or because you fear stock prices will nosedive. As long as you are investing cash that you can afford not to dip into for five years or longer—in other words, as long as you'll have enough time to recover from a market setback—you are better off seeking the higher returns that stock funds have shown they can generate.

Sorting through Stock Fund Choices

Although all the 3,300 or so stock funds that operate today invest in stocks, not all invest in the same *kinds* of stocks. Some, for example, specialize in finding fast-growing companies, while others don't look at profit growth so much as the value of the companies' underlying assets. Many managers are willing to take big risks to grab outsize returns; others settle for more modest gains while protecting shareholders' capital. Needless to say, things can get confusing when you start sifting through the thousands of funds out there to find ones whose investing strategy jibes with your goals. To bring at least a bit of order to the chaotic fund scene, fund ratings firms over the years have divided funds into a variety of categories and investing styles that attempt to reflect the investment objectives of different funds as well as the methods they use to reach those objectives. The idea has merit: by putting similar funds into the same categories, you can see how your fund stacks up against others that invest the same way and have the same goal.

On a practical level, however, the execution of this idea isn't as clear-cut as you might think. For one thing, not all the fund rating services use the same category names. What's more, as the number of funds has skyrocketed, so has the variety of categories. One premier ratings service, Morningstar Mutual Funds, separates funds into no fewer than 37 distinct categories (and that's not including broad categories that comprise several smaller ones).

As if the lack of standardization and proliferation of categories didn't make things complicated enough, there's a more central problem with pigeonholing funds into categories—namely, funds in the same category can have different investing strategies or styles that produce drastically different returns and subject investors to dramatically different degrees of risk. So, for example, you could have two growth-and-income funds whose performance differs radically because one fund gets its combination of capital growth and current income by buying volatile small-company stocks and long-term bonds while the other invests primarily in large, established firms that pay steady dividends.

Even though this system of categories and styles is far from perfect, however, it's the best fund investors have to go on for now—and if nothing else, it at least provides a way to narrow down the constantly expanding universe of funds into somewhat more digestible chunks. To help you choose the stock funds that are right for you, the rest of this chapter will describe the major stock fund categories, explain how funds within those categories operate, and suggest when funds in each category are appropriate. (International funds as well as index funds, which attempt to match the returns of a standard market benchmark, will be discussed separately in Chapters 7 and 11, respectively.) At the beginning of each category I'll include a brief statistical portrait that will reveal at a glance how funds in that group have performed. After going over the categories, I'll outline the importance of also looking at a fund's investing style or the strategy a fund uses to achieve the objective described in its category name, and then I'll explain why fund investors should invest in a mix of funds with different categories and styles.

For the names of specific funds you might consider buying, check out pages 273–280 in the appendix. As I note there, these are not the "best" funds, nor are they the only funds you should consider investing in. And you certainly shouldn't panic if funds you already own don't show up on this list. Rather, these are funds that, by virtue of their consistently solid performance in the past, are worth a look from investors seeking reliable performers. In short, think of the funds listed in the appendix as candidates you might consider along with other choices you come up with on your own. In any case, I don't recommend buying any fund on my (or anyone else's) suggestion alone. Rather, you should apply the principles outlined throughout this book and in particular the guidelines detailed in Chapter 9.

Aggressive Growth Funds

% Average Annual Gain[1]

Volatility	3 Years	5 Years	10 Years	Highest Annual Gain/Year[2]	Lowest Annual Gain or Loss/Year[2]	Worst Quarter/ Year[2]
Very high	17.2%	16.8%	12.8%	53.9%/'91	-14.4%/'84	-25.5%/'87

Source: Morningstar, Inc., Chicago. [1]To April 1, 1996 [2]Calendar year or quarter since 1976

Like drag-car racers who keep the pedal to the metal, aggressive growth funds try to speed to big gains while taking on some sizable risks. Result: These funds often lead the pack in average annual returns over long periods of time—as well as over shorter periods when the stock market is booming—but they also have some crack-ups along the way. Take the Twentieth Century Ultra Investors fund, for example. Over the 10 years to 1996, this fund gained 19.8% a year on average, a record that includes a staggering 86.5% gain in 1991. But over the years investors have had to hang on through some frightening slides as well. In 1984, for example, this fund lost 19.5% and during the fourth quarter of 1987 it dropped 26.7% in value. Clearly not a choice for the faint of heart.

Aggressive growth funds achieve their gains by investing in growth stocks, or shares of companies whose revenues and profits are growing at a rapid rate, often 15% or more a year. Although many aggressive growth funds home in on shares of small and medium-size companies, other funds in this group will invest in fast-growing companies of any size. Some of these funds may also engage in somewhat risky investing strategies such as borrowing money to buy securities, making bets on stock market indexes or options, or selling short—that is, borrowing securities, selling them at the market price, and then hoping to profit by replacing those securities after buying them back at a cheaper price in the future. Since growth companies pay no dividends, or very small ones, aggressive growth funds rarely make income or dividend distributions. Their returns consist almost entirely of the capital gains that result from increases in the share prices of the stocks they own. If investors become disenchanted with growth stocks—say, for not delivering expected profit increases—they dump them quickly, which can lead to sudden steep losses in aggressive growth funds. And unlike some other types of funds, aggressive growth funds rarely take defensive measures—such as increasing the amount of cash reserves in the fund—even if stock prices look as though they're ready to tumble. As a result, aggressive growth funds usually do worse than the market overall during market downturns, often falling twice as much as stock prices in general.

Best for: Investors who can afford to put away their money for at least five years and who won't bail out when faced with downdrafts of 20% or more.

Not suited for: Anyone looking for a fund that generates regular income or risk-averse investors who blanch at the thought of double-digit setbacks.

Growth Funds

% Average Annual Gain[1]

Volatility	3 Years	5 Years	10 Years	Highest Annual Gain/Year[2]	Lowest Annual Gain or Loss/Year[2]	Worst Quarter/Year[2]
High to very high	13.7%	13.7%	12.1%	38.1%/'80	-4.5%/'90	-21.1%/'87

Source: Morningstar, Inc., Chicago. [1]To April 1, 1996 [2]Calendar year or calendar quarter since 1976

Growth funds also invest in shares of rapidly growing companies that may range in size from very small to very large. Generally, though, growth funds are more likely than their aggressive growth siblings to concentrate on medium- to large-growth companies, including corporate giants like Coca-Cola, McDonald's, and Disney. As a result they tend to mirror the returns of the overall stock market in both rising and falling markets. Many, but not all, growth fund managers will also build up a cash reserve if they feel stock prices are getting frothy. Because of their holdings of somewhat more established companies and willingness to move into cash, growth funds typically won't zoom to the huge gains that their aggressive cousins do in bull markets—but they tend to hold up better than aggressive funds when the market heads south. These funds can still get hit for sizable temporary losses, though, as demonstrated by the 21.1% decline growth funds overall suffered in the fourth quarter of 1987.

The best-known (and largest, with some $56 billion in assets in mid-1996) growth fund in the United States is Fidelity Magellan, which racked up spectacular gains under legendary investor Peter Lynch in the seventies and eighties. While growth funds typically diversify among a wide range of industries, in recent years many growth funds have focused more of their holdings in the technology sector.

At one point in 1995, for example, Jeff Vinik, Magellan's manager at the time, had sunk 42% of the fund's assets in tech stocks. While Vinik played the tech boom masterfully, he later shifted nearly 20% of the fund's assets into bonds, a move that dragged the fund's three-year return below that of the Standard & Poor's 500-stock index. Amid an orgy of second-guessing by the financial press, Vinik left Fidelity in June 1996 to start his own investment firm, and Robert Stansky, a more traditional Fidelity growth-stock picker, assumed the reins of the fund. Such a concentration in technology, bonds, or any other area shouldn't necessarily scare you off a particular growth fund. Just remember that moving a big portion of assets from one sector to another can make a fund highly volatile—and could lead to subpar returns if the manager's call turns out to be wrong.

Best for: Investors seeking long-term growth of capital who can tolerate the normal ups and downs of the stock market, as well as some potentially severe declines in a bear market. For most long-term investors, growth funds should be a core holding around which the rest of their portfolio is built.

Not suited for: Anyone who doesn't have the time or temperament to ride out a prolonged market slide or conservative investors whose primary need is current income (although such investors should definitely think about stashing at least a bit of their money in a fund that provides growth).

Small-Company Funds

% Average Annual Gain[1]

Volatility	3 Years	5 Years	10 Years	Highest Annual Gain/Year[2]	Lowest Annual Gain or Loss/Year[2]	Worst Quarter/ Year[2]
Very high	15.7%	16.5%	12.5%	49.2%/'91	-10.1%/'90	-22.9/'87

Source: Morningstar, Inc., Chicago. [1]To April 1, 1996 [2]Calendar year since 1976

As the category name suggests, funds in this group invest in shares of small companies. The reason for this focus: Over the long term, small-fry stocks that are often overlooked by Wall Street analysts can sometimes outgain their big-company counterparts by one to two percentage points or so a year. In the investment world, that's a Grand Canyon–size gap. Problem is, there's no hard-and-fast standard for what size stocks small-company funds can actually invest in. Some buy only the smallest of the small—that is, companies with market capitalizations below $250 million. (**Market capitalization, or market cap,** is just a fancy term meaning the total market value of all of a company's outstanding shares. If a corporation has two million shares of stock outstanding that trade at $50 apiece, then that company has a market cap of $100 million.) Other small-company funds may also invest in so-called midcap companies—ones with market capitalizations of $250 million to $1 billion—or even corporations with market caps above $1 billion. (To put this market cap issue in perspective, a very large company like IBM has a market capitalization in excess of $50 billion.)

In general, the smaller the companies the fund owns, the bigger the potential rewards and the more the fund's returns will fluctuate both up and down. Funds within the small-company category can also differ dramatically in how they achieve their gains. Consider, for example, two small-company funds offered by the same fund company, T. Rowe Price. At the T. Rowe Price New Horizons fund, manager Jack Laporte snaps up shares of small to midsize companies with profits that are zooming along at an above average pace.

Meanwhile T. Rowe Price Small-Cap Value manager Preston Athey is more likely to pass on such highfliers and, instead, stock his portfolio with shares of very small companies (typically market caps well below $250 million) that are undervalued—that is, selling at a discount to their true worth. Two small-company funds in the same fund family, two dramatically different strategies. Whichever approach appeals to you, remember that small-company and large-company stocks tend to play leapfrog—that is, small stocks will outperform large shares for a few years, and then the big guys will jump into the lead again for a while. So don't be surprised if small-cap funds appear to stall occasionally on their way to superior long-term gains.

Best for: Seekers of long-term capital gains who can tolerate temporary pullbacks of 20% or more and investors looking to expand beyond mostly large-company stock fund holdings.

Not suited for: Income-oriented investors or anyone too impatient to wait out extended periods where small-company stocks lose out to large-stock funds.

Growth-and-Income Funds

% Average Annual Gain[1]

Volatility	3 Years	5 Years	10 Years	Highest Annual Gain/Year[2]	Lowest Annual Gain or Loss/Year[2]	Worst Quarter/ Year[2]
Moderate to high	13.3%	13.1%	11.3%	31.6%/'95	-4.5%/'90	-19.2/'87

Source: Morningstar, Inc., Chicago. [1]To April 1, 1996 [2]Calendar year since 1976

Equity-Income Funds

% Average Annual Gain[1]

Volatility	3 Years	5 Years	10 Years	Highest Annual Gain/Year[2]	Lowest Annual Gain or Loss/ Year[2]	Worst Quarter/ Year[2]
Moderate	12.3%	13.2%	10.8%	31.2%/'76	-5.8%/'90	-15.1%/'87

Source: Morningstar, Inc., Chicago. [1]To April 1, 1996 [2]Calendar year since 1976

Balanced Funds

% Average Annual Gain[1]

Volatility	3 Years	5 Years	10 Years	Highest Annual Gain/Year[2]	Lowest Annual Gain or Loss/ Year[2]	Worst Quarter/ Year[2]
Moderate	10.0%	11.4%	10.5%	28.7%/'82	-2.9%/'94	-11.2%/'87

Source: Morningstar, Inc., Chicago. [1]To April 1, 1996 [2]Calendar year since 1976

These three types of funds—collectively sometimes called total return funds—have a common goal: providing steady long-term growth of capital while simultaneously throwing off reliable dividends. They achieve that goal, however, in slightly different ways. And I mean slightly—in some cases it's really a judgment call as to which of these groups a particular fund falls into. Growth-and-income funds typically invest in a combination of dividend-paying stocks and **convertible securities** (bonds or special types of stocks that pay interest but can also be converted into the company's regular shares). Some growth-and-income funds may also leaven their mix with bonds. Equity-income funds invest in a similar mix of securities, but they usually emphasize stocks and convertible securities that pay above average dividends and are more likely than growth-and-income funds to also hold bonds. As a result, equity-income funds generally have higher annual yields—essentially the amount of dividends they pay divided by the fund's net asset value—than growth-and-income portfolios.

Balanced funds split their portfolios between stocks and interest-paying securities such as bonds and convertibles. Typically, balanced funds strive to keep anywhere from 50% to 60% of their holdings in stocks and the rest in bonds, although the prospectus usually gives the manager the leeway to alter that mix to as little as 25% of stocks or bonds at given times. Due to their generally higher investments in bonds and convertibles, balanced funds typically have higher dividend yields than growth-and-income or equity-income funds and, indeed, are usually among the highest-yielding stock funds.

Growth-and-income funds, on the other hand, concentrate their mix more toward growth than balanced and equity-income funds do, so they generally have the lowest yields within the total return group. Because the dividends and interest payments their holdings throw off provide a cushion of sorts when stock prices slide, all three types usually hold up better than growth funds when the market turns sour. These funds lag behind more aggressive funds in a raging bull market, however.

Best for: Risk-averse investors and anyone seeking current income without forgoing the potential for capital growth. Total return funds are also a great choice for beginners who want to wade slowly into the mutual fund waters, as well as for investors who plan on holding only one or two funds.

Not suited for: Anyone who needs maximum capital growth. These funds would be considered a bit too conservative for younger investors who are salting away money for retirement.

Specialty and Other Types of Funds

In addition to the six major categories just noted, a variety of other smaller categories of stock funds cater to more specialized needs. For example, about three dozen so-called socially responsible funds try to avoid investing in companies that engage in objectionable behavior such as polluting the environment or mistreating their employees. That idea appeals to many individual investors, but it has two hitches: first, not all funds (not to mention investors) agree on what's socially responsible; second, aside from a few notable exceptions like the Parnassus Fund, most funds with a conscience don't perform as well as conventional funds.

There are also sector or specialty funds that, rather than diversifying their holdings across many industry groups, concentrate their assets in a particular sector of the market. For example, nearly 30 funds home in on shares of technology companies, while roughly 20 specialize in health care stocks. By narrowing their focus to only one part of the market, specialty funds can sometimes score huge gains—in just the first nine months of 1995, for example, some technology funds soared to returns of 60% or more.

But one year's top sector may be a cellar dweller the following year, as was the case with funds that specialize in gold and other precious metals stocks, many of which plummeted to losses of 15% to 25% in 1994 after topping the charts the previous year. If you want to own a fund that sticks to a particular sector because you believe it has superior long-term growth potential—which is how many pros feel about technology companies—that's fine. But limit such a specific bet to a small portion of your holdings. Similarly, if you're looking for a bit more protection from inflation, there's nothing wrong with putting a small amount of your money—say, 5% to 10% of your overall investment in stock funds—into a natural resources or precious metals sector fund. But don't try hopping from one sector to another in an attempt to land in next year's winner. Few, if any, investors can pull off such a feat on a regular basis. Don't waste your time and money trying.

The Importance of Style

Maybe you couldn't care less whether hemlines are long or short, double-breasted suits are in or out, or rap or rock music dominates the airwaves. But it is crucial that you get to know a fund's investing style before you sink money into it. Why bother learning about a fund's style if you already know what category it's in? Because the category name usually tells you only what the fund's objectives are—aggressive growth, growth, or growth-and-income, for instance. But it's the fund's investing style that tells you *how* the manager hopes to achieve those aims. Furthermore, understanding fund styles isn't merely a matter of academic interest. Studies show that investment style accounts for at least 75% of a typical stock fund's return.

There are two basic questions you must answer to determine a fund's style: (1) Does the fund invest primarily in large or small stocks or something in between? and (2) Does the manager take a growth or value approach to investing?

1. Does the fund invest primarily in large or small stocks or something in between? Fund managers generally stick to stocks of a particular size. Some fund skippers, for example, prefer large-company stocks—that is, shares of big, established corporations with total market values in excess of $5 billion. One reason to favor such issues is that they can generate steady profits and hold up well during recessions and other times of economic turbulence. Large-company stocks—aka blue chips or large-caps (short for "large capitalization")—also appeal to many managers because Wall Street securities analysts generate tons of detailed financial information on them, making it easier to analyze their prospects. On the other hand, because so many people follow these companies, it's hard to unearth undiscovered opportunities that may lead to spectacular gains.

Other managers prefer homing in on shares of small firms, generally those with market capitalizations below $500 million. These often young and often entrepreneurial businesses are capable of explosive gains—plus over long periods of time very small shares can outpace their bigger brethren by one to two percentage points or so a year. But they are also somewhat riskier than large stocks since their share prices can drop farther when the stock market skids.

Still other managers play the middle ground by investing in so-called midcap stocks—total market values between $500 million and $5 billion—or by buying stocks of various sizes. The best way to tell if a fund that claims to invest in small-cap, large-cap, or midcap stocks actually does is to check out the fund's median market capitalization. If a fund has a median market cap of, say, $1 billion, that means roughly half the fund's assets are invested in shares of companies with market values above $1 billion and half below. A representative of the fund should be able to provide that figure, but if a rep can't, you can get information about the market cap of shares in a fund's portfolio by consulting publications such as *Morningstar Mutual Funds* and *Value Line Mutual Fund Survey,* which are described in Chapter 13.

2. Does the manager take a growth or value approach to investing? Size aside, the chief style distinction is between growth and value managers. Growth investors search for companies whose revenues and earnings are growing rapidly, usually at a 15%-or-better annual pace. Such successful companies generally command top prices, however, and if they don't meet their rosy profit projections, their share prices can quickly go into a tailspin.

Growth stocks will typically have an above average **price-earnings ratio,** or **P/E** in Wall Street parlance. To get a stock's P/E ratio, you take the company's current stock price and divide it by the company's most recent year's earnings per share. So if a stock trades at $40 and the company's earnings for the last four quarters were $2 a share, the stock would have a P/E of 20. A high P/E ratio usually shows that investors are enthusiastic about the future prospects of a company and are willing to pay a high price for a company's future earnings. P/E ratios can vary substantially over time, but the average P/E ratio for the stock market overall generally hovers around 14. It can get as low as 6 during recessions and zoom above 20 during an economic expansion. Growth stocks typically have P/Es of 20 or higher, which reflects the lofty expectations investors have for such stocks. To see if a growth fund truly invests in growth stocks, check out the average P/E ratio for the stocks it holds. If a fund representative can't (or won't) give you this figure, you can find it in the Morningstar or Value Line publications.

Value managers, conversely, are bargain hunters who scour the investing landscape for companies trading at prices that don't reflect the true value of their assets or earnings ability. Often the companies they invest in are ignored or disdained by other investment pros, which depresses their share prices. Value managers are essentially contrarians, then. They buy stocks that the conventional wisdom says are lousy bets. Like browsers at a flea market, they sift through companies other investors are eager to unload, hoping to find true bargains that have been thrown out with the trash. Unlike growth investors, value managers tend to buy stocks that have low P/E ratios—a sign that investors don't have much confidence in these companies.

Another barometer value investors use for stocks in some industries is a low **price-to-book value ratio**. This figure—which is the stock price divided by the value of a company's assets per share after subtracting its liabilities—shows what kind of value investors place on a company's assets. In general, the lower a stock's price-to-book ratio, the less investment pros believe the company is worth—and the more likely a value investor is to be attracted to the stock. As with a P/E ratio, you can find the average price-to-book value ratio for all the stocks in a fund in the Morningstar or Value Line publications. A fund representative isn't likely to be able to provide you with this figure.

But using P/Es and price-to-book ratios can be difficult and even misleading at times. Some stocks, for example, could still be value plays despite having a high P/E or price-to-book ratio. So for most fund investors the easiest and probably most accurate way of determining a fund's investing style is to refer to the so-called style boxes that are found in the one-page synopses for each fund in publications such as *Morningstar Mutual Funds* and the *Value Line Mutual Fund Survey*. (To see what the style box looks like, take a look at the *Morningstar* page reproduced on page 240.) By simply glancing at the style box, you can get a decent idea of what kinds of stocks a fund actually owns, which may or may not jibe with the impression created by the fund's category label or its name. (The Dean Witter American Value fund, for example, actually invests for growth.)

Once you ascertain where a fund comes down on the size and growth vs. value issues, you will have a good idea of what kinds of stocks the manager buys and how the fund is likely to behave in different markets. You'll also be better able to compare the fund's performance with that of similar funds. For example, if you own a small-company stock fund that uses a growth strategy, you should compare the fund with other small-cap growth funds. Similarly, if a manager invests in beaten-down shares of large companies, you should evaluate his or her success in pursuing that strategy by stacking the fund up against other large-cap value funds.

Why You Need a Mix of Investing Styles

If you knew that one style tended to outperform the others, you might be tempted to put all or nearly all your money in funds that use that style, right? Well, guess what. Studies show that over very long periods of time, certain styles do perform better. As I've already noted, over many decades small-cap stocks generally outperform their larger counterparts by roughly two percentage points annually. And other studies show that value investing edges out growth. Trinity Investment Management in Cambridge, Massachusetts, for example, found that over the 24 years from 1969 to 1992 value stocks bested growth shares by the hefty margin of 2.6 percentage points a year.

So why not put all your money in small-cap value funds? A few reasons. First, although many investment pros believe small-cap stocks will continue to win out over very long periods, there's always the chance that the tables could turn and growth could kick value's butt over the next 20 to 30 years. Second, academic studies are one thing and the real world is another. Translating small-cap stocks' outperformance into real returns to fund investors is often difficult because of the higher research and transaction costs involved in buying small-cap shares. Third, over shorter time periods the race between growth and value and small- and large-cap stocks is much more of a seesaw affair in which different styles take turns in the lead for periods of approximately two to five years. Growth stocks, for example, often dominate in stagnant economies or during recessions when investors are particularly drawn to companies that can post big profits. Value stocks, on the other hand, usually win out when the economy is pulling out of a recession and the stock market outlook is especially uncertain.

As for the race between small- and large-cap stocks, their respective fortunes tend to ebb and flow over longer periods based, in part, on their popularity among large institutional investors. So you'll have periods such as the six years from 1977 through 1982 when small-cap stocks clobbered the big guys, followed by an eight-year stretch from 1983 through 1990 when large-cap stocks ruled the markets. Since few, if any, investors are putting away *all* their money for the 20 to 30 years it might take for small-value stocks to assert their dominance, you want to be able to reap the benefits of different styles when they're on top.

Unfortunately, trying to predict which style is about to dominate is as difficult as predicting what next year's music or wardrobe fashion fads will be. So while the notion of surfing from one style to the next and riding each for peak returns is appealing, your chances of pulling it off are somewhere between zero and zilch. A far better strategy is to own several funds with different styles. That way you'll be able to take advantage of whatever investing fashion is in, and you'll smooth out some of the ups and downs that result when the market shifts gears and one style falls out of favor and another begins to pick up speed. The number of funds and styles you will need depends largely on how long you plan to put away your money, your appetite for risk, whether or not you're depending on your funds to generate income for everyday expenses, and how much time you're willing to spend creating and monitoring a fund portfolio. The portfolio-building strategies outlined in Chapter 10 will help you sort out these issues and create a mix of funds that makes sense for you. Once you've settled on the right mix, you can then turn to page 273 in the appendix for some suggestions on individual funds that can help you carry out your strategy.

CHAPTER 6

Investing for Income with Bond Funds

Bond Funds Can Reduce but Not Eliminate Risk

Mutual funds that hold bonds have long had a reputation as an ideal investment if you want to earn more on your money than you would at a bank without subjecting your stash to the sometimes wild fluctuations of the stock market. And by and large, bond funds have provided security while generating decent returns. From 1980 to 1996, for example, government bond funds overall have returned about 9.6% annually, while slipping into the red only one year during that span. That ability to spin out gains and sidestep losses no doubt accounts for the popularity of bond funds, which have grown from just over 300 with $135 billion in assets in 1985 to nearly 3,500 funds with just over $800 billion in assets by early 1996.

But even stodgy bond funds can have a wild side, as many investors discovered in 1994. During that year, the Federal Reserve Board hiked interest rates six times to slow down the economy and ward off inflation. As a result, many bond investors found themselves swimming in red ink. For example, long-term government bond funds—those that invest mostly in bonds that mature in 20 or more years—dropped roughly 6% in value as long-term Treasuries posted their worst loss in more than 25 years. And even some supposedly ultraconservative short-term bond funds—ones that typically stick to issues that mature in less than four years—got whacked with losses. PaineWebber Short-Term U.S. Government Income, for example, lost 5% in 1994 largely because rising interest rates devastated the value of the volatile derivative investments the fund had loaded up on to boost its yield. The lesson: No investment is entirely risk-free, not even supposedly stodgy bonds.

What 1994's reality check makes clear is that before sinking your money in bond funds, you should first understand the forces that drive their returns. This chapter will outline the rewards and risks of investing in bond funds, help you sort through the wide variety of bond fund choices available, and then give advice on how to choose funds that suit your financial needs. In addition to bond funds mentioned favorably in this chapter, on pages 277–280 you will find the names of other bond funds you might consider investing in based on their record of above average long-term performance.

Who Needs Bond Funds? Probably You

Bond funds deserve at least a supporting role in almost all investors' portfolios. Specifically, here are four reasons you might want to own one or more:

1. You need regular income. Since bond funds pay monthly dividends that you can reinvest or take in cash, they are ideal for people relying on their investments to provide income for living expenses. To get an idea of how much income a fund will generate, check out its yield. There are a variety of ways to calculate yields, but you should ask a fund representative for its **SEC yield**. Also called a **30-day yield,** this figure, calculated according to a standard formula derived by the Securities and Exchange Commission, essentially projects the fund's most recent 30-day payout into the future and eliminates tricks some funds employ to inflate their yields artificially. The higher that figure, the more income the fund throws off. But keep in mind that funds with the highest yields generally carry the highest risks—that is, their principal value is most likely to fluctuate widely up or down.

2. You'll need to dip into your investment stash soon. If you are investing for a short-term goal—such as buying a car within a few years—you should also consider bond funds. That's because even over relatively short periods of time you are far less likely to lose money in bond funds than in stock portfolios. It would be rare, for example, to lose money in intermediate-term government bonds if you hold them for at least five years.

3. You would like to dampen the volatility of your portfolio. Bond funds are not a substitute for stock funds; they simply don't have the growth and inflation-fighting power. But because bonds don't always move in sync with stocks, adding a bond fund or two to your stock fund lineup can tame the fluctuations of your portfolio overall. For example, a portfolio invested solely in blue-chip stocks would have earned an average return of 14.5% for the 20 years from 1976 through 1995 and experienced a worst monthly loss of 21.5% (in October 1987). A portfolio with 60% in blue chips and 40% in government bonds would have earned slightly lower average returns of 12.7% but would have suffered a monthly loss no worse than 11.4% (also in October 1987).

4. You're looking for tax-exempt income. Given the recent emphasis on narrowing the federal budget deficit, tax-advantaged investments are rapidly becoming an endangered species. But municipal bond funds continue to pay out dividends that are free of federal taxes and, in some cases, state and local levies as well. You should never assume you're better off in a tax-exempt rather than a taxable bond fund. But with federal tax rates ranging as high as 39.6% in early 1996, the odds are that high-income investors will fare better in munis once the tax benefits are taken into account (unless, of course, the flat tax or some other tax reform erodes munis' privileged status).

Sizing Up Risk and Reward

To reap the advantages of bond funds, however, you must first understand the two main factors that account for bond funds' returns as well as the swings in their share prices—namely, credit risk and interest-rate risk.

1. Credit risk. When you invest in a bond, you are essentially lending money to the bond issuer, whether it is a government or a corporation. Ultimately, then, bonds are nothing more than the promise of that issuer to make timely interest payments to you and to repay the face amount, or principal, of the bond at the end of its term. Credit risk measures the likelihood of the bond issuer making good on that obligation or, looked at from the pessimist's view, the chances that the issuer will default on its promise. The risk of default is zero for bonds backed by the U.S. government. Uncle Sam pays his debts. (Actually, you and I do, but it amounts to the same thing.)

Similarly, the risk of default is very low when it comes to bonds issued by top corporations, although the odds of a default increase as you move down to the ranks of smaller or struggling companies. The credit-worthiness of municipal bonds—those issued by states, cities, and a variety of state and local government agencies—can vary widely depending on the financial health of the state, city, or government agency that backs the issue.

To evaluate the creditworthiness of bonds, fund managers typically rely on credit analysts who work for the fund's investment adviser and also on the ratings issued by independent ratings firms such as Standard & Poor's and Moody's Investors Service. For example, Standard & Poor's issues bond ratings that start at AAA for issues least likely to default, go to AA, A, BBB (all of which are still considered investment grades), and then get into noninvestment-grade ratings of BB, B, CCC, CC, C, and D (in default). Generally, funds that focus primarily on bonds with ratings of A or higher are considered high-quality funds, while those that emphasize bonds with ratings of A and BBB are considered investment grade but medium quality. Funds that invest primarily in noninvestment-grade bonds are known as **junk bond funds,** though the fund industry prefers the euphemistic moniker of high-yield bond funds.

As you would expect, bonds with the lowest ratings entice investors to buy their bonds by paying higher rates of interest than higher-quality bonds. Similarly, funds that focus on lower-rated or speculative-grade bonds generally have the highest yields. Risk-averse investors are better off keeping all or most of their money in high-quality corporate or government bond funds. But you wouldn't be living too dangerously by sticking a bit of your money in medium-quality or even junk bond funds, since the higher yields such funds pay generally offset the occasional defaults.

2. Interest rate risk. This is the far more potent danger, and one that is all the more pernicious because many investors are completely blind to it. At the heart of interest rate risk is this immutable law of the bond market: As interest rates rise, the prices of outstanding bonds fall. The reason for this is simple. If I buy a bond paying, say, 7% interest for 30 years and decide to sell it 10 years later when new 20-year bonds are paying 8% interest, no one's going to pay the same price for my 7% bond as for a new 8% issue. I can't change the payments my bond makes; the rate most bonds promise to pay is fixed, which is why you often hear bonds referred to as **fixed-income investments**. So the only way I can get someone to buy my lower-yielding bond is to sell it at a cheaper price than a new issue, which compensates the buyer for the lower interest payments. The longer the buyer will be locked in to those inferior interest payments—that is, the longer it is until my bond matures or repays its principal—the more I have to cut the price.

Of course, the process also works in reverse. If interest rates fall to, say, 6%, the higher payments on my 7% bond become valuable and boost the price of my bond. If the fund sells that 7% bond at a profit, the fund gets a capital gain. If it holds on to that bond, the increase in its value is reflected in a higher net asset value or share price. So bond prices and interest rates have a see-sawlike relationship. As interest rates on the one side go up, bond prices at the other end go down. The longer the maturity of the bond, the more dramatic those swings in price will be as rates rise or fall.

The alchemy of interest rates, bond prices, and maturity explains why short-term bond funds—those whose bonds have an average maturity of four years or less—hold up much better in times of rising interest rates than long-term funds—those with average maturities of 10 years or more. For example, if interest rates move up one percentage point, a short-term fund might lose just 2% to 3% of its value vs. 7% to 10% for a long-term fund. To get a precise fix on how much a fund might lose or gain in response to climbing or falling interest rates, however, you should check out the fund's duration. (In case you missed it, an explanation of duration appears on page 57.)

Investors unaware of interest rate risk have been shocked at various times over the years when their government bond funds were rocked with price declines following upward spikes in interest rates. Since government bonds are backed by the U.S. Treasury, some investors mistakenly believed their funds were fully protected from all losses. Not so. Even Uncle Sam must bow to the immutable rules of interest rate risk.

The Dangers of Chasing High Yields

One of the biggest mistakes bond investors make is judging a bond fund solely by its yield (which essentially measures only the income a fund produces), while ignoring total return (a more comprehensive measure of performance that takes into account increases or decreases in the value of the fund's shares as well). One problem with homing in only on yield is that bond funds often resort to a variety of ways of calculating their yields to make them appear fatter than they are. For example, some funds quote distribution rates or 12-month average yields, which measure the amount of dividends the fund has paid out over the past year. That figure can be inflated, for example, by buying so-called premium bonds, or high-yielding issues selling for more than their face value. The interest rates premium bonds pay are higher than average, but that's because the price of the bond will fall as it nears the end of its term. Net result: A portion of the dividend payments from a bond fund that loads up on premium bonds amounts to a return of your own principal.

That tactic boosts the distribution rate but may eventually lower the share price of the fund. You can sidestep these problems by insisting that the fund quote you its SEC yield, which is the only yield figure funds can advertise. This figure, which is calculated according to a standard formula used by all funds, eliminates yield-enhancing tricks.

But even relying on SEC yields alone can be a dangerous way to choose a fund. Knowing that income investors are drawn instinctively to high yields, many funds try to get the edge on competitors by buying lower-quality issues or by buying bonds with longer maturities. For example, if the manager of an intermediate-term bond fund buys bonds with maturities averaging 10 years, his fund will generally have a higher yield than another intermediate-term fund that sticks to bonds with maturities of five to seven years, since the longer a bond's maturity, the higher a yield it usually has. Problem is, a fund with more low-quality bonds would likely experience more defaults than one without such issues. And if interest rates soar upward, the share price of the fund with the 10-year bonds is likely to take a bigger hit than one with five-to-seven-year bonds.

In short, aside from lowering the fund's operating expenses, the only ways one fund can post a higher yield than another are by buying lower-quality bonds or investing in bonds with longer maturities, both of which involve taking on more risk. (A manager can also dabble in certain types of so-called derivative securities, but they come with their own set of perils.) For all practical purposes, then, higher yield almost always means higher risk. And the handiest way of gauging whether those higher risks have paid off, at least in the past, is by comparing the fund's total return over several time periods with that of similar funds. Total return will show you how investors fared after accounting not just for the fund's income (or yield), but also for any capital gains or losses in bonds the fund sold, plus any rise or fall in the fund's net asset value.

Perusing the Menu of Bond Fund Choices

Now that you're familiar with the dynamics of bond fund returns and the dangers of chasing high yields, let's take a look at the bond fund choices that await you. As I did with stock funds in the previous chapter, I'll give a brief statistical portrait of each bond fund category, describe how funds within that category work, and then suggest when funds within that category are appropriate. For the names of specific funds within these categories you might consider investing in, see pages 277–280 in the appendix. One caveat: With the exceptions of 1994 and 1987, bonds and bond funds had some spectacular years in the 1980s and early 1990s, largely because of sharp declines in interest rates. Don't assume you'll get the same generous returns in upcoming years.

U.S. Government Bond Funds

% Average Annual Gain[1]

Volatility	3 Years	5 Years	10 Years	Highest Annual Gain/Year[2]	Lowest Annual Gain or Loss/Year[2]	Worst Quarter/ Year[2]
Very low to moderate	4.6%	7.1%	7.5%	28.0%/'82	-3.5%/'94	-7.9%/'80

Source: Morningstar, Inc., Chicago. [1]To April 1, 1996 [2]Calendar year or quarter since 1976

These funds invest primarily in bonds issued by the U.S. Treasury or federal government agencies, which means you don't have to worry about credit risk. Because of their higher level of safety, however, their yields and total returns tend to be slightly lower than those of corporate bond funds with comparable average maturities.

Government bond funds that limit themselves to Treasury bonds can often close much of that gap, however, since interest from Treasury obligations is exempt from state and local taxes in nearly all states. As I noted earlier, government bond funds are still subject to interest rate risk, so the value of your fund can plummet if interest rates climb. But you can at least match the level of risk you are comfortable with by choosing a fund with the appropriate average maturity.

Thus, if you can't tolerate swings of more than a few percentage points in the value of your fund shares, stick to short-term government bond funds. If fluctuations of 5% or so don't cause you to break out in a cold sweat, then you can pick up a bit more yield by tiptoeing out on the average maturity scale to intermediate-term government bond funds. If you plan to hold on to your bond fund for several years and don't mind seeing the value of your shares bounce up or down by 10% or more occasionally, you can grab even higher yields by investing in long-term government bond funds. (There are times, such as just prior to a recession, when yields on long-term bonds may fall below those of intermediate- and short-term issues. But this situation, known as an **inverted yield curve,** is a temporary phenomenon.)

Within this category there are also more specialized funds that buy securities made up of pools of home mortgages that are backed by such government-sponsored firms as the Government National Mortgage Association (GNMA or Ginnie Mae) and the Federal National Mortgage Association (FNMA or Fannie Mae). These funds, often called GNMA or Ginnie Mae funds, typically have yields one-half to a full percentage higher than those on regular government bond funds. But in return for the higher level of income you subject yourself to prepayment risk—the risk that as interest rates fall, mortgage holders will refinance their loans at lower rates. When that happens, the old mortgage-backed securities are repaid and the fund must reinvest the money at lower prevailing rates. Result: GNMA funds have little of the upside but all the downside of other government bond funds. Refinancings prevent them from collecting capital gains when interest rates fall, but GNMA funds still get clobbered if rates rise (homeowners don't refinance to get *higher* mortgage rates).

In recent years a number of government funds have begun buying a variety of derivatives that invest in new versions of mortgage-backed securities that go by arcane names like POs (principal-only securities), IOs (interest-only securities), and kitchen-sink bonds (a term referring to the fact that these hodgepodge securities contain everything but the proverbial kitchen sink). Although these securities can boost both a fund's yield and, possibly, its return, they are essentially bets on which direction interest rates will head. Thus they add an additional element of risk that many investors don't expect to find in government funds. A fund representative should be able to tell you how much of the fund's assets, if any, are invested in such securities and how much the fund's value would drop if interest rates rose, say, one percentage point. Although certain types of derivatives actually lower the risk in a fund, conservative investors will probably want to avoid funds that put more than 5% to 10% of their assets in derivatives used primarily to pump up a fund's yield.

Best for: Investors looking for reliable income and returns with a high level of safety.

Not suited for: People who require higher returns than government securities can offer and who can stomach higher levels of risk.

Corporate Bond Funds

% Average Annual Gain[1]

Volatility	3 Years	5 Years	10 Years	Highest Annual Gain/Year[2]	Lowest Annual Gain or Loss/Year[2]	Worst Quarter/ Year[2]
Very low to moderate	5.3%	8.0%	8.1%	31.6%/'82	-3.0%/'94	-7.2/'80

Source: Morningstar, Inc., Chicago. [1]To April 1, 1996 [2]Calendar year or quarter since 1976

Funds in this category buy the bonds issued by corporations that may range from well-known household names to relatively obscure widget makers most of us have never heard of. Many corporate funds also put a small portion of their money in government securities. High-quality corporate funds invest the bulk of their assets in bonds rated A or higher; corporate general funds invest in bonds with a wide range of quality ratings, although they still keep the majority of their assets in investment-grade issues. Nonetheless, corporate general funds do dabble in below investment-grade bonds.

For example, the Strong Corporate Bond fund may invest up to 25% of its assets in noninvestment-grade issues. (Strong, by the way, is the name of the fund family founded by investment adviser Dick Strong, not a term to describe the fund's performance, which coincidentally does happen to be strong as well.) Overall, by dint of the high quality of their issues and by diversifying their holdings among an average of 50 or so different issues, high-quality corporate and corporate general funds offer investors a shot at higher yields and returns than government bond funds while taking on only slightly more credit risk. As with government bonds, corporate bond funds come in a variety of maturities ranging from short to long, so you can tailor the maturity somewhat to suit your tolerance for risk. If you like the prospect of those higher yields, but blanch at the thought of defaults wreaking havoc with your investment, consider sticking a small portion of your bond fund stash into high-quality corporate funds or a combination of high-quality and corporate general portfolios.

Best for: Investors who want more income than government funds offer and don't mind moving a notch or two up the risk scale.

Not suited for: Anyone who is comfortable only with the highest level of safety.

High-Yield Bond Funds

% Average Annual Gain[1]

Volatility	3 Years	5 Years	10 Years	Highest Annual Gain/Year[2]	Lowest Annual Gain or Loss/Year[2]	Worst Quarter/ Year[2]
Moderate	8.6%	13.9%	9.0%	36.6%/'91	–10%/'90	–8.8%/'80

Source: Morningstar, Inc., Chicago. [1]To April 1, 1996 [2]Calendar year or quarter since 1976

Let's spare the euphemisms. These are junk bond funds. They invest in the debt of fledgling or small firms whose staying power is untested as well as in the bonds of large, well-known companies that no longer have the financial wherewithal to command top ratings, such as U.S. Steel and computer system designer Unisys. Junk bonds have a much higher potential for default than investment-grade corporates. In any given year, for example, the chances of an investment-grade bond defaulting are roughly 0.1% vs. 4.3% for junk issues. But since junk funds typically own more than 100 issues, a default here and there won't capsize the fund. (Besides, the price of a bond that defaults doesn't drop to zero. Since even junk bonds represent some claim on the company's assets, a bond usually retains about 40% or so of its value right after defaulting—and holders of defaulted bonds often eventually recover a higher percentage of their investment.) Given the higher level of risk they present, junk bonds pay higher yields than government or investment-grade corporates—typically three to 10 percentage points more, depending on the health of the economy.

These funds tend to shine when the economy is on the rebound and suffer when the economy is fading. In the 1990 recession year, for example, junk funds overall lost 10%. But in the five years of recovery that followed, these funds gained more than 16% annually, or more than double the returns for government and nonjunk corporate bond funds. Junk funds have had their spells of lousy performance, but over the past 15 years investors who have hung on through these turbulent periods have been rewarded with superior returns. Nonetheless, these funds aren't the right place for any but the most Rambo-like of investors to put all or even a large portion of their money. You might, however, consider putting a small portion of your bond fund money—say, 10% or so—into junk to grab some of those high returns. If you do decide to dabble in these funds, stick to those with a solid track record for fashioning above average returns from the corporate junk heap while taking acceptable risks, such as those listed in the appendix.

Best for: Investors who want to boost their income and total returns and can tolerate losses of 10% or so during periods of economic turbulence.

Not suited for: People who are looking to bond funds as a safe refuge.

Municipal Bond Funds

% Average Annual Gain[1]

Volatility	3 Years	5 Years	10 Years	Highest Annual Gain/Year[2]	Lowest Annual Gain or Loss/Year[2]	Worst Quarter/ Year[2]
Low to moderate	5.1%	7.4%	7.2%	35.5%/'82	-10.5%/'80	-12.0%/'80

Source: Morningstar, Inc., Chicago. [1]To April 1, 1996 [2]Calendar year or quarter since 1976

Tax-exempt bond funds—better known as muni bond funds—invest in the bonds issued by cities, states, and other local government entities. As a result, they generate dividends that are free of federal income taxes. The income from single-state muni bond funds—those that limit themselves to the bonds of one state—is also exempt from state and local taxes for resident shareholders. (Note: Muni funds can also make capital-gains distributions if they sell bonds that have risen in value. Such distributions, as well as any gain you get if you sell your muni fund shares at a profit, are fully taxable. Only the interest payments are tax-free.)

As a result of their tax-advantaged status, muni funds often offer better yields than taxable government and corporate funds once you factor in their tax benefits. This is particularly the case for affluent investors in the 28% or higher tax brackets. Of course, munis' tax benefits depend on how the tax laws are written. Thus, if tax rates are raised or lowered—or more sweeping changes are made in our tax system—investors will have to re-examine whether munis make sense for them.

As with other bond funds, the farther you move out along the average maturity scale, the higher the yield you can grab—and usually the bigger the setback you'll experience if interest rates go up. Although the overwhelming majority of muni funds buy long-term muni bonds, there are enough funds out there that keep their average maturities in the intermediate or short range that you shouldn't have trouble finding a muni fund that doesn't exceed your appetite for interest rate risk.

You can squeeze as much as a full percentage point of extra after-tax yield by investing in a single-state muni that buys the bonds of the state in which you live or by buying the muni equivalent of corporate junk bonds—that's right, junk, or high-yield, munis. By forgoing geographic diversification in a single-state fund, you bump up credit risk somewhat, as investors in California-only muni funds found in 1994 and 1995, when some California bond issues were rocked after Orange County, California, declared bankruptcy following an estimated $2 billion loss in the county's investment fund.

Similarly, since high-yield munis dip into low-rated issues—often those offered by industrial development agencies or hospitals—the odds of bonds in the portfolio defaulting increase slightly. Overall, however, the additional payoff probably outweighs the extra risk. (Indeed, because of their higher yields, high-yield muni funds have sometimes held up better than regular muni funds through periods of rising interest rates.) Nonetheless, conservative investors who are easily rattled by temporary losses or the threat of such losses, as well as investors who have a significant portion of their investable cash tied up in muni funds, might want to limit single-state and high-yield funds to a small percentage of their holdings, say, no more than 15% or so. And if you do decide to invest in single-state or high-yield portfolios, you are better off sticking to funds run by large fund companies, such as Vanguard, T. Rowe Price, and Fidelity, that have the financial resources to support teams of seasoned muni analysts who can separate the good junk from the bad and the ugly.

Other Types of Bond Funds

There are also a few more specialized categories of bond funds. Convertible bond funds, for example, hold preferred stocks and bonds that can be converted into shares of stock in the issuing company. They typically pay lower yields than conventional corporate funds, but they offer a shot at capital growth if the price of the underlying stock rises. Another group, known as multi-sector funds, diversifies across a broad range of different types of debt, including U.S. government bonds, foreign bonds, and high-yield corporates.

While funds within these categories can certainly produce decent returns, they aren't a terrific choice if you are trying to put together a diversified portfolio that includes specific percentages of certain types of stock and bond funds. For example, by putting $2,000 of your $10,000 bond-fund stash into a high-yield fund, you may think you've limited junk bonds to 20% of your bond holdings. But if the manager of the multisector fund in which you've also put $8,000 suddenly moves half the fund's assets into junk, you've effectively upped your high-yield stake to 60% of your bond-fund portfolio without even knowing it. If you're going through the effort of putting together a portfolio of funds—the approach I strongly recommend—you're better off investing in funds that limit themselves to one type of bond issue within a certain range of maturities, as is the case with the four major categories just described.

Choosing the Right Bond Funds for You

Now that you know the ground rules of bond fund investing, let's move to the issue of finding funds that jibe with your goals. We're not talking quantam physics here; it's pretty simple. There are four things you ought to do in order to select the right bond fund:

1. Decide how much risk you're willing to assume. If you'll need to tap into your principal within the next three years or so—or if you simply prefer not to have the value of your fund shares dip down more than a few percentage points—then you should stick to short-term bond funds. However, if fluctuations in the value of your principal on the order of 5% to 10% don't bother you—or bond funds are part of a diversified portfolio you will hold for the long term—you should consider shares of intermediate-term portfolios. You should invest in long-term funds only if you don't plan to touch your principal for at least five years or if you could handle seeing the value of your shares decline 10% or more over a short period of time.

As for credit quality, try to match the fund's risk profile to your own tolerance for risk. If you're a risk avoider who places a high premium on security of principal, then you should stick with government funds exclusively or a combination of government and high-quality corporates. (If you're a candidate for muni funds, as described on the next page, then stick to high-quality national muni funds.) But if you don't mind taking on a small amount of extra risk for the prospect of higher returns, you can tilt your mix more toward corporates—and possibly even put a bit of money in a junk corporate or muni fund.

2. Determine how much current income you need. Once you've decided which types of funds to buy based on the amount of volatility you can stand, review your plan to see if it jibes with your need, if any, for current income. For example, your gut may tell you to buy only short-term government bond

111

funds. But if your checkbook says that short-term governments don't throw off enough dividends for you to make ends meet, consider investing at least some money in corporates, and if that doesn't generate enough cash, look into funds with longer average maturities. Similarly, you might consider making high-yield junk funds a part of your portfolio. Ultimately, of course, you've got to balance your need for income with the level of risk you feel comfortable with. But with the variety of fund qualities and maturities available, you have considerable maneuvering room to come up with an acceptable mix.

3. Answer the taxable or tax-exempt question. Depending on your income tax bracket and what munis are yielding relative to taxable bonds, you may be better off putting all or most of your bond stash in tax-exempt muni bond funds. As a rule of thumb, it doesn't pay to buy munis unless you're in *at least* the 28% federal bracket, although they occasionally make sense for people in lower tax brackets.

Remember too that the spread between taxable bonds and munis can vary according to the maturity of the bonds. In 1995, for example, talk about a flat tax drove down the prices of long-term munis so much that they were terrific buys. Flat tax concerns hardly dampened the demand for short-term munis, however, so they weren't nearly as good a buy. So just because long-term munis might be a buy for someone in the 28% bracket doesn't necessarily mean that short-term munis are.

To decide whether you're better off in taxable or tax-exempt funds, you should figure the muni fund's taxable equivalent yield. This tells you what the taxable fund would have to pay to give you as much money after taxes as the tax-free fund. By translating the muni's yield to a taxable equivalent, you can then compare muni and taxable bond fund yields to see which is higher. Make sure you're comparing funds of the same duration or average maturity, so you're comparing apples to apples. The calculation is pretty straightforward. First, subtract your federal tax bracket (we'll assume it's 28% for this example) expressed as a decimal, from 1. That gives you 0.72. Then take the tax-free muni fund's yield (we'll assume that's 5%), and divide it by 0.72. That gives you a taxable equivalent yield of 6.9% (5% ÷ 0.72). So a taxable fund would have to yield at least 6.9% to pay as much after taxes as the muni fund.

In lieu of breaking out your Hewlett Packard 12C or firing up your Pentium "Approxium"-powered PC, you can consult the table of tax-exempt yields and their taxable equivalents on page 270–272 in the appendix. Things are slightly more complicated if you want to calculate the taxable equivalent yield for a single-state fund because you must allow for the federal tax deduction for state and city taxes. My view is that if a single-state fund doesn't compare well solely on the basis of your federal tax bracket, it's probably not compensating you with enough extra return given its added risks. But if you wish to calculate the taxable equivalent yield for a single-state fund, follow the five steps outlined in the appendix on page 272.

4. Opt for bond funds with low expenses. When buying real estate, think location, location, location. When choosing bond funds, however, your mantra should be expenses, expenses, expenses. Fact is that virtually all bond funds within the same category are pretty much buying the same bonds that react largely the same way to interest rate movements. So it's difficult for any one bond fund manager to get much of an edge on competitors by virtue of superior bond-picking skill.

But the one factor that more than any other does account for differences in bond funds' returns is annual expenses—that is, the yearly cost of paying the fund manager and operating the fund. The reason expenses are so crucial is that they directly reduce dollar for dollar the amount of income that goes to you. Let's say two funds hold identical portfolios of bonds that yield 8%, but one fund has an annual expense ratio (its annual operating costs as a percentage of assets) of 1.5%, while the other has expenses of 0.8%. Well, your yield from the lower-expense portfolio after expenses would be 7.2% (8.0% minus 0.8%) vs. just 6.5% (8.0% minus 1.5%) for the higher-expense fund. Essentially, bond funds with low expenses have a head start on their peers. And unless you believe some managers can predict future interest rates, the only way the higher-expense funds have of catching up with the low-expense ones is by buying riskier bonds—that is, bonds with lower-quality ratings or with longer average maturities.

In general, therefore, you are *almost always better off* investing in a bond fund with below average expenses. For taxable U.S. government and corporate bond funds, that means looking for funds with annual expense ratios below 1.0% or so and roughly 0.9% or lower for muni bond funds. In a few categories where the bonds are less homogeneous, such as in the junk and international markets (which will be discussed in the next chapter), a manager's skill can generate higher returns, but even there you should opt for funds with expenses above the average (about 1.4% for junk funds and 1.5% for international bond funds) *only* if the fund consistently rewards shareholders with above average returns. Similarly, you are almost always better off investing in no-load bond funds—that is, funds that do not charge sales commissions. But if you absolutely feel you need the help of a financial planner or broker in choosing a fund—which means you will pay a commission or fee one way or another—at least stick to funds that hold down their operating expenses.

Fortunately it's easy to find low-expense bond funds. A fund representative should be able to provide you with a fund's annual expense ratio, which you can then compare with the category averages provided in the Morningstar and Value Line publications. Alternatively, you can ask a fund rep for the five-year expense projection all funds are required to post in their prospectus or the fund's expense ratio and compare either of those figures with the comparable data **MONEY** magazine provides on more than 2,500 stock and bond funds in its semiannual February and August fund ranking issues. Other publications such as *Kiplinger's Personal Finance* magazine as well as *Barron's* and the *Wall Street Journal* also provide such information periodically.

But if you have things you'd rather be doing other than poring over expense ratios, there is a simpler way to invest in low-cost bond portfolios—namely, opt for bond funds that are part of families that tend to be miserly when it comes to expenses. In 1995 **MONEY** magazine identified these four families as having the lowest bond fund expenses among the 30 largest fund sponsors:

Fund Families with the *Least* Expensive Bond Funds			
Fund Company	Average expense ratio[1]	Number of bond funds	Telephone (800)
Vanguard	0.25%	32	851-4999
USAA	0.45%	11	382-8722
Benham	0.56%	21	331-8331
Franklin Templeton	0.68%	93	342-5236

[1]Average expenses and number of funds from *Morningstar OnDisc* as of April 1996

These four families aren't the only parsimonious ones. Other fund families that hold the line on bond fund expenses include Dreyfus, Fidelity, T. Rowe Price, Scudder, and Strong. Of course, no one can guarantee that the funds in penny-pinching fund families—or, for that matter, in any low-cost bond fund—will definitely outperform ones with fatter expenses. But I do know that more of your money will be working for you in such funds and that their low expenses give them an edge over their competitors. Given those two factors, I'd say your odds of getting above average returns increase if you stick to bond funds with below average costs.

CHAPTER 7

Going International

Buy Foreign to Boost Returns and Reduce Risk

When it comes to investing, most U.S. mutual fund shareholders act like isolationalists: they're reluctant to get involved in financial markets beyond their home shores. Indeed, when ICR Survey Research Group polled fund shareholders nationwide for **MONEY** magazine in 1995, only 22% of those queried owned one or more of the nearly 700 international stock funds open to investors, and a mere 11% held shares in any of the 200 or so international bond funds vying for investors' cash.

That wariness is understandable, considering that as recently as 1994 some international funds that specialize in volatile emerging markets such as Latin America plunged more than 20% in value, partly because of the devaluation of the Mexican peso. Besides, most people have enough trouble keeping up with the gyrations in the U.S. market without adding the complication of keeping abreast of what's going on in foreign bourses around the world.

But investors who shy away from international funds are giving up two huge advantages that international investing can offer.

1. International funds give you a shot at higher returns than those available in domestic funds. A 1994 study by G. T. Capital Management found that the longer you stay invested in foreign shares, the better your chances are of earning U.S. market-beating returns. For example, foreign stocks have only a slightly better than even chance of beating U.S. stocks in any given year. But the odds increase to 70% over a five-year time period, and if you extend your investing horizon to eight or more years, foreign stock markets surpass their U.S. counterparts 95% of the time. What's more, over periods of a decade or longer, international stocks can outperform U.S. shares by two to three percentage points a year.

2. International funds generate their superior returns while simultaneously making your overall portfolio safer. Yes, it seems paradoxical—you're getting higher returns with less risk. But here's why: Prices of foreign shares don't always rise and fall in lockstep with U.S. stocks. This means that foreign shares have what securities analysts would call a relatively low **coefficent of correlation** with domestic stocks—in other words, foreign shares often zig when U.S. shares zag and vice versa. The result is that you can significantly reduce your portfolio's overall volatility by diversifying into foreign funds. If in 1985, for example, you had put 70% of your money in U.S. shares and split the rest evenly between shares of foreign emerging and industrialized nations, by the end of March 1995 you would have gained nearly 16.0% annually versus 14.4% for an all-U.S. portfolio. *And* you would have reduced the volatility of your portfolio by roughly 10% compared with a portfolio composed only of domestic stocks.

Given these two major pluses, most investment advisers believe fund investors should put roughly 20% to 30% of their portfolio into international funds. While that is the consensus among advisers, that doesn't mean you have to jump up to that level immediately. Indeed, if you're a novice fund investor—or you already own funds but not international portfolios—you can begin by investing a small amount in a broadly diversified international stock fund to see what it's like. Once you feel comfortable, you can increase your holdings in a widely diversified fund and then decide whether or not to branch out into some of the more specialized foreign stock funds that offer a shot at even higher gains.

Ideally, investment advisers say you should keep half to three-quarters of the money you devote to international stock funds in diversified funds, while splitting up the rest among funds that invest in faster-growing emerging markets. But if you simply want a bit of international exposure to round out your portfolio and don't have the time or inclination to sift through specialized international portfolios, don't worry. You will still grab the benefits of foreign investing by owning one or two international stock funds that invest in a diverse range of global markets.

This chapter will help you sort through the three different categories of international stock funds from which you can choose and then move on to international bond funds that can help you diversify your fund holdings even further. When you are picking an international fund, it's especially important to stick to fund families that have extensive experience in international investing (or have their international funds managed by investment firms with such experience) and that have the resources needed to research and monitor companies and stock markets around the globe. A few fund companies that have such a reputation for international expertise include (but are not limited to) Fidelity, Scudder, Templeton, T. Rowe Price, and Vanguard. For the names of specific international stock and bond funds beyond those mentioned in this chapter that you might consider adding to your fund portfolio, turn to pages 276 and 280 in the appendix.

A Word about Currency Risk

Before we get down to the nitty-gritty of examining international funds, though, you should be aware of one element of risk
in international investing that you won't find in domestic markets—currency risk, or the chance that a rising dollar will erode
the value of your international stock or bond fund.

Why, you may ask, would a *strengthening* dollar—the very
thing that would enhance your purchasing power if you were
traveling overseas—hurt the value of your foreign investment?
Consider this: Let's say that when a dollar is worth 1.4 German
marks you convert $1,000 into 1,400 German marks, and then
invest those 1,400 marks in 100 shares of a German stock selling
at 14 marks a share. A year passes, during which the price of your
German stock has increased 14.3% to 16 marks a share and the
U.S. dollar has risen 21.4% to a value of 1.7 marks. How did you
do on your investment?

Well, the stock's price has definitely increased 14.3%. But let's
see what happens when we convert that gain back to U.S. greenbacks. If you sold your 100 shares at 16 marks apiece and converted the 1,600 marks back into U.S. dollars at the new
exchange rate of 1.7 marks per dollar, you would wind up with
$941 and change (1,600 divided by 1.7). In short, the rising dol-
lar would have turned a 14.3% gain into a 5.9% loss. (Actually, if
you take brokerage commissions into account, you would have
fared even worse.) Had the dollar dropped, say, to 1.2 marks, you
would have enjoyed an extra gain. Your 1,600 marks would have
fetched $1,333, boosting the stock's 14.3% gain to a 33.3%
return in dollar terms for you.

Of course, when you're investing in international funds, you
don't actually have to convert your money into German marks,
Portuguese escudos, Polish zlotys, Korean won, or any other currency. You buy your shares in U.S. dollars and you get good old
Yankee greenbacks when you redeem your shares. What's more,
such fluctuations in currency values tend to even out over peri-

ods of, say, a decade or longer. So if you're in for the long haul, there's no reason to agonize every time the U.S. dollar rallies against another currency (or celebrate when it takes a beating). What's more, some international funds try to dampen currency-related fluctuations by engaging in a variety of sophisticated hedging techniques, such as trading futures and options in non-U.S. currencies or buying offsetting positions in a variety of different foreign currencies. While these strategies can reduce volatility, they're hardly foolproof—and the cost of pursuing them shaves a bit off a fund's return. Your best bet, therefore, is to think of whatever international funds you buy as long-term investments. If you do that, you can concentrate on long-term performance and not get swept up in the often short-term roller-coaster ride of currency swings.

Now let's move on to your major options for international investing in funds, starting with three major kinds of international stock funds—diversified international funds, diversified emerging markets funds, and regional emerging markets funds—and concluding with an overview of the international bond fund market.

Diversified International Funds

Diversified funds should make up the core holding for most U.S. investors looking to diversify abroad and may represent the entire foreign stock stake for investors who aren't interested in taking a more venturesome foray into international investing. By divvying up their assets among a wide number of both large and small foreign markets (typically 20 or more) around the globe, diversified international funds reduce your chances of getting bushwhacked because stock prices take a dive in one or two countries. Typically, funds in this category invest in stocks of large foreign companies, although some managers will shoot for higher gains by sprinkling in shares of medium and small companies.

Two solid performers that are good examples of how funds in this group pursue their goals are Warburg Pincus International Equity and Vanguard International Growth. Investors who jumped aboard manager Richard King's Warburg Pincus International fund in 1994 hoping for a reprise of 1993's 51.3% gain would have good reason to be disappointed—not necessarily because the fund eked out only a 0.2% gain in 1994, but because this perennial top performer appeared to be slipping behind its peers.

Not to worry. Most fund observers feel that seasoned international stock picker King will reassert his record for producing long-term above average gains. A seasoned value investor, King seeks out companies that are selling at discounts to their underlying asset values or for less than their future earnings power suggests they're worth. One of the advantages of this fund is that investors pick up shares of companies not just in major industrialized nations, but in emerging markets, too. At one point in 1995, for example, about a third of the fund's assets were in European stocks, just under 30% were in Japanese shares, and the rest were spread liberally around the globe, including almost 15% in emerging Asian and Latin American countries. Overall, his disciplined value approach and nimbleness in moving through volatile emerging markets—not to mention his impressive long-term track record—have earned King a reputation as one of today's preeminent international managers.

Vanguard International Growth, managed since 1981 by Richard Foulkes, invests in upward of 175 or more stocks and in recent years, at least, has kept most of its assets in Europe and Japan. In 1995, for example, Foulkes homed in on growth companies such as Dutch brewer Heineken and Japanese retailers like supermarket chain Ito-Yokado, which could benefit when Japan eventually snaps out of its lingering recession. That same year the fund also held about a fifth of its assets in emerging markets in Asia.

This diversified approach has led to consistently solid gains since Foulkes began managing the fund in 1981. For example, Vanguard International Growth has beaten the average return of its peers in seven of the 10 years from 1985 through 1994 and outgained the average international stock fund by more than a full percentage point over that decade-long stretch. Of course, in addition to Foulkes's managing skill, the fund had another advantage going for it over this period—razor-thin expenses. While the average international stock fund levies annual expenses of roughly 1.8% of assets, Vanguard International Growth's annual expense tab is a third of that amount, a miserly 0.6%.

Diversified Emerging Markets Funds

Once you've invested in one or two diversified international funds, you might consider shooting for even higher international gains by putting 5% to 10% of your stock fund portfolio into funds that invest in a broad range of emerging markets. The reason investment pros believe emerging markets such as China, India, and Thailand in Asia, and Argentina, Brazil, and Chile in Latin America should be able to generate long-term returns 20% higher than those you can get in U.S. shares is simple: Developing countries' economies are growing at a much faster pace than those of major industrialized countries. For example, the World Bank projects that between the years 1997 and 2000 the economies of developing nations will grow at a 6.3% pace— that's more than twice the 2.7% rate forecasted for industrial countries.

But don't even *think* about investing in one of these funds unless you've got the stomach for a wild ride—and you're willing to strap yourself in for a minimum of five years, preferably longer. That's because funds that specialize in emerging markets can soar to glorious heights one year and come crashing back to earth with a sickening thud the next. Take the Fidelity Emerging Markets fund, for example. In 1993 it zoomed to a staggering 81.8% gain. But investors who jumped aboard hoping for a repeat of that splashy performance the next year would have gotten a severe reality check. Because of turmoil in emerging markets in various places around the world, the fund lost 17.9%.

If you can handle those kinds of gyrations, though, these funds can produce spectacular gains. What's more, even though they're highly volatile, they at least offer a bit of diversification by investing in a variety of emerging markets rather than sticking to a single country or region. So you're not depending on the performance of only one highly volatile area, as you are in the regional emerging markets funds described next. Thus if, say, India and Indonesia tank, there's at least the chance that the fund's holdings in Peru or Chile or Brazil could buoy the fund's returns.

Most diversified emerging markets funds haven't been around long enough to establish much of a long-term track record. But investors willing to tolerate the inherent volatility of these funds for the prospects of U.S. market-beating returns might consider these two funds that are often recommended by fund experts: Templeton Developing Markets and Montgomery Emerging Markets.

With roughly $2 billion in assets, Templeton Developing Markets is the largest of the diversified emerging markets funds and generally considered the bellwether of the category. Although the fund carries the name of the renowned octogenarian international investor John Templeton, it is actually managed from Hong Kong by Mark Mobius, another seasoned foreign stock picker who has racked up superior gains at other portfolios he's managed. A value investor who tends to buy and hold stocks over the long term rather than trading constantly, Mobius scours the globe for stocks selling at bargain prices in such diverse markets as Argentina, Hong Kong, Mexico, Brazil, and Turkey. When he can't find values he likes, he's not afraid to keep a significant portion of the fund's assets in cash equivalents (essentially ultrashort-term money-market securities). At one point in 1995, for example, upward of 40% of the fund's assets were in cash equivalents. This fund comes with a relatively hefty 5.75% sales charge, but many fund experts believe that Mobius's skill is worth the price of admission.

At the Montgomery Emerging Markets fund, managers Brian Sudweeks and Josephine Jimenez employ a variety of quantitative measures and forecasts each month to decide which markets to invest in. The managers then seek out the best stock values—including shares of very small companies—within the markets they've targeted. Typically the fund owns upward of 250 stocks in some 25 to 30 countries that, in recent years, have included Malaysia, Taiwan, South Korea, and South Africa. In the past the managers have displayed a knack for dodging dicey markets just at the right time. In 1994, for example, they cut back the fund's Mexican stock holdings prior to the peso's devaluation, which held the fund's 1994 loss to 7.7%, or about half of what its peers lost. A relatively modest decline, yes, but still quite a drop from 1993's 58.6% gain. It's in the nature of these funds to produce huge swings in return, so keep that in mind going in.

Regional Emerging Markets Funds

By limiting their investing to emerging markets in specific areas such as Latin America or the Pacific Rim, these funds offer you a shot at the highest gains—but also carry the greatest risk. What elevates the risk level in these funds is that they're investing in highly volatile markets to begin with, and on top of that they are breaking the cardinal rule of diversification by concentrating their assets in one region. Thus, if you had invested solely in Latin American equities between 1985 and 1995, for example, you would have earned a return of roughly 23% a year. But you would also have had to suffer through some scary downturns along the way, such as the 22% drop in December 1994.

Given the prospect of such downdrafts, most investors should probably limit themselves to small doses of these funds—generally no more than 5% to 10% of their stock fund holdings, if that—and turn to them only after they've already chosen a diversified international fund and a diversified emerging markets fund. You also shouldn't consider a regional emerging markets fund unless you plan to hold it at least 10 years. Conservative investors might prefer to keep away from these funds altogether. After all, you can gain sufficient international exposure simply by buying a broadly diversified international fund. And if it's excitement you're after, a small holding in a diversified emerging markets fund can provide cheap thrills. So don't feel obligated to buy into one of these meteoric funds—or guilty about not investing in one—just because I'm including them here or because you read about their phenomenal returns in the newspaper or a personal finance magazine.

However, for those adventurous (or greedy) souls who are interested in shooting for the lofty long-term returns these funds have to offer, here are a few funds in this group that a variety of fund experts have recommended: Colonial Newport Tiger, T. Rowe Price New Asia, and Scudder Latin America.

The first two funds, as you might guess from their names, home in on shares of companies in Asian emerging markets, and neither fund invests in Japan. Colonial Newport Tiger is one of the oldest funds in this relatively young category, with a track record going back to 1989. Manager Jack Mussey generally concentrates the fund's holdings in a relative handful (often under 50) of shares of blue-chip companies located for the most part in the region's more established markets, such as Hong Kong. Conversely, T. Rowe Price New Asia lead manager Martin Wade focuses on stocks of fast-growing small- and medium-size companies such as Technology Resources Industries, a Malaysian mobile telecommunications firm that's signed up a half million mobile phone customers in just three years. Given the nature of the markets they invest in, both funds' returns can gyrate wildly. In 1993, for example, Colonial Newport Tiger and T. Rowe Price New Asia were up 75.2% and 78.8%, respectively, only to post losses of 12.0% and 19.2% the following year.

As for Scudder Latin America, manager Ed Games eschews the jumping-bean approach of flitting from one country to another in favor of a long-term buy-and-hold strategy. The fund's ultra-low 22% annual portfolio turnover rate is only a third that of the average international fund. (The portfolio turnover rate measures the amount of trading a fund manager does relative to the size of the fund's assets. A 100% turnover rate means the fund's trading volume in a single year equals the value of the fund's assets, suggesting that the fund holds its stocks for one year on average. An annual rate of more than 100% implies a holding period of less than a year; a rate below 100%, a holding period of more than a year.) The fund, which in early 1995 had the bulk of its assets in Brazil, Mexico, and Argentina, isn't afraid to build up a defensive cash stash that can provide a small safety cushion when volatile Latin emerging markets turn sour: in 1994, for example, the fund lost 9.4%, compared with more than 20% for some of its competitors. But Scudder Latin America can also ride a bull market, as its 74.3% return in 1993 attests.

You can make even finer geographical distinctions by investing in a single-country fund—that is, a fund that, as its name suggests, limits itself to the securities of only one nation, such as the Brazil, Korea, or Italy fund. With few exceptions, single-country funds are so-called closed-end funds—that is, funds that issue only a specific number of shares, which then trade on a stock exchange. If existing shareholders wish to sell—or new ones wish to buy into the fund—they do so through a stockbroker, just as if they are buying or selling a stock. Unless you have some expertise in the economy of a particular country, I'd suggest staying away from single-country funds. Of course, you could diversify by buying a handful of single-country funds. But why bother? For a lot less time and expense you can get immediate diversification by buying the diversified funds described in this chapter.

International Bond Funds

Much like international stocks, international bonds can give you a shot at higher returns while reducing the overall level of risk in your porfolio. One reason is that over long periods of time the bonds of many foreign countries outperform U.S. bonds. Over the nine years from December 1985 through December 1994, for example, the bonds of such countries as Australia, Belgium, Denmark, France, Germany, Japan, the Netherlands, and Great Britain all posted annual average returns at least three percentage points higher for American investors than did U.S. bonds. What's more, because international bonds don't always move in unison with American stocks *or* American bonds, they provide a measure of diversification that can help smooth out the ups and downs of the U.S. market.

That's the theory, anyway. And based on that theoretical framework, some investment advisers suggest investing anywhere from 10% to 40% of the bond portion of your portfolio in international bond funds. But there are some complications when fund investors try to put that theory in action. For one thing, the return-enhancing, volatility-reducing effect of international bonds isn't all that huge if you already have a mix of U.S. and foreign stock funds plus domestic bond funds. For example, if in 1987 you had invested 50% of your money in U.S. stocks, 10% in international shares, and 40% in U.S. bonds, you'd have earned an 11.1% annual average return by the end of 1994, according to investment firm Rowe Price-Fleming, International. But if you had kept the stock portion of your portfolio the same but cut back your U.S. bond holdings to 30% and added a 10% position in international bonds, you would have boosted your return to 11.5% and lowered the level of risk by roughly 1%. An improvement, yes—0.4% a year more in return with a slight decrease in volatility—but hardly one that'll have you slapping high-fives.

Furthermore it's difficult to achieve even that small benefit.

Why? Because it's hard to find a true international bond fund. Today these funds go by the name *worldwide* or *world* bond funds because most tend to invest not just in foreign bonds, but also in U.S. issues. Many regularly keep 20% or more of their assets in U.S. bonds, and some worldwide bond funds have loaded upward of 75% of their portfolio in domestic bond issues. (Similarly, global stock funds will invest in both foreign and U.S. shares, while international stock funds limit themselves to foreign markets.)

My advice: Don't make international bond funds a huge priority. If you've put together all the other elements of your fund portfolio—U.S. stock funds, U.S. bond funds, and international stock funds—and you still have some money left and aren't totally burned out on picking funds, then fine: add an international bond fund to your mix. (For the purists, I've included international bond funds in the model portfolios in Chapter 10.) Three possibilities with below average expenses and solid performance: T. Rowe Price International Bond (which invests only in non-U.S. issues), Scudder International Bond (which is prohibited from investing more than 35% of its assets in U.S. issues), and Warburg Pincus Global Fixed Income (which has no set limits on the amount it can invest in the United States but typically keeps its domestic holdings below 10%). But if you don't have the time, cash, or inclination to be an asset allocation purist, don't sweat it. Your portfolio isn't going to fall apart because you've left out international bonds.

One final caveat: If someone suggests you buy a short-term world income fund, turn around and start walking the other way. These funds were launched in the late 1980s and early 1990s as allegedly safe alternatives to CDs and money-market funds. They were supposed to produce fatter yields by capitalizing on high short-term interest rates around the globe while dampening risk through a variety of complicated hedging techniques. In reality, they were—and, I think still are—more a marketing gimmick than a savvy investment. In 1992, when Europe's Exchange Rate Mechanism went kaflooey (in non-technical terms that means it broke down), many of these funds were rocked for double-digit losses. Over the past few years these funds have tried to reinvent themselves in various ways, but it's their premise, not the packaging, that's flawed. These funds simply haven't proven themselves as worthy custodians for your money, so give them the Nancy Reagan treatment: Just say no.

CHAPTER 8

Don't Get Fleeced
by High Costs
and Fees

Take a Hard Look at Fund Expenses

Mutual funds are clearly one of the great investment values available to small investors. After all, for a cost of about $1.40 a year for every $100.00 invested in a diversified domestic stock fund and about $1.00 for the same amount in a bond fund, investors get the expertise of a professional money manager as well as an array of services ranging from 24-hour access to fund prices and performance, periodic account statements, semiannual and annual reports, check-writing privileges, and the ability to switch money around from fund to fund by telephone.

The question is, though, should funds be an even *better* value?

A handful of mutual fund executives and industry observers, the most prominent of whom is Vanguard funds former chairman and low-expenses zealot John Bogle, argue that fund companies could easily trim fund expenses, but don't because fund groups are more interested in maintaining or increasing profit margins. These critics point out that although the amount of money invested in stock and bond funds has exploded upward nearly fortyfold over the last decade and a half—from a mere $49 billion in 1979 to just over $2 trillion by 1996—fund companies generally have not lowered their fees to reflect the economies of scale that come from managing larger sums of cash.

Several recent studies of fund expenses by **MONEY** magazine support this criticism. While fund assets between 1979 and 1995 zoomed upward, **MONEY** magazine found that expense ratios rose rather than fell. Expense ratios for diversified stock funds, on average, climbed roughly 35% over this period, while those of taxable bond portfolios increased 14%. Muni bond funds were the lone exception: their average expenses dropped by about 12%.

But many fund execs, as well as the fund industry's main trade association and lobbying group, the Investment Company Institute, contend that fund expenses have increased because of the ever-rising level of services that funds must offer to satisfy investors. Automated telephone lines, sophisticated computer equipment, newsletters to shareholders—all add to the expense of running a mutual fund. Indeed, the often repeated refrain from the industry camp is that comparing a fund in 1979 with one today is like equating a Model T with a Ford Taurus. Of course, the Taurus costs more, but it probably comes with air bags, antilock brakes, and air-conditioning.

Whichever camp you side with—I believe that fund companies could and would pare expenses *if individual investors raised more of a fuss about costs*—the fact is that you can probably improve your bottom line by paying more attention to fund costs. Why? Because the amount you pay in fees and expenses reduces dollar for dollar the amount of the fund's gains that wind up in your pocket. As a result, investors who stick to funds with below average expenses generally earn higher returns over time than those who invest in more costly funds.

The aim of this chapter is to help you understand the variety of expenses you are paying for in a fund—and to show how avoiding high expenses can improve your returns. Toward that end, I'll outline the main fees and expenses that investors face when investing in funds, starting with the most obvious—the sales commissions that many funds charge—then moving on to the ongoing annual operating expenses that all funds levy, and winding up with a look at the fast-growing charge known as a 12b-1 fee, which many investors aren't even aware that they're paying.

You Are Better Off in No-Loads, But . . .

Almost 60% of stock funds and about 65% of bond funds are what are known as **load funds**. Sold through brokers, financial planners, insurance agents, and others who earn their living on sales commissions, load funds carry a sales charge or load that generally ranges between 2.00% and 5.75%, which investors must pay when they buy or redeem shares in the fund.

It's fashionable for financial journalists and other fund experts to thunder vehemently that *under no circumstances should you ever, ever pay a load!* Rather, these pundits claim, you are always better off in **no-load funds**—that is, ones that don't levy sales fees. And they are right—up to a point. The sales charge you pay is, for the most part, split between the salesperson and the firm he or she works for. Not a cent of it goes to the fund manager, so a load can't boost a fund's performance by providing an incentive for the manager to do a better job. Indeed, as far as investors are concerned, sales charges undoubtedly lower the effective return on investable cash.

Let's say you've got $10,000 to invest. If you put that 10 grand in a no-load fund that earns 10% annually, you'll have $25,937 in 10 years. If you invest in a fund that charges an up-front sales load of, say, 5.75%, then $575 of your money will go to sales commissions, leaving you $9,425 to put into the fund. Assuming the load fund also earns 10%, after 10 years you would have

$24,446, or $1,491 less than in the no-load fund. In other words, $575 of your money that could have been racking up 10% annual gains for you has instead gone to a salesperson. So you are out that money as well as any gains it would have generated.

Theoretically, therefore, you are always better off in a no-load fund. But in the real world people sometimes feel the need to turn to a broker or a planner or someone else for advice when choosing a fund. And advice, at least good advice, doesn't come free. (Unfortunately bad advice isn't free, either, and admittedly, it can be hard to distinguish between the two.) In the case of funds, most of the time that means the broker or planner will recommend only a load fund in which a portion of the sales charge goes to the salesperson as compensation for spending time with you. You can get advice and still invest in no-load funds if you deal with one of the growing number of fee-only financial planners—that is, ones who instead of collecting sales commissions charge a flat hourly rate or collect a fee based on the percentage of your money they're helping you manage. (To find such a planner in your area, call the National Association of Personal Financial Advisors at 800-366-2722.)

There may even be other reasons for occasionally paying a load. One such reason is that some very good funds happen to have loads. Many Fidelity funds carry loads, such as the 3% toll levied by the Magellan fund. And on the theory that some investors might want to consider a load fund with solid performance—even if they ultimately reject it in favor of a similar no-load—I've also mentioned some good load funds in this book.

So my position on the load vs. no-load debate boils down to this: I think investors can and should opt for no-load over load funds whenever possible and *especially* when buying bond funds. And for most investors I think "whenever possible" should be all or pretty nearly all the time. If you're willing to spend even a little time researching funds by reading magazines or plowing through a book like this, then I think you can probably set an investing strategy and pick funds as well as or better than many of the fund salespeople I've run across.

But if you need a bit of hand-holding—even if it's just until you get started—then face up to the fact that one way or another you will be paying for the advice. Then make sure that you get your money's worth for the load or, in the case of a fee-only planner, the fee that you're paying. The best way to do that is to demand that the planner or broker fully disclose in writing exactly what you're paying, give you the choice of a few different funds with similar investing styles that have different-size loads, and justify to you why, on the basis of its track record vs. both no-load and load funds and its possible future performance, you ought to pay a fee to get into these funds.

Will the Real No-Loads Please Stand Up?

Over the last few years, however, as load fund companies have sought to make their sales charges more palatable to cost-conscious investors, it's gotten more difficult to distinguish between load and no-load funds. To win over investors who would balk at paying a 5% load up front, for example, some funds charge back-end loads, also known as **contingent deferred sales charges**. You don't pay a sales fee to buy into the fund, but you will be slapped with a sales charge if you cash out early. Typically, the charge declines each year until it vanishes in the sixth or seventh year. For example, a fund with a 5% back-end load would charge you 5% of the original price or current market value (whichever is lower) of the shares you redeem during the first year, 4% the next year, 3% the next, and so on until the charge expires in the sixth year.

Don't think that by hanging in you've entirely escaped sales fees, however. To pay the brokers and planners who sell back-end load funds, fund companies typically tack on to the fund's annual operating expenses extra annual distribution charges that can inflate a fund's expenses by 0.25% to 1.00% a year.

Even more confusing, most major load fund sponsors now offer two to four (sometimes more) versions of the same fund in the form of multiple classes of shares, typically A, B, and C shares. Each share represents a piece of the same portfolio, but each has a different set of fees and expenses and, therefore, different returns. As of yet there are no generally accepted standards for how fund companies can set fees for various classes, but a typical arrangement would go something like this: A shares carry an initial sales charge of 4% to 6% plus annual fees of, say, 0.7% to 1.5%; B shares carry higher annual expenses (often upward of 1.5% to 2%) plus an exit fee that starts at 4% to 6% and phases out gradually over six to eight years (once the back-end load disappears, B shares often convert to A shares); C shares, also known as level-load shares, typically carry a small front-end sales charge of 1% or 2% and then have annual expenses a bit higher than those carried by B shares.

Which shares are you better off in? The answer depends on how long you plan to hold the fund. Generally, A shares are best for investors planning to hang in seven years or longer, while C shares tend to be better if you plan on owning the fund just a few years. Because of their relatively high exit fees and ongoing expenses, B shares are the most difficult to figure. Usually they're the best bet only if you'll be in the fund five to seven years. The exact answer depends, however, on the specific structure of fund expenses. So if you're considering investing in a fund with multiple shares, ask the broker or planner to provide hypothetical examples showing the holding period at which each share class wins out. Alternatively, you can ask the salesperson to provide a prospectus that includes a fee table for each share class, showing projected expenses for one, three, five, and 10 years. Whichever class has the lowest expenses over the length of time you're likely to hold the fund is the right class for you. Better yet, you can completely avoid dealing with this confusing alphabet soup of multiple shares by sticking to plain old no-load funds.

Unfortunately some brokers have been capitalizing on this confusion by peddling load funds without up-front sales charges as no-loads—a practice that is illegal. Such misrepresentation has been so widespread, in fact, that in 1993 the SEC sent a notice to fund sponsors telling them that representing funds that contain distribution or service fees in excess of 0.25% as no-loads "may constitute a violation of the anti-fraud provisions of the federal securities laws." In SEC language that's a strong warning. So remember. Just because a fund doesn't have an up-front sales charge doesn't necessarily make it a no-load. If you want a no-load, make sure the fund also doesn't charge a back-end sales charge and that it doesn't carry a service or distribution fee (also known as a 12b-1 fee) that's higher than 0.25%. Better yet, try to limit yourself to funds that don't charge 12b-1 fees, period.

Checking Out a Fund's Expense Ratio

While you can easily sidestep sales charges by limiting yourself to no-load funds, no investor can avoid the annual management and shareholders' servicing expenses that all funds, load and no-load alike, pass on to shareholders. These annual fees are disclosed in the fund's prospectus and are bundled together in a figure called the **expense ratio,** which expresses your fund's total annual expenses as a percentage of the fund's assets.

Management fees, also known **investment advisory fees,** make up the biggest chunk of the expense ratio—often accounting for half or more of the typical stock and bond fund's total yearly expenses. The management fee represents the amount of money the fund's investment adviser—the company the fund manager works for—receives for choosing and monitoring the securities that go into the fund's portfolio. Management fees of stock and bond funds typically run between 0.4% and 1.0% annually, although they sometimes fall outside that range.

Another 0.2% or so each year goes to the fund's transfer

agent, which handles investors' questions, tracks shareholders' accounts, processes shareholder deposits, and mails out redemption checks. A fund must also pay another 0.1% or so each year for other services, such as having a bank custodian hold the fund's securities for safekeeping, hiring lawyers to make sure the fund is adhering to securities laws and other regulations, and printing prospectuses, annual reports, and other material for fund investors. On top of these costs, load funds layer annual marketing expenses, such as the cost of advertising and the expense of selling the fund through brokers, planners, and other salespeople. Such marketing costs can add anywhere from 0.25% to 1.00% annually to a fund's expenses. All of these expenses are reflected in the fund's expense ratio.

Funds that invest in stocks and certain other securities also incur brokerage commissions. These costs typically amount to 0.1% to 0.2% of assets annually—though they can be two to three times higher than that if a fund trades frequently. Brokerage fees are not included in the expense ratio, although they are divulged in a report called the **statement of additional information, or SAI,** which you can request from the fund company. Even though trading costs are not part of the expense ratio, a fund's returns nevertheless include the effect of trading expenses, since brokerage commissions effectively raise the price the fund pays for securities and lower the amount the fund gets after selling. Some funds also engage in so-called **directed brokerage agreements,** under which the fund pays higher than normal brokerage commissions in return for the broker providing investment research or administrative services. This practice effectively shifts a portion of research and administrative costs that would otherwise be included in the fund's annual expense ratio into brokerage costs that aren't included in the expense ratio. As a result, directed brokerage arrangements can make a fund's expense ratio appear lower than it really is. Under new SEC rules, however, funds that use such arrangements must disclose in the prospectus's fee table how much directed brokerage has lowered the expense ratio.

All these expenses chip away at the fund's assets year after year after year. As a result, abnormally high annual expenses can have a much bigger effect on your fund's long-term performance than a onetime sales charge. Just how much can high fees erode a fund's performance? Take a look at the chart presented here, which shows that, on average, low-cost funds generate superior returns compared with their pricier competitors. Over the 10 years to January 1, 1996, for example, U.S. diversified stock funds with below average expenses returned 13.4% annually versus just 11.6% for those with expenses above the average.

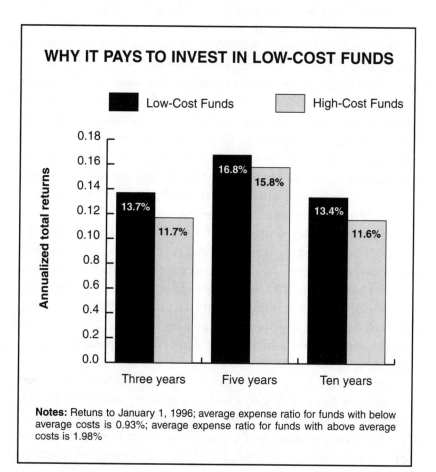

WHY IT PAYS TO INVEST IN LOW-COST FUNDS

Low-Cost Funds   High-Cost Funds

Annualized total returns

Three years — 13.7% / 11.7%
Five years — 16.8% / 15.8%
Ten years — 13.4% / 11.6%

Notes: Retuns to January 1, 1996; average expense ratio for funds with below average costs is 0.93%; average expense ratio for funds with above average costs is 1.98%

As the chart shows, you would have been better off in the funds with low expense ratios. One reason for this is that the less the fund deducts for its management fee and other expenses, the more return is left for you. If two funds hold exactly the same portfolios over the same period of time, but one deducts 1.0% of assets in expenses while the other soaks you for 1.5%, then the lower-cost fund's return will be a half percentage point higher. But there's something else at work that's less obvious. Often, funds with higher expenses trade their securities more frequently than low-expense funds, probably in an attempt to overcome the drag of a fatter expense ratio. Unfortunately, more trading generates lofty transaction costs, making it difficult for these funds to generate enough extra returns to wipe out the extra trading costs, let alone the higher expenses they set out to overcome in the first place. So high expenses can be a sword that cuts investors' returns two ways: first, by simply lopping off a bigger chunk of the fund's raw gains; second, by forcing the manager to adopt trading strategies that generate more transaction costs than extra profits, which puts the fund further in the hole.

Keeping expenses low is especially important in bond funds, where high fees are virtually certain to lead to subpar returns. For one thing, bond funds' returns tend to be lower than those of stock funds. So annual expenses eat up a higher percentage of your returns. What's more, bond fund managers don't have many ways to outperform other bond fund managers. All the managers in a given category (such as government bonds or corporate bonds) are essentially buying very similar securities. It's extremely difficult, then, for bond fund managers to overcome the drag of high fees with superior bond picking skills. In fact, I'd say it's close to impossible, which is why I would be especially wary of investing in bond funds with above average expenses.

Of course, I'm not saying that you should automatically reject a fund just because it has a higher expense ratio than its competitors. That would be foolish, especially if a fund's expenses were, say, only a quarter of a percentage point higher than those of similar funds, or if a fund with elevated expenses regularly paid off with exceptional returns. What I am saying, though, is that you should factor fees into your selection of funds—especially bond funds—and that if you are choosing between two funds of the same type with comparable records, you should probably opt for the one with lower expenses. To make that determination, you can compare the expense ratio of any fund you're considering to the average expense ratios for the 11 stock and bond fund categories below. (A fund representative should be able to give you a fund's expense ratio; otherwise check the expense ratios in each Friday's mutual fund listings in the *Wall Street Journal*.)

Type of Fund	Average Annual Expense Ratio
Aggressive growth	1.75%
Growth	1.44%
Small-company	1.52%
Growth-and-income	1.26%
Equity-income	1.37%
Balanced	1.32%
International stock	1.82%
U.S. government bond	1.08%
Corporate bond	0.92%
High-yield corporate	1.41%
Tax-exempt bond	0.93%

Source: Morningstar, April 1996.

Exposing the Hidden Load: 12b-1 Fees

If the sponsor of a mutual fund in which you owned shares asked you to fork over your money to bring more investors into the fund, would you object? Probably. After all, new investors who put more money into the fund primarily benefit the sponsor, who rakes in bigger management fees as fund assets swell.

But in 1980 the SEC approved a new type of charge called a **12b-1 fee** (the name refers to an SEC rule) that allows fund sponsors to pass along marketing, advertising, and sales costs to the shareholders who are already in the fund. Supporters of these fees argued back in 1980 (and some still argue today) that spending shareholders' money for advertising and marketing would lure more investors into funds, increase funds' assets, and create economies of scale that would actually lower costs to fund shareholders—sort of a variation of the wage-war-to-win-peace theory. In practice, however, 12b-1s have been a gold mine for fund companies—nearly 3,000 funds collect an estimated $2.7 billion a year overall from 12b-1 fees that usually range from 0.5% to 1.0%—and not much of a bargain for fund investors. Over the past 15 years fund assets have grown, but expenses on average have gone up, not down.

What's especially galling about 12b-1 fees, though, is that they tend to go unnoticed by many investors, which is why 12b-1s are sometimes called **hidden loads.** Unlike an up-front sales charge, you don't pay them in a chunk of cash when you buy the fund. Instead they take a slice of your investment's value year after year. And some brokers even push funds with 12b-1s as no-loads, which is illegal if the 12b-1 exceeds 0.25%, as is usually the case.

And if that's not reason enough for you to avoid these fees, consider this: 12b-1 fees can distort the way a fund manager invests the fund's money, largely by making the manager take on bigger risks to compensate for the extra baggage of a 12b-1 fee. This is especially the case in bond funds. If you look only at total returns, bond funds with 12b-1 fees sometimes seem to do pretty well. For the five years ending January 1, 1996, the return for bond portfolios with 12b-1s was actually a smidgen *higher* than the return for funds without this charge. (For one, three, and 10 years, however, the 12b-1 funds lagged in performance.) How is it possible for these funds to outperform when, on average, they levied a 0.6% 12b-1 charge? Simple. The managers of the 12b-1 funds boosted the performance of their funds by investing in riskier bonds—in this case bonds with average maturities of 13 years vs. 10 years for funds without 12b-1s. If interest rates spike up, however, the shouting will really begin among shareholders in 12b-1 funds, since, because of their longer average maturities, these funds will lose more money than those not saddled with 12b-1s. So there you have it. Lots more risk with very little (if any) extra return. Not a good combination—and a good reason to avoid funds with 12b-1 fees (especially large ones) whenever you possibly can.

CHAPTER 9

How to Pick
Winning Funds

Paring Down Those 8,000 Fund Flavors

Imagine for a moment that when you walk into an ice-cream parlor you find not 28 choices but 100, 200, or even 300 times that many. More than 8,000 different kinds of ice cream! And instead of flavors you're familiar with, like chocolate, vanilla, and strawberry, you find descriptions that don't give you a clue as to what the ice cream tastes like: Ben & Jerry's Bombastic Blend, Sealtest Special Swirl, Baskin-Robbins Tastee Treat, or Breyer's Big-Taste-Low-Calorie Concoction.

Well, substitute ice-cream flavors for mutual funds and it's understandable why so many people feel dazed and confused when faced with the more than 8,000 stock, bond, and money fund choices available to them. Presented with this overload of funds—most of which claim to be terrific performers by one self-serving standard or another—some people no doubt wind up fleeing from funds. Paralyzed by indecision, they trudge down to the local bank and put their money in a savings account or CD.

Others try to sort through this plethora of funds by enlisting the help of a stockbroker or financial planner—a plausible plan, assuming the broker or planner actually knows how to pick the right funds for you and isn't just selling whatever generates the juiciest commission. Still other investors have another way of dealing with today's mind-numbing multitude of funds: they turn to one of the "top performer" lists that newspapers and magazines churn out with frightening regularity and pick the fund that had the highest return over the past three or 12 months. These people certainly wind up with yesterday's greatest hits, but not necessarily with tomorrow's, as people who bought precious metal funds on the strength of 1993's 85% average gains found out when those same funds lost 12% of their value the following year.

So many funds, so little money and time. What's an investor to do?

Well, you can start by taking some of the pressure off yourself. First off, far, far too much emphasis is placed by newspapers, magazines, and the growing field of quasi personal finance experts on finding the best fund—as if only one of the 8,000 or so choices out there can get the job done for you. That's simply not true. There are many fine funds that can help you achieve your financial goals. (Indeed, as I explain in the next chapter, the way you divvy up your money among different kinds of funds has a greater impact on your long-term financial success than the individual funds you choose.)

Second, picking good funds really isn't all that difficult—if you're willing to do a bit of homework. (And I truly mean a bit; you don't have to devote your life to the mutual fund cause to be a successful investor.) As with many things in life, choosing mutual funds comes down to focusing on what is important to you and not letting yourself get overwhelmed by extraneous details.

That universe of 8,000 funds, for example, can be whittled down to a manageable number pretty quickly just by making a few choices. Let's say that (for the moment, at least) you're interested only in stock funds. Chop! You've cut the field to roughly

3,500 funds. Then, suppose you want to consider only funds whose portfolio manager has at least three years tenure. Wham! You've just weeded out another 2,300 or so portfolios. Limit your search further to funds that invest primarily in shares of small-growth stocks, and you're down to just over 60 funds. Eliminate those open only to large institutional investors and specialty funds that restrict themselves to a particular industry, and you're down to just over 40 choices. So you've quickly gone from 8,000 funds to 40—and you haven't even begun weeding out candidates on the basis of risk or performance. You don't necessarily need a formal process of elimination as I've laid out here. But whether you're choosing a bond fund, stock fund, or money fund, the key is to come up with some criteria that makes sense for your situation and use them to whittle down your choices to a number you can work with.

Whatever you do, don't get bogged down by the worry that you might somehow overlook a great fund. That will probably happen no matter what you do. Remember, your job as an investor isn't to find *all* the terrific funds you might invest in. It's merely to put together a portfolio of funds that perform well. If the funds you choose rack up above average returns over the long term, you should be satisfied. If they wind up in the top 25% or so of performers, you should be ecstatic—and humble enough to attribute a bit of your success to luck as well as your investing prowess. But the fact is, even average performance will make your money grow at a healthy rate. For example, if you had invested $10,000 in 1980 in a stock fund that achieved the 14.8% average rate of return for all domestic equity funds over the following 15 years, your original 10 grand would have grown (before taxes) to $90,940. Hey, you could do a lot worse.

Of course, everyone wants to beat, not meet, the averages. And in this chapter I will give you some tips on how to increase your chances of earning better returns than the average fund investor. I want to stress, however, that there is no system or formula or screening device that guarantees you will end up with the crème de la crème of funds. And if you approach fund investing with the idea of finding a fund picking Holy Grail aimed at landing you in the funds that will appear on some expert's top 40 chart, I believe you will ultimately become frustrated—and possibly poorer. Instead, in this chapter I will suggest some sensible ways to go about choosing solid performers, give some advice on comparing funds, share some insights on how to make the best use of a fund's past performance, and present other tips that can help you exercise your own critical judgment to come away with a group of good funds. And beginning on page 274 in the appendix, you'll find a list of funds of various types that you could consider as possible candidates for your money or as benchmarks against which you might compare funds you've come up with on your own.

Past Performance Matters . . . Up to a Point

Before getting into the nitty-gritty of fund picking, let's first take a quick look at the issue of past performance. Virtually every advertisement that touts a fund's returns also carries in fine print a message warning that past performance is no guarantee of future returns. Similarly, countless fund experts constantly caution against relying on past performance when picking funds, likening it to driving a car by looking in the rearview mirror. On the other hand, magazines devote scads of space to funds' returns, while financial planners and other experts don't hesitate for a second to point to past performance as evidence of a fund manager's investing prowess. What gives? Should you consider past performance when picking funds or not?

The answer is yes, you should—but not exclusively. At least three studies in the past few years contend that a fund's past track record can offer a glimpse into its likely future performance. The most comprehensive, published in 1994 by Yale finance professors William Goetzmann and Roger Ibbotson, examined the relationship between past and future returns for 728 stock funds over a variety of successive periods beginning in 1976. For example, Goetzmann and Ibbotson compared returns for 1976 through 1978 with those for 1979 through 1981 and then compared results in 1982 through 1984 with those of 1985 through 1987. After examining the results for these periods, the professors found that funds that ranked in the top quarter in the initial three-year periods had a 72% chance of finishing in the top half and a 41% shot at making the top quarter again in subsequent three-year periods. Funds that had been in the second quartile originally had about a 51% chance of finishing in the top half in subsequent periods and an 18% chance of moving up to the top quarter. On the other hand, funds that were in the bottom quartile initially had only a 13% likelihood of climbing into the top half in the following periods. The professors, who plan to release a follow-up study on the same issue covering more funds through 1994, found similar results when they looked at performance over shorter periods of time.

These results strongly suggest that winners and losers alike are apt to repeat. But superior returns definitely do not guarantee future success. Even the top performers have nearly a 30% chance of later racking up below average results, according to the study. And funds in the second quartile have barely more than a 50-50 shot at repeating their success. Remember too that this study examines a particular period. It's possible that the relationship between past and future success might not hold as much, or for that matter at all, in other past periods or in the future.

The upshot: You should definitely take past performance into account when choosing funds and lean toward funds with successful track records. But you should also consider factors beyond a fund's returns, such as its risk level, fees, whether the fund has switched managers lately, and whether its investing style is right for you. What's more, I don't want to suggest that you should never invest in a fund that's been a laggard. Indeed, just as some great hitters go into slumps and great actors and actresses occasionally give lousy performances, good funds may stumble now and then. But if you plan to invest in a fund that's posted stretches of subpar performance, you should have good reasons why you expect the fund to outpace its peers in the years ahead.

The Right Way to Choose Funds

Now that we're agreed that performance is important but only one of many factors you should consider, let's turn to some specific guidelines you can use for picking funds.

• **Identify the types of funds you need:** That's right, forget about performance for a minute. And ignore those funds you see in the newspapers and magazines with those mouthwatering gains. You should launch your fund search by asking the question What kinds of funds do I need to help me meet my goals? Ultimately your aim should be to build a portfolio, as described in Chapter 10, that includes stock and bond funds with a variety of the investment objectives and investing styles described in Chapters 5 and 6. But, of course, you will pick these funds one at a time, beginning, say, with a balanced fund or a growth-and-income fund or a growth fund that invests primarily in large-company stocks, or whatever.

The important thing is that restricting your search to a specific type of fund with a precise investing objective and style helps focus your attention. You automatically screen out irrelevant information such as which fund streaked to the biggest gains over the past 12½ weeks or what category of funds is on top for the past year and which group is bringing up the rear; instead you can set your sights on finding a solid performer within a given investment objective and investing style. If you begin your search this way—not just for a fund, but for a specific *type* of fund—many of the steps described in this section fall into place much more easily. Once you've finished this process for one type of fund, you can repeat it for other types (large-company growth funds, short- or intermediate-term bond funds, and so on) until you've chosen however many funds you feel you need to round out your portfolio.

• **Compare apples to apples:** One of the most common traps investors fall into is choosing a fund that appears to have superior performance because it's being compared to a fund with a completely different investment objective or investing style. Let's take an admittedly extreme example. In 1993 the MFS Gold and Natural Resources fund gained a seemingly impressive 48.1%, while Fidelity Disciplined Equity returned a much more modest 13.9%. On the basis of those returns, an inexperienced investor might assume that MFS Gold is clearly the better fund. Hardly. What's really going on here is that we're comparing apples and pomegranates. MFS Gold and Natural Resources, as its name implies, invests in precious metals and other inflation hedges, while Fidelity Disciplined Equity is essentially a growth fund whose manager uses a computer program to home in on fast-growing large and small companies. And in 1993 gold and other precious metals funds zoomed to abnormally large gains, while growth funds had a good but not spectacular year. This means apples overall had far higher returns than pomegranates that year.

But if you compare MFS Gold with its peers—in other words, with other precious metals funds—its 48.1% gain wasn't very impressive—in fact, it was a full 36.9 percentage points below the 85% average gain for all precious metals funds in 1993. Fidelity Disciplined Equity's 13.9% 1993 gain, on the other hand, outpaced the 11.6% average return for its peers, which are other growth funds. What's more, if you examined their records further, you would find that Fidelity Disciplined Equity regularly ranks in the top quarter to top half of all growth funds, while MFS Gold tends to be a cellar dweller in its group.

I like to think that most investors would probably know that

151

comparing a gold fund's returns to those of a growth fund (or virtually any other fund besides another gold portfolio, for that matter) won't tell you much about the relative merits of the two funds. But other cases might not be as apparent. For example, I can easily envision investors choosing an aggressive growth fund over a growth or a growth-and-income or a balanced fund in a raging bull market because aggressive growth funds' returns typically lead the pack when the market is sizzling. Of course, aggressive growth funds' returns tend to be much more volatile than those of the other types I've just mentioned. This means the aggressive fund is likely to get hit a lot harder if the market retreats. So make sure that you are using a level playing field when comparing the performance of two funds.

Ideally you should make sure you are comparing funds that have not only the same investment objective, but the same investing style as well. Thus if you are considering a growth fund that invests primarily in undervalued shares of large companies, you would want to compare that fund's results against those of other growth funds that employ a large-company value style. Similarly, if you are comparing two bond funds, be sure they both invest not only in the same types of bonds (U.S. government bonds or high-quality corporates or junk), but also in bonds of similar maturities. Comparing the returns of a short-term government bond fund vs. a junk bond fund can certainly tell you which fund posted the higher gain over the period you're examining, but it won't tell you a thing about which fund excelled versus its peers, which is what you really want to know.

• **Look for superior performance over a variety of periods:** When examining a fund's performance, you should look at its long-term investing record versus that of its peers as well as how the fund has fared over shorter stretches. With few exceptions I won't consider a fund unless it has at least a three-year performance record, and I generally like to see a five-year or longer record. (The exceptions: I'll consider a new fund if it's run by a manager who has an established track record or if the fund is part of a group, such as funds that invest in foreign emerging markets, that hasn't been around very long.) The reason you want to examine a minimum of three years' worth of returns is that, by and large, market cycles take at least that long to unfold, and you want to get an idea how the manager handles a variety of market conditions.

While you certainly want to look at a fund's annualized total return over the most recent three, five, and (if available) even 10 years, you should also look at the fund's year-by-year results, as well as how the fund did during market downturns. Why? For one reason, annualized returns over a long time frame can mask some dramatic fluctuations within the period. That's because annualized total returns don't tell what the fund actually gained each year within a given period. Rather, annualized returns give you an average return that smooths out ups and downs. (Technically, annualized returns represent not a simple average, but the *compound* annual return—in other words, the amount the fund's value would have to increase on a yearly basis to achieve its gains over the entire period. But virtually all investment advisers use the terms "annualized return," "average annual return," and "compound annual return" interchangeably these days.) Thus, two funds can have the same annualized return but vastly different annual results. For example, a steady fund that gains 10.5% one year, 12.0% the next, and 10.0% the third year would have a three-year annualized return (or compound annual return) of 10.8%—the same annualized return as a fund that gained 21% the first year, lost 10% the next, and rebounded for a 25% gain the third year.

What's more, a fund could have a terrific long-term record but actually be a laggard in recent years. The IDS Managed Retirement fund, for example, ranked among the top growth-and-income funds for the 10 years to January 1, 1996. But if you look at the three-year period ending that same date, you will find that the fund had slipped into the bottom 15% of growth-and-income funds. Similarly, it's possible that what appear to be impressive long-term results could mostly be due to exceptional recent performance. Results from a single time frame—no matter how long—cannot give you a complete picture of a fund's performance. You are always better off examining performance over many periods of time.

In general I favor funds that more often than not rank in the top half of similar funds for long periods and for each year. If I can find funds that usually rank in the top 25% for those periods, so much the better. (The Morningstar fund research service, described in Chapter 13, provides percentile rankings for funds within specific investment objectives. Many magazines also provide the average returns by investment objective so you can compare individual funds versus the averages for a variety of periods.)

I fudge with the phrase "more often than not" because many perfectly good funds have an off year that pushes them below average for a given year and, possibly, longer. So you don't want to be unrealistically rigid in setting performance criteria. For example, Ken Heebner's CGM Mutual fund (to paraphrase another great and volatile performer, Frank Sinatra) has been up, down, over, and out any number of times during the past decade. The fund's results can be erratic because Heebner often takes big postions in certain sectors of the market. Nonetheless, like Ol' Blue Eyes, CGM Mutual has displayed real staying power, generating 15.4% annual returns for the five years to January 1, 1996, and 14.0% average annual gains for 10 years, placing the fund in the top 11% and 6%, respectively, of all balanced funds in those periods. In other words, don't be afraid to forgive occasional stumbles in performance if the fund makes up for it in competitor-beating gains over a variety of periods.

• **Factor in risk:** A fund's returns, of course, are just one side of the coin. The other side is risk: How did the fund achieve those gains? Did it reliably churn out decent returns year in and year out, rank consistently in the top half of similar funds, and hold up as well as or better than competitors during market squalls? Or did it streak to big gains, then get hit with stomach-wrenching losses and bounce up and down on the performance rankings scale like an out-of-control elevator in a high-rise?

How did the fund fare in lousy markets? Did it pull a real el foldo—or hold up pretty decently compared with its peers? Most people put a premium on consistency. That's understandable; we all like predictability, especially when it comes to investments. But there's nothing wrong with investing in a fund that posts erratic gains and that falls behind its peers from time to time—provided you are compensated for that uncertainty with outsize gains. After all, why put up with the anxiety usually associated with roller-coaster-like volatility if you're not doing any better than you would with a plodder that produces steady returns?

Keep in mind, too, that some types of funds are risky by their nature. Aggressive growth funds generally buy shares of fast-growing companies that often get hammered if the firm's earnings fall short of projections or the stock market overall drops. The value of small-company funds typically fluctuates more than that of funds that stick to corporate behemoths because small stocks are generally more flighty than their big brothers. The important thing to look for in such cases is how such funds behave compared with similar funds, not with steadier performers like, say, growth-and-income or balanced funds. I believe a well-rounded portfolio should have some risky funds that can produce extra-large returns. Devoting a portion of your portfolio to highly volatile funds makes intellectual sense. Then again, some people can't emotionally handle volatility. If you know that you're one of them—that is, you're sure to panic and sell if a fund takes a 20% hit—you should probably opt for a tamer fund that you can hold for the long term. So before investing in any fund, don't be swayed solely by alluring returns. You should also take a look at how it stacks up on the various measures of risk discussed in Chapter 3.

• **Determine if the fund maintains a consistent investing approach:** Even if a fund has a decent record and you feel comfortable with its level of risk, you want to make sure the manager hasn't switched to a new investing style. For example, basing your investment decision on a fund's past performance and risk measures that were generated when the fund held small-growth stocks won't give you much of a clue of how the fund might behave if the manager has recently loaded up on undervalued companies. Generally funds don't make radical switches in their investing styles, but some do bounce around a bit. One example: The Crabbe Huson Special aggressive growth fund has pretty much limited itself to small stocks, but it has adopted a growth investing approach in some years, a value style in others, and a blend of growth and value in still other years. That doesn't mean the fund manager is misleading you—in fact, some managers pride themselves on being able to switch back and forth between styles depending on which is on the ascent. But it is harder to predict the behavior of a fund that switches styles because you can never be sure when the manager might shift gears.

Similarly, if you are trying to build a portfolio that includes funds with a variety of styles, adding a fund whose manager changes investing styles can throw your portfolio out of whack. Let's say, for example, you put 10% of your money into a small-company growth fund and another 10% into a small-company value portfolio. If, for whatever reason, the value manager suddenly switches to small-growth stocks, you will wind up with far more growth and far less value than you wanted—not the biggest problem in the world, but something to consider if you are putting together a fine-tuned portfolio.

One easy way to verify a manager's current style is to check the investing style boxes provided by Morningstar and Value Line and described in Chapter 13. Morningstar also tells you what style the manager adopted in past years. Additionally, a fund's investing style can give you a good idea of how risky the fund is. A recent study by Morningstar found that investing style was a pretty good indicator not just of the present relative riskiness of funds, but of future risk as well, with funds becoming more volatile the more they tilt their style toward growth over value and toward small stocks over large.

• **See if the fund invests the way you think it does:** While examining the fund's style, you should also make sure the fund does what you think it does. Many domestic stock funds routinely spice their portfolios with foreign stocks. And to boost their returns, many diversified funds in recent years have made big bets on high-flying technology stocks. The Fidelity Emerging Growth aggressive growth fund, for example, let its tech-stock holdings grow to upward of 70% of its portfolio in 1995, according to Morningstar. There's no denying the fund has performed well, but investors should also realize that if the high-octane technology sector runs out of gas, so could the fund. Bond fund investors should also make sure they have a good idea of what the fund is buying. Rather than sticking to mundane goverment securities, some U.S. government bond funds may invest in derivative securities that could make the fund riskier than its U.S. government status implies. Reading the fund's prospectus or a write-up in a service such as Morningstar and Value Line can often alert you to potential risks you wouldn't be aware of if you scan only past performance data.

• **Make sure the manager who posted the terrific track record is still in charge:** If the manager responsible for a fund's track record has retired or moved on to another fund, you have to be especially careful about using past performance as a predictor for the fund's future behavior. Reason: The new manager may react completely differently from his or her predecessor to similar market conditions, which could dramatically change the fund's performance and risk profile. The effect of a manager change, however, can vary widely depending on how the fund is managed. If the fund invests in a relatively formulaic or highly structured way—for example, if it invests only in companies whose dividends are rising at a specific rate each year—then a new manager might have little material effect on the fund's strategy. In that case the old track record might still give you a good idea of how the fund is likely to perform in a given set of market conditions. Similarly, if the fund is run by a team of managers or a lead manager who works closely with several co-managers, then the exit even of the manager most closely associated with the fund may not represent a big shift in the fund's direction.

However, if the fund is run by a manager who truly puts his or her personal stamp on the selection of securities—which is the case for most funds—then the arrival of a new manager effectively wipes the fund's performance slate clean. Thus, for example, anyone considering investing in the Vanguard Windsor fund, managed from 1964 through 1995 by renowned value investor John Neff, would have to give little weight to the fund's stellar performance history under Neff, even though Neff's successor, Charles Freeman, helped Neff run the fund some 25 years. That doesn't mean Freeman can't take Windsor to the same heights that Neff did—or that existing investors should bail out just because the fund has a new skipper. It does mean, however, that investors already in Windsor—or any other fund whose manager exits—should be keeping a close watch to see how the fund fares under its new leader.

If the manager has proven herself at another fund with a similar investing objective and style, you can give at least some consideration to the track record at the former fund. For example, Carlene Murphy Ziegler launched the Artisan Small Cap fund in March 1995, which means Artisan has no track record to speak of. Ziegler did, however, distinguish herself at another small-company fund, Strong Common Stock, for several years prior to launching Artisan. Thus Ziegler's performance at Strong Common Stock should provide at least some clues as to how Artisan might perform under her tutelage. In general, however, if a fund has a manager who hasn't established a credible performance record of *at least* three years, you would probably be better off continuing your search until you find one that has.

• **Evaluate the fund's costs and expenses:** As we saw in Chapter 8, you are generally better off opting for funds that don't have sales commissions and that keep their ongoing operating costs low. Before you invest in any fund, therefore, I think you ought to compare its sales load, if any, as well as its expense ratio with those of similar funds. If its expenses are abnormally high, I would try to find a similar fund with comparable performance and lower expenses. In the case of bond funds, I would be especially reluctant to pay a sales commission or above average expenses, since I think it's particularly difficult for bond fund managers to overcome the drag of lofty fees and expenses. (Indeed, I believe you're almost always better off opting for bond funds that pare expenses to the bone.)

That said, however, I wouldn't automatically jettison a solid-performing fund just because it had a sales load or above average expenses, particularly if the expenses were only a bit above the average for similar funds. A handful of managers are good enough to compensate for bloated expenses—and even worth forking over a sales commission so you can get into their fund. In short, all other things being equal, I think you should give the nod to the fund with lower costs, but you should also realize that there will inevitably be rare cases when a truly great fund happens to have above average costs. (P.S.: If you happen to invest in a fund with elevated expenses, I suggest writing a letter to the fund's independent directors complaining about the costs. It might not help, but, hey, it can't hurt.)

Does Size Really Matter?

As if you don't have enough other factors to consider when picking funds, many magazines and fund experts caution against investing in funds whose assets are growing quickly. Similarly, many pundits warn about funds becoming too big for the manager to run effectively. Once a fund reaches a certain size, these Cassandras warn, the manager can't make nimble moves; the fund, presumably, becomes like a giant oil tanker that can no longer maneuver in the perilous straits of the financial markets. A chorus of critics have recently begun accusing $56-billion-and-growing Fidelity Magellan of being too big for its britches. Of course, similar criticisms were aired back in 1989 when the fund had swollen to the then-unbelievable size of $10 billion.

So should you give much consideration to a fund's size and the amount of money it's attracting? I'd say that in most cases size and asset growth are something to consider but nothing to obsess about. For one thing, it's not often that so much money comes cascading into a fund's coffers that it presents the manager with a real problem. And to the extent this does happen, paradoxically enough, assets are probably ballooning because investors are rushing into the fund after magazines and experts have been breathlessly touting the fund—in other words, the same people who are later shooing you away. Yes, a fund's performance may falter after the fund receives a huge slug of new money. And once a fund's coffers swell to the extent Fidelity Magellan's have (and performance falters as Magellan's did in early 1996), common sense requires that investors keep close tabs on its results. But a stumble in performance that follows a significant increase in a fund's size doesn't necessarily mean the new money was the cause of the subpar showing. (Does *post hoc, ergo propter hoc*— "after the fact, because of the fact"—ring a bell?) The manager could simply have made a lousy call about the direction of markets or interest rates, for example. Indeed, since new money is likely to chase funds with big recent gains, chances are that the fund has just come through a period in which its investing style has been hot. When a different style starts to take off—for example, when growth stocks begin to outstrip value or small shares leap ahead of large stocks—then you would expect the once-hot fund to cool. In other words, to the extent you should avoid funds because of their size or asset growth, it's often because these funds are being overly hyped by the personal advice crowd.

On the other hand, if you find that a fund's performance *relative to that of its peers* is flagging after it's gone through a growth spurt, then you should be concerned. Perhaps the fund is having trouble digesting the new money or perhaps the manager has lost her touch or made some poor investing decisions. Whatever the case, you should consider finding a fund with more consistent performance.

Now, there are times in which a size spurt is more likely to present a problem. One example is small-company funds. Identifying truly good small companies is tough—so tough, in fact, that the manager might have a hard time finding enough investment-worthy small firms to sop up all that new cash. As a result, that new money might languish in alternative investments such as Treasury bills until the manager can zero in on small firms he likes. Or, in an effort to put the cash to work in small stocks, the manager might end up buying shares of small companies he would otherwise have rejected or investing in stocks of larger companies, which can more easily absorb higher levels of investment. Whatever moves the manager makes, they will likely result in a departure from the fund's original mission and, therefore, figure to alter the fund's performance. Similarly, managers of value-oriented funds might have a hard time finding enough stocks selling at bargain prices to accommodate the new money investors have poured into the fund. Indeed, that's why you will occasionally see value managers such as Michael Price temporarily close his Mutual Series funds to new investment.

Therefore I would be wary of jumping into a small-company or value fund very soon after it has received a flood of new money. I'd also be wary of buying a small-company fund once its assets go very far over the $500 million mark. Why? Because I would be concerned that in order to invest the fund's assets, the manager might buy larger companies than he or she ordinarily would. So if I were in a small-company fund that had grown above $500 million—or were considering investing in one—I'd check to see if the market capitalization of the stocks the manager buys has been increasing in recent years. (You can get the median market capitalization for a fund's stocks from the Morningstar reports described in Chapter 13.) After all, if I've bought a fund because I want exposure to very small companies, then a fund that has been investing more and more in medium-size companies isn't filling my needs. In that case I would consider getting out of the fund (or at least not putting more money into it) and investing in a true small-company portfolio.

If the fund has remained true to its investing style despite its larger asset base, I'd look to see if the manager has still been able to perform in line with similar funds. If performance has begun to falter, then, using the guidelines outlined at the end of this chapter, I would monitor the fund's returns and, if necessary, replace it with a better performer.

Taxing Questions

In recent years the question of tax efficiency—the proportion of a fund's gains you actually get to keep—has gotten a lot of attention in fund circles. Specifically some fund experts and personal finance magazines have claimed that merely looking at a fund's returns before factoring in what you pay in income tax on your gains isn't helpful—or may even be blatantly misleading. These experts contend that because some funds' returns consist more of interest, dividend, or capital-gains distributions on which shareholders must pay taxes (as opposed to appreciation in the fund's net asset value or share price, which wouldn't be taxable until the fund is sold), funds' *after*-tax performance rankings can be significantly lower than their standing before taxes are taken into account. In short, the suggestion is that analyzing funds on the basis of the pretax returns provided by personal finance magazines and fund research companies may be seriously flawed and that we all ought to be putting even more effort into choosing funds by slogging through a variety of tax considerations.

Frankly I think the case for after-tax returns is largely overstated—and I believe that investors are better off simply trying to choose good funds using the guidelines just outlined than by spending their time judging funds both on pre- and after-tax returns. That's good news, since taxes, in addition to being one of the most boring subjects on earth, can also be one of the most complicated. In any case, here's why I don't think you have to agonize over tax issues when choosing funds.

No one doubts that there's a distinct advantage to getting your gains in the form of a rising fund share price rather than through taxable distributions—namely, you don't have to pay income taxes on the appreciation in the price of your fund shares until you actually sell them. Since you don't have to hand over part of your gains in taxes each year to the IRS—as you do when you receive taxable distributions—you have more of your money actually invested and working for you. But it's important to realize that you are not *avoiding* taxes; you are postponing them. When you sell your fund shares, you will pay taxes on the appreciation in the fund's share price.

What this means is that in addition to the level of tax rates, three other factors largely determine your after-tax return: the amount of taxable distributions the fund throws off each year; what proportion of those distributions are taxed at ordinary income tax rates (as interest, dividends, and short-term capital-gains are) versus generally lower capital gains rates (as long-term capital-gains payouts are); and how long you hold the fund shares before selling them. All these factors, therefore, play a part in determining how much your fund's pretax return will vary from its after-tax return. (You don't have to take any of this ~~crap~~ vital information into account if you are buying funds for a tax-deferred account such as a 401k employer retirement savings plan or an individual retirement account. Unless Congress decides differently, all gains in such accounts are taxed at ordinary income tax rates only when they're withdrawn.)

So the big question is, How do these factors play out?

Well, the *No-Load Fund Analyst* newsletter did a study to find out. The editors examined the pre- and after-tax performance rankings of stock mutual funds, assuming that they were held for three, five, or 10 years and then sold. (There were 91 funds in the three- and five-year holding periods and 75 funds in the 10-year period.) What they found was that the longer the funds were held before selling, the greater were the differences between pre- and after-tax rankings. No surprise there—a longer holding period means someone who owns funds that derived more of their gains from a rising share price would postpone tax payments, allowing that money to remain invested and generate yet more gains. But guess what? Even with the 10-year holding period, the difference between pre- and after-tax rankings was modest—less than 5% up or down on average—and the biggest changes occurred among funds that had mediocre peformance both before and after taxes. The differences were even smaller, on average, for the shorter holding periods. In other words, unless you owned mediocre funds to begin with, taxes didn't cause a major shift in the funds' relative performance rankings.

The editors also found that funds that throw off high dividend payments are also more likely to slip in the after-tax rankings, at least for investors in high tax brackets. This suggests that types of funds geared toward making regular dividend payouts—growth-and-income, balanced, and equity-income funds, for example—might not fare as well on an after-tax basis as they do in pretax rankings. Then again, the very fact that these funds can provide steady payouts (not to mention lower levels of risk) probably compensates for their decline in after-tax standings.

Bottom line: Don't make tax analysis one of your main criteria for screening funds. But you might consider using tax efficiency as a tiebreaker of sorts. If you have narrowed down your choice to a few good candidates and one is clearly more tax-efficient—that is, it does not consistently pay out big distributions—then you can give the nod to that fund. (Since tax efficiency is moot in tax-deferred instruments such as individual retirement accounts, you could always use the other funds for these accounts.)

The editors at *No-Load Fund Analyst* did make one tax-related suggestion, however, that will save you money—and that you can follow easily: Don't buy shares right before the fund makes a large capital gains distribution. (Most stock funds distribute capital gains in December, although some funds may do so more frequently. A fund sales representative can usually tell you when a fund distributes capital gains.) At first glance, having a gain paid to you immediately after investing in the fund may seem like a bonanza. But it's not. That's because when a fund distributes gains all it's really doing is giving you money you already had. (The gain didn't materialize out of thin air, after all; its value was already included in the fund's share price.) For investors who have been in the fund, that gain represents a return on money they invested a while ago. Newcomers, however, are effectively getting back in the form of a capital gain the money they just put in. The downside to that: Unless you're investing for your IRA or other tax-deferred account, you now owe taxes on the distribution (in other words, the money on which you really haven't earned anything yet). So if you had invested $10,000 yesterday, for example, and the fund paid a $2,000 capital-gains distribution today, you would owe tax on $2,000.

To avoid that immediate tax bite, try not to make large investments in a fund right before it pays its capital-gains distributions. (However, I wouldn't hold off making regular investments that are part of a dollar-cost-averaging plan, as described in Chapter 11, since the effect on a relatively small investment would be minimal for long-term investors.)

Tracking Your Funds' Performance

Once you've made the effort to choose superior funds, you might as well take a little time to check that they are continuing their winning ways. There's no need to be a fanatic about this. I'm not suggesting that you pore over the financial pages every day or put the fund company representative's phone number on speed dial so you can pepper her with questions every time the Dow takes a dive. I'm merely proposing some prudent monitoring to make sure that your funds haven't ventured off course since you bought them.

The most important thing to do is periodically to compare the total return of your funds versus the returns of funds with

similar investment objectives and investing styles. It also would-
n't hurt to see how your fund is doing compared to an appropriate market benchmark, such as the Standard & Poor's 500
stock index (if your fund invests primarily in large-company
stocks) or the Russell 2,000 (if it mostly sticks to small and medium-
size companies). Other indexes you might consult: the Morgan
Stanley EAFE index for diversified international stock funds; the
Morgan Stanley emerging markets index for foreign emerging
market funds; and the Lehman Brothers aggregate bond index
and municipal bond index, respectively, for taxable and tax-
exempt bond funds. Many personal finance magazines list the
results for these indexes, as does the Morningstar mutual fund
research service.

How often should you perform this checkup? Once at the
end of each calendar quarter ought to do it, but even if you manage it only semiannually, that's okay, too. You should find it pretty easy to monitor your fund's progress at the end of a quarter or
half year, since virtually every personal finance magazine and
newspaper business section these days gives quarterly or semiannual performance figures for all or most categories of stock and
bond funds as well as results for large numbers of individual
funds. Of course, you can also track your fund's performance
monthly (or more frequently if you have nothing better to do).
But if your decision to stay in a fund is going to be based on one
month's performance, I think you need to reexamine your
approach to funds.

One of your goals in these periodic evaluations is to see how
much money you've made (or, horror of horrors, lost) over a
given period. After all, you're probably investing to reach a certain goal, and you want to see if you're getting closer or sliding
back. From an investing standpoint, however, you should be
interested not just in whether your funds are making money, but
whether they are performing in line with similar funds. If your
aggressive growth fund is down 10% for the quarter, for example, that is certainly not welcome news. But if aggressive growth
funds on average are off by the same amount, chances are that

stock prices overall have fallen or that growth stocks have taken a beating. In that case the cause of the loss is probably weakness in the market, not a lapse by your fund manager.

If, on the other hand, the value of your aggressive growth fund has declined 20% while its competitors are off just 10%, you should be calling the fund company (or checking one of the sources listed in Chapter 13) to find out what's going on. Did the manager make a big bet on shares of a company that went belly up? Has the fund embarked on a risky new investing strategy that backfired? Has the fund switched investing styles? Did the original manager run off to join a heavy-metal band and hand over the reins to some 23-year-old whiz kid with an MBA but no experience managing a fund? Enquiring minds (especially those with money invested in the fund) want to know.

By the way, you should also be suspicious of unusually spectacular performance. I'm talking about your fund really clobbering competitors, not just beating them by a few percentage points. For example, if your growth-and-income fund gains 35% for the year when most growth and income funds are up just 15%, chances are pretty good that the manager is taking on a lot more risk than his competitors. That doesn't mean you should necessarily bail out of the fund. But you may want to rejigger some of your holdings to account for the fact that some of your money is sitting in a much more volatile portfolio than you originally believed.

When to Hold 'Em, When to Fold 'Em: Five Reasons to Dump a Fund

Sometimes, despite your assiduous research and the manager's herculean efforts, the best-laid investment strategies go awry— and that terrific fund you picked turns out to be a dud. Don't despair. Even the most successful investors screw up occasionally. What's tough, though, is figuring out whether a fund is going through a rough period from which it will recover or whether you've got a turkey on your hands.

You don't want to overreact to a short-term performance lapse. Just because a fund slips below its peer group for 90 days, or even longer, doesn't mean you should automatically jettison it from your portfolio. Indeed, if the fund has a history of lagging for a quarter or two but recovering to post a good record over longer periods, this may be its normal behavior. So when faced with a troubling stretch of returns over a quarter or so, your first thought should be that no moves are good moves. (That's right, don't just do something, stand there!)

Sometimes, however, an investor has got to do what he's got to do—and dump a fund. Here are five valid reasons for bailing out:

1. The fund consistently underperforms its peers. Occasionally even good funds will stumble. By stumble, I mean not just lose money—you have to expect that will happen if the financial markets overall head south—but fall behind the returns for comparable funds. Sometimes even good funds will have a horrendous quarter or year, much as some of us will go through a period at work or home where we're not our usual exceptional selves. In such cases you should try to find out why the fund's performance is suffering and then monitor it closely, going to quarterly (if you're not already there) or even monthly checkups to see if the fund shows signs of reviving. Generally I would give the manager at least a year but no more than two years to bring the fund's performance back in line with that of its peers. If that doesn't happen—and an immediate turnaround isn't in sight— I'd bail out.

2. A new manager isn't doing the job. Any time a new manager takes over, you should pay more attention to performance. Yes, you want to give a new skipper time to prove herself, but if the fund's performance is slipping, you can't hang in forever. Two years is time enough. If the new manager hasn't shaped up by then, you should ship out.

3. The fund has switched strategies. If you've put together a mix of funds with different investment objectives and investing styles as described in the next chapter, then the success of your portfolio depends on each manager doing his job. The large-cap growth manager should be buying large-cap growth stocks. If, instead, the manager is building up a huge horde of cash to guard against possible market declines or is dabbling in highly speculative tech stocks, then your overall asset mix is out of whack. If the fund manager isn't doing what you hired him to do, fire him and find a manager who will.

4. Your needs have changed. Maybe 15 years ago when Tiffany was a toddler and you were investing for four years of engineering school at MIT, an aggressive growth fund was an ideal choice because it gave you the double-digit gains you knew were needed to meet hefty tuition bills. But now that Tiffany is an art appreciation major at Sarah Lawrence, you can't afford to take big risks with the money you'll be shelling out for tuition and board over the next few years. Remember, each fund you pick should address a specific need. If a fund no longer fits your needs (kind of like a college), look for one that does.

5. You would like to create a tax loss. Tax considerations should never dictate your investment strategy, so I think this last tip for dumping a fund should be used sparingly, if at all. That said, there are times when you might be able to lower your tax bill by dumping a losing fund yet still pretty much maintain the asset mix within your fund portfolio. For example, if you own shares in a large-cap stock fund that are now worth less than you paid for them, you can sell those shares to establish a loss. You can then use that loss to offset capital gains on other investments. If your loss exceeds those gains, you can apply what's left against $3,000 of other income, such as wages and investment income. (If you *still* have a loss after these two steps, you can carry forward what remains and apply the same offset procedure in future years until you write off the entire loss.) So that you don't upset the equilibrium in your portfolio, you can then reinvest the proceeds in a similar large-cap stock fund. Essentially, then, what you've done is make the best of a loss by lowering your taxable income while at the same time maintaining your asset mix.

Unfortunately, tax regulations can sometimes complicate this otherwise straightforward maneuver. For example, if you buy shares in the fund you're selling within 30 days of the sale, the IRS will disqualify all or part of your loss, depending on the number of shares you've bought, in accordance with what are known as the "wash-sale" rules. By the way, any shares you acquire through reinvested dividends during the 61-day wash-sale window—30 days before the sale, the day of the sale, and 30 days after—count as an additional purchase. There are also rules that restrict the amount of a short-term loss you can claim if you sell shares that you've held six months or less and you receive a capital-gains distribution from the same fund during that period. Similarly, if you receive a tax-free dividend from shares of a muni bond fund that you've owned six months or less and then sell for a loss, you can deduct only the part of the loss that exceeds the amount of the tax-free dividend. (If these last two sentences don't convince you that we desperately need to simplify the tax code, you must be an accountant.) So if you're going to try some fancy tax footwork, I suggest you at least order the free publications the IRS provides that deal with mutual fund taxation (call the IRS at 800-829-1040) and, better yet, sit down for a scintillating discussion with your tax adviser.

CHAPTER 10

Building a Winning Portfolio of Funds

The Right Mix Is All

Many fund investors—novices and veterans alike—put most of their effort into trying to pick funds that will one day zoom to the top of some newspaper's or financial magazine's hot-performer list. That's a mistake. Over the long term only a very few managers outdistance their competitors by more than a few percentage points a year—and it's difficult, if not impossible, to identify those superior skippers in advance.

Instead, investors hoping to achieve long-term financial success should devote less energy to picking individual investments and more toward what investment pros call **asset allocation,** or the process of divvying up your holdings among stock, bond, and money-market funds. Why? Because the *types* of funds you own and the *proportion* in which you hold them play a much more important role in determining the returns you will earn than the individual funds or securities that you choose.

171

Indeed, a seminal 1991 study of pension fund performance by consultant Gil Beebower and money managers Gary Brinson and Brian Singer found that asset-allocation accounts for roughly 92% of a typical investor's return. Another 5% comes from fiddling with that mix in response to changing market conditions. And what of those stocks, bonds, or funds that you took so much time and effort to choose? Well, they contributed, too, but barely, accounting for a measly 3% of the typical investor's gains. To paraphrase that weird disembodied voice in the Kevin Costner film *Field of Dreams:* If you create the right mix, the returns will come.

In this chapter I will show you how to create a mix of funds that will help you achieve your financial goals. I'll begin by explaining how and why asset allocation works and then warn you about a few mistakes investors commonly make, such as buying too many similar funds. I'll then take you through the steps you should follow to create and properly monitor your own asset mix. Finally, so that you will have a guide for putting together your own portfolio of funds, I asked Gibson Capital Management, a Pittsburgh investment research firm that specializes in asset allocation, to design four model portfolios for investors with typical goals such as saving for a down payment for a house in five or so years, investing for a child's college education in 10 or more years, accumulating money long-term for retirement, and investing for both income and capital growth during retirement. Once you've settled on the ideal mix for you, you can begin choosing funds to fill out your portfolio by turning to the suggestions listed in the appendix on pages 273–280 or, better yet, by searching for your own funds using the principles outlined throughout this book.

What Makes Asset Allocation Tick?

The idea behind asset allocation (technically known as **modern portfolio theory**) is really no more complicated than putting your eggs (in this case, funds) in several different baskets (asset classes). Since different investments don't move up and down entirely in sync, diversifying your holdings among a variety of assets or funds allows gains in one area to offset losses or poor returns in another. For example, when domestic stocks funds tumbled nearly 6% in 1990, government bond funds gained more than 8%. Similarly, when stock funds eked out a mere 1.2% gain in 1987, international funds managed a respectable 10.9% return. Of course, diversification among different types of assets or funds doesn't guarantee you'll never lose money. In 1994, for example, both domestic and international stock and bond funds ended up in the red. But since such instances are rare, asset allocation usually assures that at least some part of your portfolio is chugging along, which reduces the overall level of risk in your portfolio.

In general, asset-allocation specialists try to figure out how you can get the best return for whatever level of risk you are willing to take. To determine that efficient mix of risk versus reward, investment research firms such as Gibson Capital Managment begin by looking at **correlation,** which is a barometer of how different assets perform compared with one another over varying market cycles. To measure correlation, investment analysts use a scale that ranges from 1.0 (two assets move exactly in sync) to -1.0 (the two move in opposite directions). To assure that your portfolio generates steady returns, you want to assemble a collection of assets or funds that are weakly correlated to each other. That way your portfolio won't be decimated by having all your investments decline in value at exactly the same time.

Another advantage of combining different assets that don't all move in lockstep is that you can invest some of your money in funds that, on their own, you might consider too risky. That's because their volatility is muted by the offsetting movements of other holdings in your portfolio. Thus, for example, had you invested in a portfolio with half its assets in blue-chip U.S. stocks, 40% in corporate bonds, and 10% in U.S. Treasury bills, you would have earned an annual return of roughly 10% over the 22-year period from 1973 through 1994.

But if you had split your bond holdings equally between domestic and international bonds and also divvied up your 50% stock holdings to include small-company shares, international stocks, small positions in real estate–related investments, and a gold fund, you could have boosted your return to nearly 12% annually, while taking on about 12% less risk than the all-U.S. portfolio. This seemingly unachievable alchemy of lower risk and higher return is possible because you are combining investments with a range of different correlations. Small stocks, for example, have a 0.79 correlation to large domestic shares, which in turn have only a 0.39 correlation to domestic bonds. Foreign equities, meanwhile, have only a 0.47 correlation to U.S. blue chips and a 0.38 correlation to small U.S. stocks.

In determining an asset mix, most asset-allocation specialists also take into account the risk of each asset class. In most cases that means looking at the volatility of the investment using a measure such as standard deviation for stocks and duration for bonds. (These and other risk measures are explained in Chapter 3.) It's crucial to incorporate risk into your asset mix because the tendency over the short term for a particular asset class, such as stocks, to experience sharp setbacks has a direct impact on your odds of reaching your goal within the time you've set to achieve it. Allocation pros also rely not just on the historical performance of various asset types, but on estimates of their potential future returns based on the relative performance of various asset classes.

How to Figure the Right Mix for You

By assessing variables such as correlation, risk, and potential future returns, the computers used by asset-allocation pros can churn out thousands of possible returns for different portfolios. The pros themselves can then sort through various permutations and, using the expected returns and risks for each allocation, choose a mix that provides the highest possible return for any given level of risk. Sounds complicated—and it can be. Fortunately, though, individual investors can use more of a seat-of-the-pants approach that, combined with the model portfolios provided later in this chapter, can lead to a portfolio mix that provides the most important benefits of diversification. Here are the four steps to take:

1. Figure out your investment time horizon. Many financial publications suggest you base your mix of stock, bond, and money funds on your age. Wrong. The length of time you have before you must tap into your investment stash—also known as your time horizon—is the single most important factor in determining the right allocation. If you are going to need your money within a few years, you will want to minimize big short-term swings in your portfolio's value. Why? Because you don't want to be forced to sell your investments after their value has dropped and before they've had a chance to bounce back. In search of higher returns, some investors decide to take the risk of putting all their money in stocks even if they know they'll have to tap their holdings soon. That risk might pay off, but if stock prices take a big hit, these investors could find themselves short of the money they need. To insulate themselves against such setbacks, short-term investors should tilt their mix toward more stable investments such as money-market and short-term bond funds.

If, on the other hand, you are salting away money for an investment goal that's a decade or more away, you can afford to ride out short-term swings in the market. As a long-term investor, your primary goal is to grow the value of your portfolio and keep ahead of inflation. You will need higher returns than those available solely through bond and money-market funds. So the longer your investment horizon, the more you should load up on various types of stock funds. In general, if your time horizon is 10 years or longer, you should be putting 60% or more of your holdings in stock funds.

2. Realistically evaluate your appetite for risk. Modern portfolio theory can tell you how your fund holdings should be split among stock, bond, and money funds, given these investments' risk characteristics, correlations, and potential future returns. But the theory can't tell you whether you have the stomach to hang on through a bear market without panicking and selling your stocks after prices have bottomed out. So take your emotional makeup into account as well when deciding on your portfolio allocations.

If you reach for the Mylanta every time stock prices dip 5% or so, you might want to scale back the equity portion of your portfolio by five or 10 percentage points. Yes, you will be sacrificing some return. But you're better off doing that than bailing out during a market setback and effectively undoing the benefits of a diversified portfolio (and blowing your chance of realizing stocks' higher long-term returns). Conversely, don't overdo it on the safety side. Sure, you might feel warm and fuzzy inside knowing your life savings are stashed in funds that invest in Treasury bills backed by Uncle Sam's full faith and credit. But you won't feel so great 20 years from now when prices have probably doubled but your investment stash, after taxes and inflation, isn't worth any more than it is today.

3. Diversify among a wide range of funds. At a bare minimum, you must own all three broad classes of fund types— stock, bond, and money-market. But to reap the full benefits of a diversified portfolio, you should also branch out into even finer categories. The stock fund portion of your holdings, for example, ideally should include international and small-company funds. And since investing styles drift in and out of favor without warning, you should include funds that invest primarily in growth stocks as well as ones that home in on value stocks. (If you want to cut down on the number of funds in your portfolio, choose a blended fund—that is, one that buys both growth and value shares.)

As for bond funds, you want to protect yourself from upward swings in interest rates. To gauge a bond fund's sensitivity to interest rate movements, check out its average maturity or, better yet, its duration. (Both measures are explained in Chapter 6.) The longer a bond fund's duration (and, generally, average maturity), the more its value will fall if interest rates rise and climb if rates fall. To insulate yourself from interest rate swings, most advisers recommend holding a combination of short-term and intermediate-term bond funds.

4. Don't mess with your mix. Once you've settled on an allocation that's right for you, let it be regardless of what's going on in the market. You might be tempted to capitalize on the higher returns generated by some high-flying sector of the market, but you should resist the urge to jump around. Your chances of riding a hot sector, jumping out before it crashes, and landing in the next soon-to-be-torrid area are minuscule. More likely you'll just undo the benefits of diversification.

Inevitably your portfolio mix will get out of whack, as some parts of your portfolio gain more than others. So once a year you should rebalance your holdings. If the proportions are off by only a few percentage points, you can simply put the new money you invest into the parts of your portfolio that have trailed over the year, thus bringing them back to their proper proportion. (This way you can continue to defer taxes on unrealized gains in your winning funds.) Otherwise you should sell parts of the portfolio with big gains and reinvest the proceeds in the laggards. Besides restoring your portfolio to its proper allocations, this rebalancing act has another advantage: by investing in the trailing funds, you wind up buying shares when their prices are depressed. In short, rebalancing forces you to pursue the oft-cited but little followed strategy for success of buying low and selling high.

You may, however, have to adjust your mix if your goals change or as you grow closer to the time you'll need your money. For example, to invest for a goal such as funding a child's education in 10 or so years, you would want to create a portfolio much like Model Portfolio 2 on page 183, which recommends putting fully 60% of your holdings in stocks and 40% in bond and money funds. But as you draw nearer to the time you will tap your stash, you should begin shifting money out of stocks and into bonds and money funds. By the time you are within three or so years of needing that money, your mix should be closer to that in Model Portfolio 1 on page 182, with only 25% of your holdings in stocks. And when you are within a year of needing the money, it should be mostly in money funds and short-term bond funds and perhaps a small portion in intermediate-term bond funds.

The Pitfalls of Owning Too Many Funds

In their zeal to diversify, some investors go overboard, snapping up whatever fund happens to be hot or catches their eye and giving little or no thought to whether one holding complements another. Such investors may wind up with lots of funds, sometimes 20 or more.

But such a grab-bag lineup of funds is no more a portfolio than a used-car lot is a collection of vintage cars. Remember, to get the benefits of diversification, you must own funds with different investment objectives and investing styles in proportions that make sense given your goals and time horizon. If you have 10 stock funds but they're all small-cap growth funds, then the equity portion of your portfolio isn't diversified. You would be better off with one small-cap growth fund plus perhaps a small-cap value fund and some large-company growth-and-value funds.

So how many funds do you actually need? That depends on how much work you're willing to do to build a portfolio and monitor it. To create the model portfolios in this chapter, you would ideally use eight to 10 funds, assuming you include a money-market fund and both value and growth versions of the large- and small-cap stock funds. You could add one or two more if you wanted to include an international fund that invests in emerging markets or add an extra inflation hedge to your portfolio in the form of a real estate or natural resources or precious metals fund. But once you get beyond a dozen or so, you're virtually guaranteeing you'll have overlap in the securities your various funds own.

If you know, however, that you aren't diligent enough to keep track of such a portfolio—or put one together in the first place—you could easily cut back to five or six funds by, say, using stock funds that take a blended growth-and-value approach or by eliminating an international bond fund. Such streamlining won't cause your portfolio to self-destruct; rather, it means that your returns might not be quite as high as they otherwise would have been or you may be incurring somewhat more risk to get the same return. While that may be something to think about, it's not something to obsess over. Even if you owned simply one stock, one bond, and one money fund, you would get at least some benefits of diversification. In fact, if you really, really don't want to bother with building a portfolio, you can get by with a so-called life-cycle fund or a fund of funds, both of which amount to mini portfolios in and of themselves. You can find out more about both of these two low-maintenance options in the next chapter.

Whichever approach you take and number of funds you decide to buy, don't feel you have to get them all at once. You can build your holdings gradually to whatever number of funds you feel comfortable with. If you are just starting out and don't have much cash, you might consider starting with one of the life-cycle, fund of funds, or asset-allocation portfolios described in the next chapter (or a balanced fund, as discussed in Chapter 5) and then accumulating the others as you have more money to invest. In general, though, you want to get by with the fewest number of funds that will give you the diversity you need. And you should not invest in more funds than you feel you are willing to keep an eye on. As with risk, some self-assessment is called for in building a portfolio. Ultimately you are better off with a simple portfolio that meets your basic needs and whose returns you monitor every three months or so at a minimum than with a wide-ranging complicated one that demands attention but doesn't get it.

Model Portfolios for Typical Goals

With those tips in mind, here are four portfolios for different goals, designed by asset-allocation firm Gibson Capital Management. You should not consider the allocations in these portfolios as immutable parameters that you must follow down to the exact percentage point. Rather, think of them as general guides for creating your own mix to meet your own circumstances, including your specific time horizon, the rate of return you need to meet your goals, and your risk tolerance.

If you feel you can stomach more volatility, you can lean more toward stock funds. If your idea of living dangerously is taking 11 items through the express checkout lane in the supermarket, then you might want to shift the mix a bit toward bond and money funds. If you are in the 28% or higher tax bracket, you might also consider tax-free municipal bond funds. Similarly, while I recommend that you try to include all the different types of asset classes listed in the model portfolios, I realize that some people may find that level of work daunting. If you are among them, at least try to adhere to the overall percentages allotted respectively to the broad categories of stock, bond, and money funds in each portfolio.

One more thing: Many publications offer portfolios with various asset mixes, claiming that some are for "conservative" or "risk-averse" investors, while others are for "aggressive" investors. I specifically rejected this approach of labeling portfolios as conservative or aggressive and, instead, have identified these portfolios by the investing time horizon for which they're suited. Why? Because the so-called conservative portfolios would typically include a big slug of bonds and money funds, much like my Model Portfolio 1. But if you are investing for the long term, you should not be loading up on bonds and money funds—*even if you consider yourself a conservative or risk-averse investor.* Bonds and money funds simply won't power your portfolio with long-term inflation-beating returns. Your horizon should be your basic guide in determining your allocations, and then you can make adjustments from that point based on how much volatility you feel comfortable taking on.

Finally, before building one of these portfolios, try to set aside an emergency reserve equal to three to six months' living expenses in a safe accessible investment like a money fund. By doing so, you won't have to sell shares of your stock funds at an inopportune time should you happen to lose your job or face large unexpected expenses. The portion of your portfolio devoted to money funds and short-term bond funds can serve as part or all of your reserve, depending on how large it is.

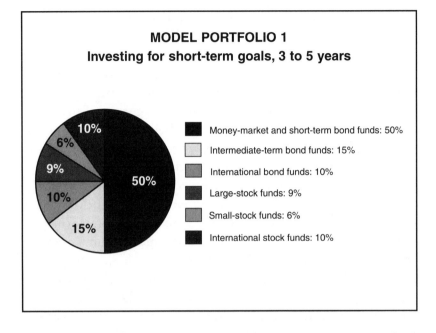

MODEL PORTFOLIO 1
Investing for short-term goals, 3 to 5 years

- Money-market and short-term bond funds: 50%
- Intermediate-term bond funds: 15%
- International bond funds: 10%
- Large-stock funds: 9%
- Small-stock funds: 6%
- International stock funds: 10%

Stock funds: 25% (large-stock 9%, small-stock 6%, international 10%)
Bond funds: 25% (intermediate-term 15%, international 10%)
Money-market and short-term bond funds: 50%

You would put together a mix of funds like this one if you were investing money, say, to accumulate cash for a down payment on a house or for any other goal that required you to tap your funds in three to five years. The aim of this portfolio heavy in bond and money funds is to provide a reasonable rate of return, while also providing a high degree of stability.

By sticking 50% of your money into money and short-term bond funds—that is, ones with a duration or average maturity of two to four years—you have a reasonable assurance that the value of at least part of your stash is always growing. (An equal mix of short-term bond and money funds should work fine for most investors, although if you are especially risk-averse, you might want to tilt the blend in favor of money funds over short-term bonds.) The 25% invested in bond funds also adds a measure of security but should give higher returns than the money fund portion.

The 25% stake in stock funds will likely generate the biggest annual gains. But since stocks are also volatile, you run the risk that the market could go into a slump and stocks could drag down the value of your porfolio, at least temporarily. Even if the stock market were stung with a major setback, however, the money fund and bond portions of this portfolio should limit the damage—and give you a large reserve of liquidity to draw on when you need it.

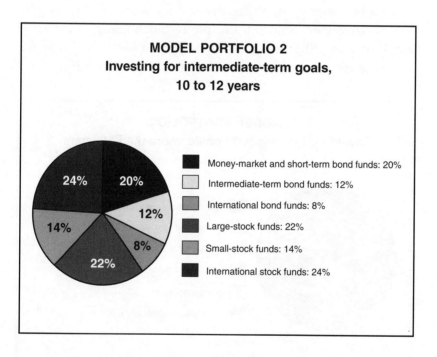

MODEL PORTFOLIO 2
Investing for intermediate-term goals,
10 to 12 years

- Money-market and short-term bond funds: 20%
- Intermediate-term bond funds: 12%
- International bond funds: 8%
- Large-stock funds: 22%
- Small-stock funds: 14%
- International stock funds: 24%

Stock funds: 60% (large-stock 22%, small-stock 14%, international 24%)
Bond funds: 20% (intermediate-term 12%, international 8%)
Money-market and short-term bond funds: 20%

If you have a longer investing time horizon—perhaps you're investing to meet your children's college education expenses 10 to 12 years from now—you can afford to shoot for higher returns by loading up more on stock funds. That is exactly what this portfolio recommends. To get the capital growth you will need, you should put the bulk of your money in a combination of large- and small-company domestic stock funds as well as in an international fund or two. To add a bit of stability, divide the rest equally between bond funds (20%) and money funds and short-term bond funds (20%).

As you near the time when you will need your money, you should gradually shift out of stocks and into bond and money funds. With its 60% stake in stock funds, this portfolio will be quite a bit more volatile than the one for short-term goals previously described. Still, you can pretty much ignore short-term stock-market setbacks since you will have plenty of time for stocks to recover and move on to stellar long-term gains.

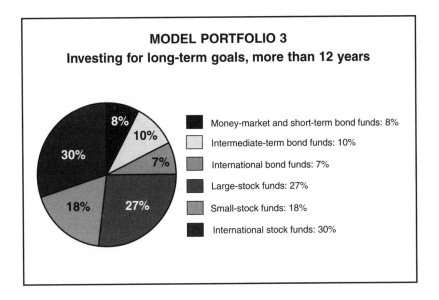

MODEL PORTFOLIO 3
Investing for long-term goals, more than 12 years

- Money-market and short-term bond funds: 8%
- Intermediate-term bond funds: 10%
- International bond funds: 7%
- Large-stock funds: 27%
- Small-stock funds: 18%
- International stock funds: 30%

Stock funds: 75% (large-stock 27%, small-stock 18%, international 30%)
Bond funds: 17% (intermediate-term 10%, international 7%)
Money-market and short-term bond funds: 8%

True long-term investors—for example, people saving for a retirement that is still a good 12 years or more away—should be focusing almost single-mindedly on stock funds. The reason: When putting away money for periods of a decade or longer, your main concern is building your capital at a faster pace than the inflation rate. What's more, with a long investing horizon, you don't have to concern yourself with the short-term ups and downs of the stock market. So you can shoot for stocks' higher returns without worrying about your portfolio's value occasionally hitting downdrafts. As a result, you can devote 75% of your holdings to stock funds, with the rest split between bond funds and money and short-term bond funds.

Now, some investment advisers and financial planners might recommend that long-term investors devote 100% of their money to stock funds. The theory behind that all-stock approach: Since stocks produce the highest long-term returns and you're investing for a very long period of time anyway, why drag down the performance of your portfolio by adding even a modest amount of bonds and money funds? Why not go with stocks alone and just hang on tight when the market slides?

To some extent, the 100%-stock approach is right. You probably will increase your returns with a stocks-only portfolio. The problem with that thesis, however, is that it probably overestimates most investors' ability to stay the course during a prolonged bear market like the 1973-74 slide when the Dow Jones Industrial Average dropped some 45%. We haven't seen such a sustained market downturn since then, so it's unclear whether investors would stay invested or bolt if stocks fell and stayed down a long time.

For that reason, Gibson Capital Management founder Roger Gibson rarely, if ever, recommends an all-stock approach, even for the longest of long-term investors. But if you are truly confident you won't start unloading your stock funds when the market hits a prolonged and deep skid, by all means increase the amount of money you put into stocks beyond the 75% recommended here. But if you later wimp out during the depths of a severe bear market, don't say you weren't warned.

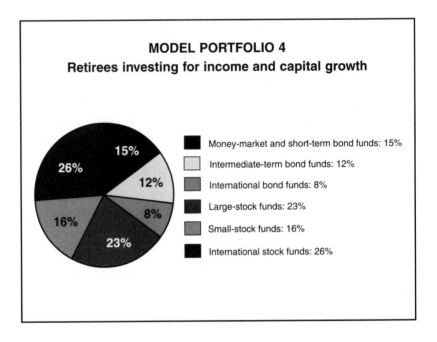

MODEL PORTFOLIO 4
Retirees investing for income and capital growth

- Money-market and short-term bond funds: 15%
- Intermediate-term bond funds: 12%
- International bond funds: 8%
- Large-stock funds: 23%
- Small-stock funds: 16%
- International stock funds: 26%

Stock funds: 65% (large-stock 23%, small-stock 16%, international 26%)
Bond funds: 20% (intermediate-term 12%, international 8%)
Money market and short-term bond funds: 15%

Retirees and other investors who rely on their portfolios to generate income for daily living expenses often stick all or near-ly all of their money in bonds or bond funds instead of salting away most in stock funds as outlined in Portfolio 4. Big mistake. Unless you're absolutely sure that you are not very long for this world, you face the risk that your investment stash will run down before you do. The fact is that most retirees and other elderly investors must invest for the long term, if they don't want to out-live their money. At age 65, for example, the average American has a life expectancy of another 17 years. Faced with that kind of an investment horizon, a portfolio of bonds alone simply won't keep the purchasing power of your investment stash ahead of inflation. As a result, unless you've got a huge portfolio to draw on, the chances are good you will run out of money before you run out of time.

To assure that you don't outlive your portfolio, most advisers recommend that retirees and other older investors resist the urge to hunker down in bond funds and, instead, keep a healthy chunk of their portfolio in stock funds. The portfolio recommended above, for example, suggests stashing 65% of your money in a variety of stock funds, while dividing the other 35% between bond funds and money and short-term bond funds. Granted, this portfolio won't generate nearly as much income as one invested mostly in bonds. But, in general, you are better off focusing on stocks and, if necessary, occasionally selling shares of stock funds to meet current expenses than you would be putting your money solely or mostly in income-producing bonds, which offer little chance of capital growth.

If you still feel you need more current income than a portfolio like this provides, however, you can make a few adjustments. For example, you can tilt your stock mix toward funds that generate dividends, such as growth-and-income and equity-income funds. You could also include some well-chosen high-yield or junk bond funds in your portfolio or even boost the portion of the portfolio going into bonds. You should be wary, though, of putting more than 50% of your holdings in bond and money funds, since you will reduce the prospects for capital growth—and increase your chances of running through your money.

CHAPTER 11

The Hands-off
Approach to
Fund Investing

In Investing, Less Can Be More

Wouldn't it be great if there were an easy way to home in on a fund that could provide reliable high-powered performance? A fund that could generate above average returns in most years and, better yet, one you could count on to outperform 70% or so of its competitors over long stretches of a decade or more? Sure would make fund picking easier. Well, guess what. Such a stalwart performer is available today. It's called an **index fund,** so named because unlike regular funds whose managers constantly buy and sell securities, hoping to beat the market averages, index funds hold all or nearly all the stocks in a standard market benchmark such as the Standard & Poor's 500 index of large-company stocks. The results from this so-called passive approach—as opposed to the regular trading of securities that goes on in actively managed funds—can be surprisingly rewarding. Over the 10 years to April 1, 1996, for example, the 13.7% annualized return of the largest S&P 500 index fund—the

Vanguard Index 500—landed the fund in the top 25% of all 402 diversified domestic stock funds with 10-year records.

But what's really amazing about index funds, given their consistently above average performance, is how few people invest in them. Less than 10% of fund investors own any type of index portfolio, and as of early 1996 the assets in index funds accounted for only about 3% of all the money invested in stock and bond funds.

In this chapter I'll cover a variety of ways you can make money in mutual funds, even if you don't want to devote a good part of your life (or, for that matter, a small part) to your investments. I'll begin with a look at one of the best-kept open secrets in the mutual fund world—index funds. My unabashed aim is to convince you to put at least a part of your money into one or more of these funds. From there, I'll move on to other types of funds—such as so-called life-cycle funds—that essentially allow you to put your fund investing on autopilot. You sit back and the fund manager decides what mix of stocks, bonds, and other securities is best for you.

Then I'll talk briefly about a relatively new but fast-growing wrinkle in fund investing called wrap accounts, which a number of brokers and financial planners are pushing (too hard, in my opinion). I'll conclude with a look at a disciplined, easy-to-use strategy called dollar-cost averaging (and its more sophisticated cousin, value averaging), which helps investors build wealth while reducing risk by taking emotion and guesswork out of investing.

The Compelling Case for Index Funds

Most investors, quite understandably, expect that the professional investment advisers who buy and sell securities for mutual funds, insurance companies, and pension funds should be able to beat the market—that is, earn higher returns than the averages posted by broad market benchmarks such as the Standard & Poor's 500, an index of the shares of 500 large U.S. companies that's considered a barometer of the overall stock market's health. After all, if a money manager who spends all of his or her time at work sifting through research reports and monitoring the stock market can't consistently identify promising stocks that will offer above average gains, why bother hiring the manager in the first place?

But as the chart on the next page shows, the majority of stock fund managers don't consistently beat the market; indeed, most have *lagged* the stock market in 12 of the 20 years from 1976 through 1995. In addition, more than half of stock fund managers have also fallen short of the stock market's average return over longer periods as well. For example, less than 20% of the 402 U.S. diversified funds that had been around 10 years managed to beat the S&P 500's 14.0% annual return for the 10 years to April 1, 1996. In other words, fund investors had far less than a 50% chance of beating the market over that 10-year span. (A chart showing bond-fund managers' returns versus an appropriate benchmark for the bond market would show similar results.)

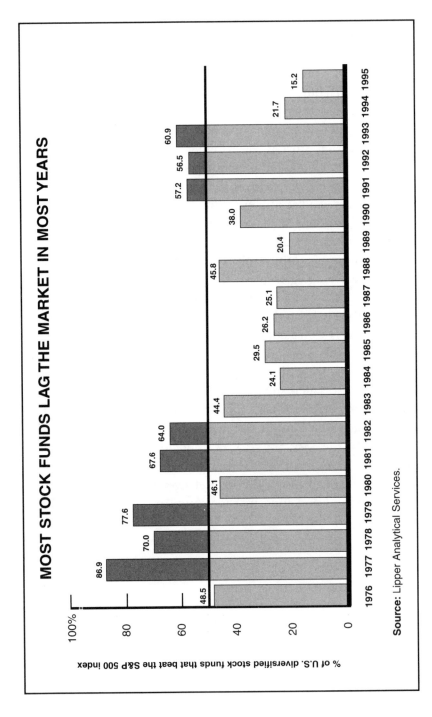

MOST STOCK FUNDS LAG THE MARKET IN MOST YEARS

% of U.S. diversified stock funds that beat the S&P 500 index

Source: Lipper Analytical Services.

You would be wrong, however, to conclude from this chart that fund managers are inept bumblers who aren't earning their considerable salaries. Rather, the reason most funds don't outpace market averages largely comes down to simple mathematics. Here's how the reasoning goes: In effect, the professional money managers at mutual funds, banks, insurance companies, investment firms, and pension funds *are* the market. The portfolios they manage constitute about half the value of U.S. stocks and account for the bulk of trading in those stocks. So their returns, overall, are the market's return. And while "all the children are above average," in radio show host Garrison Keillor's fictive Lake Wobegon community, in the real world only about half of managers can post market-beating returns. The ones who beat the market have to beat those who didn't, which means roughly 50% of the managers post returns above the market average and the other 50% fall below the average.

But there's one more thing to factor in: mutual funds' annual operating expenses. When you deduct fund's annual expenses (about 1.4% of assets for U.S. diversified stock funds and roughly 1.0% for bonds), you further winnow down the ranks of the market beaters. So how, you may ask, can a majority of managers beat the market in a given year, as nearly 87% did in 1977? Simple. Most stock funds invest in stocks that are smaller than those in the S&P 500 index. So in years when small-stock returns outpace large ones, funds often beat the S&P 500. These short bursts of superior performance aside, however, mathematics and the gravitational pull of expenses combine to keep the returns of a majority of funds below those of the market overall.

All of this adds up to a splendid reason for investing in index funds. By holding all or a representative sample of the stocks or bonds in a particular market benchmark—and by keeping annual expenses very, very low—an index fund attempts to *match* the market, not beat it. Shooting for the market averages may not sound exciting—after all, who aspires to be average at anything? But if you invest in a fund that delivers market returns, you will beat 60% to 70% of funds most years and over the long run. What's more, you will likely get to pocket a higher portion of those returns after taxes. Why? Since index funds don't trade securities as frequently as actively managed funds, they don't create as many taxable capital gains as other funds. Instead the bulk of your return is due to the appreciation in the price of your fund shares. And you pay no tax on that appreciation until you sell your shares.

When Indexing Works Best . . . and Which to Buy

You can find index funds that specialize in all sorts of stocks and bonds—small stocks, medium-size shares, international stocks, long-term or short-term bonds, and so on. But indexing usually works best in what academics call efficient markets—that is, markets such as those for large household-name stocks or government and corporate bonds, where thousands of Wall Street pros analyze securities daily, making it difficult for a fund manager to gain an edge on other players in the market. Therefore I strongly recommend that you make index funds your primary holding in the portion of your portfolio that you devote to large-company stock funds and government or high-quality corporate bond funds. (Alas, there are no index funds for municipal bonds.)

Indexing doesn't appear to work quite as well, however, in less efficient markets, such as those for small stocks and international shares, where issues aren't followed as closely by the Wall Street horde and fund managers have a shot at unearthing real bargains. For the portion of your fund holdings in these areas, therefore, you have a decent shot at superior gains by investing in actively managed funds. Nonetheless, even in these inefficient markets, index funds can still provide competitive returns, if for no other reason than the fact that index funds keep their costs down. So they're a terrific choice if you want to own funds that invest in a variety of different securities but you don't want the hassle of evaluating large numbers of funds. By choosing a good index fund in these areas, you know that you'll get solid performance.

So which index funds, specifically, should you buy? The single most important thing to keep in mind when choosing an index fund is that the lower the fees, the closer the fund will come to matching the performance of its index. And when it comes to shaving fees to the minimum, no one beats the Vanguard Group. Its 0.19% expense ratio for the Vanguard Index 500 fund, for example, is less than half the 0.45% expense ratio of the S&P 500 index funds offered by Fidelity and T. Rowe Price.

There's another reason to go with Vanguard's index funds: In certain types of index funds, Vanguard is pretty much the only choice. So unless you're willing to sacrifice a slight bit of return to keep your holdings within a certain fund family, in most cases you're better off going with Vanguard, the king of the index portfolios.

THE TOP INDEX FUND CHOICES

Fund	What It Invests In	Expense Ratio	Minimum Initial Investment	Telephone (800)
Vanguard Index 500	The large companies that make up the Standard & Poor's 500 stock index	0.19%	$3,000	851-4999
Schwab 1000[1]	The 1,000 U.S. companies with the highest total stock market value. Special feature: This fund is managed to minimize ongoing taxable gains to shareholders.	0.51%	$1,000	435-4000
Dreyfus Midcap Index[2]	Medium-size U.S. companies	0.40%	$2,500	645-6561
Vanguard Index Trust—Extended Market[3]	Small and medium-size U.S. companies	0.20%	$3,000	851-4999
Vanguard Index Small-Cap Stock[4]	Small U.S. companies	0.17%	$3,000	851-4999
Schwab International Index[5]	The 350 largest foreign companies	0.90%	$1,000	435-4000
Vanguard International Equity-Index—Europe[4]	Large companies of 13 European countries	0.32%	$3,000	851-4999
Vanguard International Equity-Index—Pacific[4]	Large companies primarily in Japan, but also in such Pacific Rim markets as Hong Kong, Singapore, Malaysia, and Australia.	0.32%	$3,000	851-4999
Vanguard Bond Index—Total Market	Representative sample of bonds in the Lehman Brothers Aggregate Bond Index, an index of U.S. government and corporate bonds. Fund keeps average maturity of roughly 9 years and is ideal for investors looking to match returns of the overall bond market.	0.18%	$3,000	851-4999
Vanguard Bond Index—Short-Term	Representative sample of a Lehman Brothers short-term bond index. With an average maturity of about 3 years, ideal choice for investors looking to beat money-market returns without assuming a lot of extra risk.	0.18%	$3,000	851-4999

Notes: All Vanguard index funds levy a $10 annual account maintenance fee on accounts below $10,000 [1]Fund charges a 0.5% redemption fee on shares redeemed within six months of purchase [2]Fund charges a 0.5% redemption fee on shares redeemed within six months of purchase [3]0.5% transaction fee on purchases to defray brokerage costs [4]1% transaction fee on purchases [5]0.75% redemption fee on shares redeemed within six months of purchase

196

Funds That Double as Portfolios

Going the index route can certainly make fund picking a breeze. But you still have the task of assembling a mix of funds with different objectives into a portfolio that reflects your goals and tolerance for risk. There are also funds that can streamline—indeed, even eliminate—the task of building a portfolio. These choices, which include so-called life-cycle funds, funds of funds, and asset-allocation funds, are essentially mini-portfolios unto themselves. When you invest in them you get a diversified group of securities, usually stocks, bonds, cash equivalents, and possibly other assets such as precious metals and real estate.

The idea behind this all-in-one-package is that it saves you from having to assemble on your own a lineup of funds with a variety of asset classes. I consider these funds a distant second choice to tailoring your own portfolio, as outlined in Chapter 10. You are essentially delegating the all-important asset-allocation decision to the manager. And no matter how well the manager does his or her job, there's no way a fund that is sold to thousands of investors can possibly cater to your needs as specifically or with as much flexibility as a portfolio you devise and fine-tune on your own.

Nonetheless, for novices who want to create a diversified portfolio with just a few thousand bucks, investors who really don't want to own more than one or two funds, or people who simply don't want to bother with the effort of creating their own portfolio of funds, these ready-made portfolios can be useful. Here's a rundown of the all-in-one funds available to you.

Life-cycle funds: Over the past few years, about 20 or so fund companies have begun offering so-called life-cycle funds that typically offer three to four portfolios with different mixes of stocks, bonds, and cash designed to fit people at various stages of life or with different risk tolerances. Sponsors typically provide booklets, charts, and other materials to help you decide which mix is best for you, given your age, goals, and stomach for risk. For example, the T. Rowe Price Personal Strategy funds consist of three separate portfolios, including, in order of lowest to highest volatility or risk, an income fund (that aims to invest roughly 40% of its assets in stocks, 40% in bonds, and 20% in money-market securities), a balanced fund (60% stocks, 30% bonds, and 10% money-market securities), and a growth fund (80% stocks and 20% bonds and money-market securities). Depending on market conditions, the fund manager can shift any of these allocations by 10 percentage points. (Thus the growth fund, for example, could go as high as 90% in stocks and 10% in bonds and money-market issues.) The fund manager also has leeway to invest in a mix of large-company, small-company, and foreign shares, as well as investment-grade, junk, and foreign bonds. Similar offerings include the Dreyfus Lifetime Portfolio, Schwab Asset Director funds, and Vanguard Life-Strategy funds.

With most of these plans you would have to shift money from one portfolio to another as your needs change. But one program, Wells Fargo's Stagecoach LifePath funds, relieves you of that task, too. You choose one of five funds based on when you intend to start withdrawing money (the choices now range from 2000 to 2040 in increments of 10 years), and the manager tilts the mix of securities in the fund away from stocks toward bonds and cash as that date approaches. The most aggressive fund—LifePath 2040—starts out with roughly 95% of its assets in stocks and the rest in bonds and will eventually work its way toward the allocation of the least aggressive fund—LifePath 2000—which starts with roughly 25% in stocks, 60% in bonds, and 15% in money-market securities. This moving-allocation approach saves you from having to shift money around on your own.

Funds of funds: This concept—a mutual fund that buys shares of other funds—has been around awhile but has gotten more attention as investors look for ways to make sense of the thousands of fund options that confront them. In some cases the fund of funds is run by a fund family. Vanguard STAR, for example, holds shares in the well-known Windsor II fund as well as eight other stock and bond funds and keeps 60% to 70% of the fund's portfolio invested in stocks with the rest in bonds and money-market instruments. T. Rowe Price has two funds of funds: Spectrum Growth, which includes shares of six equity funds, and Spectrum Income, which holds shares of five bond funds and one equity-income fund. Both funds can also put a small portion of their assets in a T. Rowe Price money-market fund. The funds also hold money-market instruments to the extent that the underlying funds they invest in hold these securities.

In the case of Vanguard STAR and the T. Rowe Price Spectrum funds, investors pay only a pro rata portion of the expenses of the underlying funds that these portfolios invest in. Effectively, then, you pay only as much as you would if you invested in the funds directly. There are other funds of funds, however, where investors wind up paying not just the expenses of the underlying funds, but an additional layer of expenses as well. For example, in the FundManager Trust, portfolio manager Michael Hirsch sorts through more than 6,000 load and no-load funds and then puts shares of nine to 12 of those funds into five separate portfolios designed to meet different investment objectives: aggressive growth, growth, growth-and-income, income, and total return.

Investors in each of those portfolios pick up roughly 0.8% annually in expenses of the underlying 10 to 15 funds, plus another 1.4% to 1.9% or so in annual expenses levied by the FundManager Trust portfolio. Similarly, investors who buy one of the three portfolios in manager Robert Markman's Markman Multifunds pay annual fees of 0.95% on top of the expenses of the eight to 12 funds in the portfolios themselves. This double layer of fees creates a serious drag on your returns, although they may still be worth paying if you would do a far worse job of picking funds on your own—or if you would otherwise avoid funds altogether.

Asset-allocation funds: The 160 or so funds in the asset-allocation category shoot for solid returns with relatively low risk by spreading their holdings among different types of assets, much as you would do in creating your own portfolio of funds. Trouble is, no two do it alike. Many asset-allocation funds, for example, limit themselves to the three major asset classes—stocks, bonds, and money-market securities. Many others, however, will also throw in an inflation hedge such as shares of precious metals or other natural resource companies. Some keep the percentages of each type of asset relatively fixed, while others can respond to changing market conditions by shifting those percentages dramatically, going almost entirely into stocks, bonds, or cash, for example. Many stick to domestic securities, while others have free rein to add foreign stocks and bonds to their portfolio. This diversity of approaches in these highly diversified funds makes it difficult to compare the results of several funds of this type and all the more important to delve into the prospectus to understand the exact strategy the manager will pursue.

If you're going to create a portfolio of funds on your own, then adding an asset-allocation fund doesn't make a lot of sense. It would mostly serve to skew the asset mix you've tried to achieve in your other funds. Even if I had decided on a hands-off approach to fund investing, I'd still be wary of putting a large portion of my money in asset-allocation funds.

In my view it's often just too difficult to know how your money is invested. That said, however, there are a number of funds in this category whose ability to generate alluring returns with below average levels of risk makes them good choices for investors looking for low-risk ways to invest in funds. Two such funds that generally get high marks from fund experts: SoGen International, a fund with an excellent long-term record that, despite its name, invests in domestic as well as foreign stocks and bonds; and Vanguard Asset Allocation, which sticks primarily to a mix of S&P 500 stocks, Treasury bonds, and money-market securities.

The Rap on Wrap Accounts

One of the fastest-growing investments in the mutual fund industry has been so-called **wrap accounts,** which now hold more than $17 billion of investors' money, up from less than $3 billion in 1992. Marketed by brokerage firms, fund companies, banks, and financial planners, wrap plans are similar to funds of funds in concept in that they are accounts that typically hold three to seven mutual funds or a combination of pools of securities that are very much like mutual funds.

In a typical arrangement, a broker or planner would sit down with an investor and, on the basis of that person's goals and risk tolerance, create a diversified portfolio of funds with different investment styles and objectives—much the same process you can do on your own using my advice in Chapter 10. The broker or planner would then track the progress of this portfolio and, if necessary, recommend changes in it, such as firing underperforming fund managers or hiring new ones should investors' goals change.

Some wrap programs stick to the funds of just one sponsor; the Fidelity, SteinRoe, and Strong fund groups, for example, offer wrap plans that use their own mutual funds. Other wrap plans will sift and choose among funds from a variety of fund groups or portfolios managed by independent managers. Most wrap accounts require investors to invest $50,000 or more initially, although a handful have minimums of $25,000 or less. Proponents of wrap accounts (mostly the people who sell them) claim that these programs provide a cost-efficient way for investors of relatively modest means to have a portfolio of funds tailored to their specific needs and then monitored by a pro to make sure the portfolio is performing as it should.

But while the wrap pitch may sound tuneful, I believe most investors should refuse to sing along. As I see it, there are three major problems with these accounts:

1. The fees are far too high. Wrap programs usually charge an annual fee of 1% to 2% *in addition* to the management fees you pay for the underlying funds. The largest wrap plan, Smith Barney's TRAK program, charges 1.50% annually and anywhere from 0.55% to 1.72% in operating expenses for the 13 different investing options it offers. That means that two to three percentage points of your returns are siphoned off each year before you see a dime. I'm sorry, but no advice is good enough to overcome that towering hurdle and still deliver competitive returns.

2. The advice you're getting isn't as personalized as you might think. Most brokers or planners selling wrap plans gauge your investment objectives and risk tolerance with a questionnaire of some sort and then devise a portfolio that is presented as if it's designed just for you. Not quite. What usually happens is that the questionnaire channels you into one of seven or so portfolios that already exist. That doesn't mean these portfolios can't be helpful; it's just that the allocations aren't tailored individually for you. So you're getting something much like a life-cycle fund, but at a much higher price.

3. You may be opening yourself up for more sales pitches in the future. In discussing your financial needs with a broker or planner for a wrap account, you will invariably divulge information such as what other investments you own and how much you have tucked away in them. Given that many brokers and planners are under considerable pressure from their firms to generate sales commissions and other fees, it's only natural that much of this information may be used to induce you to move more of your money into the wrap program or other investments sold by the firm.

My advice: If you don't feel up to putting together your own portfolio, try a life-cycle fund, a fund of funds with low expenses, or even an asset-allocation fund or two. After all, the reason you're investing in funds is to build your wealth, not some broker's.

Dollar-Cost Averaging Your Way to Riches

Speaking of building wealth, I think most, if not all, fund investors ought to consider a disciplined method of investing known as **dollar-cost averaging**. Here's how it works: You invest the same amount of money at regular intervals—say, $100 each month—in a fund or group of funds regardless of what the market is doing. When fund share prices are rising, your $100 buys fewer shares of the fund; conversely, when share prices fall, your $100 buys more shares. The table below gives a hypothetical example of how such a plan might work over the course of a single year:

DOLLAR-COST AVERAGING WITH $100 A MONTH

Month/Amount Invested	Price Per Share	Number of Fund Shares Purchased
January/$100	$7	14.3
February/$100	$9	11.1
March/$100	$10	10
April/$100	$12	8.3
May/$100	$14	7.1
June/$100	$12	8.3
July/$100	$10	10
August/$100	$8	12.5
September/$100	$8	12.5
October/$100	$10	10
November/$100	$10	10
December/$100	$12	9.3

Total invested: $1,200
Total shares purchased: 123.4
Average cost per share: $9.72 ($1,200 divided by 123.4)

Contrary to popular misconception, dollar-cost averaging does *not* guarantee you the highest returns. Over the course of the year in the table here, for example, you would have paid an average of $9.72 per share for the fund. That's better than if you had put all your money into the fund in May and paid $14 a share, but not nearly as profitable as if you had bought all your shares at January's low of $7. Similarly, dollar-cost averaging won't immunize you against losses. For example, if next year the fund's price fell to, say, $8 a share, then despite dollar-cost averaging you would be showing a temporary loss on average of $1.72 a share. (Your average cost of $9.72 minus $8). No one ever knows when it's the best time to invest, and dollar cost averaging can't change that basic fact.

But what dollar-cost averaging and other so-called periodic investment plans *can* do is take the emotion out of investing and turn it into a discipline. It's another way of putting your investing on autopilot, so to speak. By doing that, dollar-cost averaging prevents you getting swept up in the euphoria of a bull market and dumping all or most of your money into funds when the market is racing to spectacular returns but may be primed for a fall. Just as important, the discipline of dollar-cost averaging forces you to buy shares after the market has dropped, when fund shares are more likely to be bargains but when many investors are afraid to jump in.

There are also a few variations to dollar-cost averaging you might consider. In **progressive dollar-cost averaging,** for example, you increase your monthly contribution by a manageable amount every year—say, 5% to 10%—as a way to accumulate more money and to be sure to keep far ahead of inflation. There is also a more advanced version of dollar-cost averaging known as **value averaging,** in which you set a target amount by which you want your fund balance to increase each month—let's say $200—and then you invest more or less than that amount depending on how much your fund's value rises or falls. (In this plan it's even possible you might have to sell shares, if your fund's value bounds ahead very quickly.) Michael Edelson, a Harvard Business School professor and author of *Value Averaging: The Safe and Easy Strategy for Higher Investment Returns* ($22.95, International Publishing; 800-488-4149), figures that value averaging outperforms plain dollar-cost averaging about 90% of the time. It is definitely more complicated, demands a lot more attention, and, if the market drops, may require you to come up with very large monthly sums to keep the plan going. I'd advise holding off on value averaging until you've got dollar-cost averaging down cold.

No-load mutual funds are an especially good vehicle for dollar-cost averaging and other periodic investing plans. Why? Since you pay no sales charge to buy, you don't have to worry about part of your monthly investment being frittered away on commissions, as you would with load funds or with stocks. And once you've met a fund's minimum initial investment, you can usually buy additional shares in small amounts, often $100 or less. Some funds have no minimum for subsequent investments. What's more, many funds encourage dollar-cost averaging by offering systematic investing plans in which you can instruct the fund to withdraw a certain amount of money, usually monthly or quarterly, from your checking account and deposit it into the fund or, in some cases, make payroll deductions into the fund. (You'll have to be sure both the fund and your employer will agree to this.) If that's not incentive enough, consider this: Some funds will waive their usual minimum initial investment rules if you agree to participate in their systematic investing plan and tuck away as little as $50 or $100 a month. For a list of such funds, see page 264 in the appendix.

When You Shouldn't Dollar-Cost Average

Dollar-cost averaging is clearly a great way to invest money from a paycheck or other regular income. But what if you have just received a lump sum from a pension payout or an inheritance from dear Aunt Tilly? Should you throw that into funds all at once or move the money into funds gradually à la dollar-cost averaging? A few recent studies have examined this question of whether you are better off putting a lump sum into, say, a money-market account and feeding it gradually into the stock market (or stock mutual funds) or whether you'll do better just dumping it into stocks (or stock funds) all at once. The conclusion: About two-thirds of the time, simply diving in beats the wade-in-a-bit-at-a-time strategy.

But these studies aren't as earth-shattering as they've been portrayed by some personal finance publications. (Headline: NEW STUDIES CAST CLOUDS OVER DOLLAR-COST AVERAGING!) It's not surprising that putting all your money into stocks at once would beat going into the market gradually. Since the stock market rises more than it falls and usually rises more than money-market funds, it's pretty obvious that more often than not the money sitting in a money fund waiting to go into stocks will be dragging down your overall return.

In the real world, though, an investor probably isn't facing a decision with just two choices: jump into stocks all at once or dollar-cost average in. Rather, the critical issue for most investors is how to integrate new money such as a lump sum from a pension or an inheritance into the portfolio you already have (or that you will have after following the advice in this book), given your investment time horizon and tolerance for risk. Thus, if you will need to tap into Aunt Tilly's $20,000 legacy in two years to buy a house, it doesn't matter whether investing in stocks all at once beats dollar-cost averaging. You probably shouldn't be investing in stocks at all. Rather, most of it should go into money funds and short-term bond funds.

In short, once you've determined how to divide up your money among funds of different asset classes and investing styles as described in Chapter 10, the issue of what to do with a lump sum is pretty simple. You invest it pretty much according to the allocations you've decided on. So if you already had, say, 75% of your money in stock funds, 20% in bond funds, and 5% in money funds, you would divide up your $20,000 pretty much along the same lines. Sure, you could beef up your portfolio with types of funds you might have overlooked—for example, you might add an international stock fund or a foreign emerging market fund, if you don't have one. But you would pretty much invest the new money so that the mix of stock, bond, and money funds you wind up with after investing the 20 grand suits your investment goals and risk tolerance.

There are possible exceptions to this rule. For example, if you are a relative novice investing a substantial sum of money or if the lump sum you've received is huge compared to the value of your portfolio—say, Aunt Tilly left you $200,000 and your portfolio weighs in at $20,000—then you might want to put the stash in a money fund and dollar-cost average into an appropriate mix of stock and bond funds over the course of a year or two.

The reasoning: Neophyte investors and people who invest a big slug of cash and then take a quick hit when the market turns against them may get spooked and desert stock and bond funds altogether. To guard against that possibility, it can make sense for risk-averse investors and newcomers to dollar-cost average in. Yes, this approach may result in somewhat lower returns, but it will also lower your risk. And you'll certainly be better off than if you jumped in all at once and then retreated forever. Clearly this is an issue where your temperament, as much as any research study, should be your guide.

To sum up, when it comes to investing money from your paycheck, use dollar-cost averaging. If you're lucky enough to get a windfall that you must invest, let your tolerance for risk—and your overall portfolio allocations—be your guide.

CHAPTER 12

Where to Buy Funds

Here, There, and Everywhere

The marketing of mutual funds in the '90s is reminiscent of Beatlemania in the '60s. There's no escaping it. Everywhere you turn, somebody's trying to sell you a fund.

Load and no-load companies alike have hawked their wares on the tube. (In an attempt to justify paying a sales load for advice, an Alliance funds ad likened picking your own funds to doing brain surgery on yourself. I admit the commercial was funny and that investing requires some skill. But brain surgery? Gimme a break.) Brokers will cold call you to push the latest hot fund. Go to your local bank, and wedged between a teller and a loan officer you'll likely find a sales rep happily extolling the virtues of funds. Not to be left behind, many insurance agents have added funds to their arsenal of insurance and annuities. Even affinity groups have gotten into the act. The American Association of Retired Persons and the Lutheran Brotherhood, to name just two organizations, have sponsored funds for years.

So the issue isn't whether you can find someone to sell you a fund—it's determining the best way for you to buy. Where you come down on this issue will depend largely on how much of your own research you're willing to do, whether it bothers you to see some of your money go into sales commissions rather than into the funds themselves, and how high a premium you place on convenience. In this chapter we'll examine the three main ways investors buy funds—directly from the sponsor, through brokers and planners, and from banks—and also briefly discuss whether you should invest in funds that are offered through affinity groups. We'll then take a look at a fast-growing and convenient way of investing in funds—namely, by purchasing them from a variety of different sponsors without paying a transaction fee through one of the new discount broker networks such as Charles Schwab's OneSource program.

As you weigh these options, remember: Just because you start buying through one channel doesn't mean you're wed to it for life. Thus, if you already own funds you bought through a broker, but now feel confident enough to assemble an all-star line-up of funds from a variety of different fund families, don't hesitate to buy directly from a fund sponsor or one of the discount broker networks.

Buying Directly from the Fund Company

If you can do even a minimal amount of research on your own, then buying funds straight from one of the 360 or so no- or low-load fund companies that offer more than 3,100 portfolios to investors is the most economical way to go. The reason, quite simply, is that if less of your money is diverted to sales commissions, more of it can go to work for you in the fund. To invest with one of these companies, just pick up the phone, call them (usually at a toll-free 800 number), and ask for an application and a prospectus for whichever funds you're considering. (I've included a list of the 20 largest no- and low-load fund sponsors on page 265 of the appendix.) You won't get individualized advice about what specific funds to buy or how to build the right portfolio for your needs, but a growing number of no- and low-load companies offer retirement-planning workbooks as well as asset-allocation assistance.

The companies that sell direct range from big operations— like Fidelity Investments, Scudder, T. Rowe Price, Twentieth Century–Benham, USAA, and Vanguard, which have huge stables of funds—to companies that also have solid reputations but much smaller lineups, such as Berger, Janus, Mutual Series, and Neuberger & Berman. Most of the companies that market directly to consumers—usually by advertising in newspapers or personal finance publications—charge no sales commission whatsoever, although some companies may levy sales loads of 3% or so on some of their funds to help defray the cost of advertising and other marketing.

Similarly, some fund families may have certain funds that they sell directly to the public with no sales charge and others marketed through brokers or banks that carry a load. Dreyfus, for example, levies no sales commissions on funds such as Dreyfus GNMA, which it sells directly to investors, while Premier GNMA, part of a stable of Dreyfus-run funds sold through brokers and banks, charges an up-front sales load of 4.5% or a maximum back-end charge of 3%, depending on which shares of the fund you buy.

Clearly the low-cost no- or low-load alternative, already popular with savvy do-it-yourself investors, is becoming even more popular. As recently as 1991, for example, directly marketed funds accounted for only about 37% of that year's $223 billion of stock and bond fund sales. The rest were sold through brokers, planners, and other salespeople. Within three years, however, the tables had turned. In 1994 directly sold funds accounted for 56% of $435 billion in sales of stock and bond funds. This move to no- and low-load funds doesn't necessarily mean that investors have wised up to the fact that their odds of getting higher returns improve if they lower their investing costs. Rather, the trend toward directly sold funds is being driven more by the growing popularity of 401(k) company retirement plans, where Vanguard, Fidelity, and T. Rowe Price have been dominant players. Those financial planners who charge a flat fee or a percentage of assets for their fund picking and monitoring advice are also increasingly buying no-load funds through discount broker no-transaction-fee networks.

Buying Funds through a Broker or Planner

Investors who don't feel comfortable going the DIY route—or who just don't want to devote the time and effort to picking funds—have the option of buying funds through a broker or a financial planner who will help them decide which type of fund to buy and select a fund within that type. More than 3,800 funds from an estimated 190 fund sponsors are sold this way, ranging from the funds offered by major brokerage firms such as Merrill Lynch, Dean Witter, and Prudential to load funds marketed through sales forces by well-known fund companies such as Putnam, American Funds, and Franklin-Templeton. If you decide to buy your funds this way rather than directly from the fund company, you should expect to pay a sales commission or other type of fee. Typically, funds that are sold through planners and brokers carry an up-front sales charge that ranges from 4% to 6% of the amount you invest or a back-end charge that often starts at 5% and declines by a percentage point or so each year until it disappears in the sixth year or so.

Be aware that some brokers try to portray funds without up-front sales fees as no-loads. Fact is, if the broker or planner is getting a sales commission for selling it, then one way or another you are somehow footing the bill for that fee—if not through a front-end sales load, then in the form of a back-end sales charge and (in some cases or) by paying annual marketing or distribution fees that have been tacked on to the fund's yearly expenses. (These fees are explained in Chapter 8.)

A few planners and brokers *can* help you choose no-load funds, but in that case you will pay them a flat fee or an hourly rate for their advice. If you want them also to monitor your portfolio on an ongoing basis, such advisers may charge a fee of 1% or so of the amount you have invested. Several brokerage firms are also reportedly revving up plans to allow their brokers to offer no-load funds along with those that carry sales commissions. For example, Merrill Lynch has said it is exploring several options that would allow its brokers to sell clients no-load funds, possibly by charging a base annual fee of as much as 1.5% of the assets in the customer's account.

Theoretically, of course, the sales commission you pay compensates the broker or planner for providing expert advice. Nothing wrong with that—provided you get expert advice. While I'm sure that many brokers and planners do a fine job of analyzing funds and put their clients' interests first, there's also a sordid history in the load fund business of putting clients into funds that are the easiest sell or pay the highest commissions or even of moving clients in and out of funds many times to generate fees and commissions. One particularly shameful episode involved the pushing, largely by brokers, of short-term world income funds in the late '80s and early '90s as supposedly safe CD alternatives when, in fact, these funds were far more risky than CDs.

Similarly, in the past brokers have steered clients into junk bonds or other hot sectors just as the sizzle was ready to fizzle. If you're paying a commission (whether up front, with a flat or annual fee, or through annual marketing or distribution charges), make sure the salesperson or adviser earns it. Ask the broker or planner to provide performance results and other information that explains why he or she chose this particular fund, ask what alternatives were considered and why they weren't chosen, and don't be afraid to ask what commission the broker is earning and how that will be coming out of your investment dollars (and despite what anyone says, it is).

Convenience (But at What Price?) from a Bank

To keep from losing their customers to fund companies, more and more banks have been getting into the fund business themselves. About a third of all mutual funds are now available at banks, and banks account for 14% or so of annual stock and bond fund sales. An estimated 2,300 or so of our nation's 13,500 banks and thrifts now offer mutual funds to their customers. In most cases banks are simply selling—usually with a sales load—the funds of an established fund company. But in the late 1980s through mid 1990s more than 100 banks established their own funds, which they manage themselves or through a subsidiary.

So why should you bother going to this relative newcomer in the business? Convenience is about the only reason I can think of. I suppose it can be an advantage (though it doesn't seem like a very big one) to be able to invest in funds while you're making deposits to your checking account or paying the mortgage.

Beyond that rather minor plus, however, I don't see any reason to limit yourself to the funds your local bank happens to peddle. If the bank is selling someone else's funds, then clearly you're not getting something you can't get elsewhere, usually with a far wider range of choices. And if the bank is offering funds that it manages itself, the question is whether you want a bank investing your money. Some bank-run funds do have excellent records—a few of the Chase Vista funds, for example, have been above average performers. But many don't have much of a record at all.

Another potential problem: Bank sales staffs tend to be inexperienced and may not fully understand the funds they sell. And they don't appear to be providing adequate disclosure about the risks of investing in funds. A 1995 report by the General Accounting Office (GAO), which is the investigative arm of Congress, noted that when the GAO visited banks and thrifts in 12 metropolitan areas, many bank representatives didn't adequately inform them that funds are not insured by the Federal Deposit Insurance Corporation (FDIC), are not deposits, are not guaranteed by the bank, and could involve loss of principal. Let there be no doubt: a fund you buy at the bank is subject to the exact same risks and market forces as one you buy directly from a fund company or through a broker or planner. Bank funds are not guaranteed by the federal government, the FDIC, or the bank.

If you decide that you like the convenience of investing at your local bank, that's fine. But before you buy what they're selling, I suggest you compare it rigorously with similar nonbank funds and invest only if it shapes up well in the comparison.

Affinity Funds: Should Birds of a Feather Invest Together?

Among the many ways fund purveyors have of setting themselves apart from the thousands of portfolios competing for your money is by appealing to you on a social or emotional level rather than in purely financial terms. Thus the American Association of Retired Persons (AARP) hopes that you'll invest in its menu of mutual funds if you're in or nearing retirement.

What better match could there be? You're getting older and they're an organization ostensibly fighting for the rights of retirees and the elderly. Similarly, if you're a Lutheran, you'd naturally want to invest in one of the Lutheran Brotherhood funds, no? (To date, at least, there's no Our Lady of Perpetual Income fund or other offerings specifically pitched to Catholic investors like myself.) Even corporations are getting into the act. American Airlines markets its American AAdvantage funds to its passengers, and a subsidiary of a Virginia-based utility launched the America's Utility fund and marketed it by putting flyers in utility customers' bills. State Farm runs four mutual funds for its insurance agents and other employees.

My take on this: You should invest in a fund because it's performed well in the past and you expect it to do so in the future, not because you feel simpatico with the organization that's selling it. However you may feel about AARP's work on behalf of the elderly, for example, the fact remains that you are giving them your money because you expect them to earn competitive returns. On that score, a 1995 analysis by **MONEY** magazine found that AARP's stock, bond, and money funds (which are actually managed by the Scudder fund group) are a mixed bag. Three AARP funds—GNMA & Treasury, Growth & Income, and Balanced Stock & Bond—met AARP's goal of providing a good balance between risk and return. But the other five, in **MONEY** magazine's estimation, fell short on both counts. I believe that when so many good funds are available, it's a mistake for investors to limit themselves to a relative handful offered by a few organizations. If for whatever reason—loyalty to religion, an employer, a cause—you decide to invest with affinity groups, you should at least subject their offerings to the same kind of scrutiny you would give any other fund.

Discount Broker Networks:
The New Extended Fund Families

Fund investors who wanted to minimize paperwork and be able to switch easily among different funds have always had the option of keeping all their fund investments within one or two fund families. By sticking to large fund groups with a well-rounded stable of solid funds—for example, Fidelity (167 funds), Vanguard (80), T. Rowe Price (65), Dreyfus (70), Scudder (45), and USAA (32)—investors who wanted to keep it all in the family had a good shot at combining convenience with a diversified portfolio of funds with decent performance. The problem with this familial approach, however, is that it prevents you from adopting a more eclectic strategy—namely, putting together an all-star lineup of funds culled from many fund groups both large and small.

But in 1992 giant discount brokerage firm Charles Schwab revolutionized the fund industry by launching the Schwab OneSource plan. This program represented a major breakthrough in the way funds were sold because it allowed investors to buy funds from a variety of different no-load fund families without paying a transaction fee. (Previously, discount brokers would sell no-load funds, but they charged brokerage commissions much the same as if you were buying stocks.) Today, at least eight discount brokers offer a no-transaction-fee plan for buying no-loads, and a few full-service brokerage firms are reportedly considering launching similar programs. (In September 1995, for example, Prudential Securities began allowing its customers to hold no-loads in their brokerage accounts, although clients could not buy no-loads through Prudential.) These discount broker networks have become so popular, in fact, that in 1994 the two largest programs—Schwab's OneSource and Fidelity's FundsNetwork—accounted for an estimated 15% of the new money going into stock and bond funds.

The appeal of these no-transaction-fee plans is simple. By buying your funds through such a program, you get all the advantages of investing within a fund family plus access to far more portfolios—370 funds from 45 different fund families in the case of Fidelity's FundsNetwork. By contrast you would have fewer than half that number of funds to choose from if you restricted yourself to Fidelity funds only. What's more, investors who buy their funds through one of these plans can switch money from one fund family to another—redeem some shares in, say, a Gabelli fund and put the proceeds into a Neuberger & Berman fund—by making a single phone call. All your transactions and fund balances are consolidated onto a single statement, as opposed to the separate statements you would get from each fund family if you tried to duplicate this approach outside a no-transaction-fee plan. In short, by mixing and matching funds from a wide range of sponsors, you can essentially create your own fund family, or extended family, if you will.

So what do these plans cost you? That depends on what funds you choose and how you invest. Unless you frequently jump in and out of different funds (and if you do, you aren't following the advice in this book), you pay no commissions or annual account maintenance fees to buy the no-load funds offered by the plan. You can buy no-loads that aren't part of the network's lineup for a fee that starts at $27 a transaction and increases for larger investments. You can also buy load funds through these programs, but if you do, you will pay the network's transaction fee, plus the fund's usual sales load. Some discounters, however, will waive the transaction fee on funds that carry loads of 3% or more.

Not all no-load funds are available through these programs, however. For example, you can buy Fidelity's no-loads without a fee only through Fidelity's FundsNetwork plan. And some fund groups, including T. Rowe Price, Vanguard, and the Mutual Series funds managed by renowned value investor Michael Price, have not joined these networks. (Vanguard's Fund Access plan, however, lets its shareholders buy and sell other sponsors' no-loads for a flat fee of $35 per transaction.) One reason these groups haven't joined a network is that funds within a discount broker's no-transaction-fee plan usually have to pay the discounter 0.25% to 0.35% of each dollar that comes into the fund through the plan.

That payment can drive up the fund's expenses. Indeed, a survey of fund expenses by fund tracking firm Morningstar, Inc., and the *Wall Street Journal* found that no-transaction-fee funds in the three largest discount broker networks had higher annual expenses than no-loads outside the programs. What's more, these networks sometimes set a higher minimum initial investment than you would pay by investing directly in the fund family. Muriel Siebert's no-fee plan has a $5,000 minimum investment ($2,000 for individual retirement accounts), which is roughly double what most sponsors themselves demand.

These limitations nothwithstanding, you should consider investing through one of these networks if you own (or would like to own) a variety of funds from different sponsors, you tend to shift money among funds several times a year or more, and you would like to eliminate the clutter that results from getting multiple statements from different fund groups. Clearly Schwab OneSource and Fidelity FundsNetwork offer the best overall package of competitive prices, worthwhile services, and a veritable smorgasbord of different funds and sponsors from which to choose. So you can't go far wrong if you simply choose one or the other of these plans. Nonetheless it's still a good idea to think beforehand how you will use the network and then select one that provides the right mix of services and price for you. Here are a few questions you should ask yourself before signing up with a plan:

• **Does the network have the funds I want?** Don't automatically go with the network that offers the largest number of funds. Instead see if the network has the funds you own now or might buy in the future. Thus, if Fidelity funds will likely be the core of your portfolio, you should probably join Fidelity's

FundsNetwork, even though it offers far fewer funds than Jack White & Co.'s plan. Fidelity's network, on the other hand, doesn't offer the funds of the Twentieth Century and Invesco fund groups, while Schwab's OneSource does. So look for the network that includes the funds you're most likely to use. If you buy the occasional load fund, you should look into Jack White's Connect program, which lets you buy load funds directly from present shareholders rather than through the fund sponsor. The $200 transaction fee that White charges is prohibitive if you plan to invest small amounts of, say, $1,000. But the flat $200 fee would represent a $375 saving compared with investing $10,000 in a fund levying a 5.75% load.

• **Is the fee schedule right for the way I invest—and are the fund's annual expenses reasonable?** If you buy funds outside the network, commissions can vary widely from plan to plan. AccuTrade offers the lowest commission—$27 to buy or sell any number of shares. Schwab and Fidelity charge minimums of $39 and $28, respectively, for out-of-network trades, but the cost would rise to about $70 at both places on a $10,000 purchase or sale. If you think you will often buy and sell funds outside the network—or will incur trading charges by exceeding the allotted number of free switches—look for the plan that's easiest on your wallet.

Given the evidence that funds in no-transaction-fee plans may carry higher expenses than other no-loads, you should also compare the expense ratios of funds you buy through the program with those of similar funds. (For more on how to compare expenses, see Chapter 8.) If the expenses of a fund you are considering far exceed those of its competitors, you might want to consider similar, lower-cost, no-transaction-fee funds. Alternatively, if you don't switch funds frequently, you could simply choose a low-cost no-load fund that's not part of the no-fee program and pay the transaction fee.

• **Are the account statements helpful—and can I get research material to help me choose funds?** Since streamlining paperwork is probably a major reason for joining one of these networks, make sure the account statement you get details all your holdings—including not just funds, but individual stocks and bonds, if you own them—and that they are presented in a manner that's easy to understand. Fidelity's statements are generally considered the clearest and, among other things, reveal each month your cost basis in each fund—that is, what you paid for all the shares you own, including those acquired through reinvested dividends. Several of the networks, including Schwab, Fidelity, and Waterhouse Securities, send out quarterly performance rankings of the funds they offer, while for a small fee Fidelity, AccuTrade, and York Securities will provide one-page fund analyses from Chicago fund rating firm Morningstar.

• **Are the network's business hours compatible with my investing habits?** If you tend to squeeze in your investing at nights or on weekends, you might want to go with one of the three discounters whose representatives man the phones 24 hours a day: Jack White, Fidelity, and Schwab. If you prefer dealing with a rep in person, then Schwab or Fidelity is the logical choice since both have branch offices spread around the country. If you prefer to do your investing by computer, then AccuTrade, Fidelity, Schwab, and Jack White can accommodate you.

To evaluate the discount broker plans and decide which is likely to work best for you, take a look at the following chart, which summarizes the prices and services of the eight major no-transaction-fee programs. They are ranked in order of the number of funds they offer in their no-fee network.

HOW THE NEW EXTENDED FUND FAMILIES STACK UP

Fund Network Telephone (800)	Number of No-Fee Funds/ Fund Families	Number of Free Short-Term Switches[1]	Minimum Charge per Additional Switch[2]	Representatives' hours[3]
Jack White & Co. 233-3411	719/107	15	$27	24 hours
AccuTrade 882-4887	576/113	None	$27	8:30 A.M.–6 P.M.[4]
Muriel Siebert & Co. 872-0666	400/44	None	$40	9 A.M.–5 P.M.
Fidelity's FundsNetwork 544-9697	370/45	5	$28	24 hours
Schwab OneSource 266-5623	369/51	None	$39	24 hours
Waterhouse Securities 934-4443	250/41	15	$29	8:30 A.M.–12:00 A.M
Securities Research[5] 327-3156	200/13	Unlimited	None	9 A.M.–5 P.M.
York Securities[5] 221-3154	127/14	Unlimited	None	7:30 A.M.–5 P.M.

Notes: All data as of December 1995 [1]Unlimited free switches are allowed for shares held six months or longer at AccuTrade and Fidelity, three months or longer at Schwab, Jack White, and Waterhouse Securities, nine months or longer at Muriel Siebert on purchases under $10,000 (shorter periods for larger purchases); no fees on any switches at Securities Research and York Securities [2]Charge also applies to trades of funds outside network [3]By phone, Eastern Standard Time [4]24-hour trading by Touch-Tone phone [5]These programs are available only to customers who also buy and sell securities other than mutual funds at these firms.

CHAPTER 13

Resources for Fund Investors

Making Sense of the Fund Information Overload

One often overlooked but nonetheless huge benefit enjoyed by fund investors is the ability to easily scrape together a wealth of information on virtually any fund. Indeed, these days it's hard to avoid being inundated with fund coverage. Everywhere you turn—TV, newspapers, magazines, cyberspace—it seems as though you run into the most recent returns for a few thousand funds, a laudatory profile on a fund manager whose portfolio is hot (or a dressing-down of last year's poster boy, whose fund has cooled), and, of course, the inevitable lists touting yet another compilation of someone's idea of the "best" funds.

This barrage of fund information can certainly overwhelm investors, but it can also keep you up-to-date on what's going on in funds and, in some cases, even help you better choose and monitor funds. In this chapter we will look at the major sources of fund information, starting with newspapers and magazines, then moving on to more specialized publications such as newsletters and mutual fund rating services, and winding up with a look at some of the ways you can use your computer to pick and monitor funds.

My aim in each of these sections is not so much to rate specific publications or services, but to tell you what kind of information you can get from each and how you can make best use of the various sources vying for your attention and money. Remember, too, that no one person, newspaper, magazine, or rating service has cornered the market on savvy fund advice or reliable statistics. So my advice is to check out a variety of sources, read with a skeptical eye, occasionally look at past issues to see if a publication's advice is as sage as its authoritative prose makes it out to be, and, generally, try to put to use true insights wherever you find them and ignore the self-serving bombast you're also likely to encounter now and again (and again and again).

Keeping Up with Funds through Newspapers

Over the past few years the financial sections of most newspapers around the country have dramatically improved their coverage of mutual funds. Despite that improvement, however, relatively few business and personal finance sections provide enough in-depth statistical information about funds to enable you to choose or keep track of your funds based solely on what you find in the paper.

Nontheless, fund investors should definitely peruse the business and finance section of their local newspaper, if for no other reason than the fact that newspapers keep abreast of the latest trends in the financial markets and offer news about proposals the Securities and Exchange Commission and other regulators may be making that can affect the way funds are managed and sold. In 1994 and 1995, for example, most large daily newspapers did an excellent job of keeping fund shareholders informed about three major stories: funds' use of highly volatile derivative securities by supposedly conservative money-market funds and short-term bond funds; the SEC's investigation of fund managers' personal trading practices; and the effect of the bankruptcy of Orange County, California, on the portfolios of tax-exempt money-market and bond funds. I'm not suggesting that you should immediately buy or sell a fund on the basis of such coverage. You shouldn't. But keeping aware of such developments makes you a better informed investor and could spur you to go to other sources to examine more closely funds you already own or are considering buying.

What's more, as newspaper editors sense the growing appetite for fund information, an increasing number of newspapers are not only beefing up their reporting on funds, but adding investment advice to their news coverage. If you happen to live in an area whose local newspaper doesn't provide enough substantive information on funds, you could try picking up a copy of the *Wall Street Journal*, whose "Money & Investing" section has long offered an impressive combination of statistical data, breaking news, and practical advice.

How to Read Newspaper Fund Listings

Unfortunately many newspapers fall far short on the one job you would figure they could do best—namely, helping you keep track of your fund's returns on a regular basis. Yes, most newspapers do publish daily listings of fund performance. Problem is, the information is virtually useless—usually the fund listings give the fund's name, its net asset value (and sometimes the selling price if the fund has a load), and the amount per share by which the net asset value (NAV) has increased or decreased from the previous day.

For one thing, following your fund's NAV on a daily basis makes little, if any, sense. Even if you calculated the percentage change in the daily NAV (which some listings actually do), you'd know your fund's return for one day. Big deal. Actually you may not even know that. Why? Because a fund's NAV drops whenever the fund pays a distribution to shareholders, as most bond funds do monthly. (If you have distributions reinvested, the money is invested in more shares at the lower price, so you wind up with the same amount of money before and after the distribution.) So a seemingly sharp drop in the fund's NAV could represent nothing more than the payment of a distribution to shareholders.

Some newspapers, however, are publishing more informative fund listings that provide truly useful information. The fund tables in the *Wall Street Journal,* for example, give different pieces of information each day, with the most comprehensive quotations published in Friday's paper. Below is a sample of the listings the *Journal* runs each Friday along with a brief explanation of how to read the tables. What's great about these listings is that you can track a fund's progress over a variety of time periods, compare its performance with that of similar funds, and check out its sales charges, if any, as well as its ongoing annual expenses.

TOTAL RETURN

(1) NAV	(2) Net Chg	(3) (4) Fund Name	(5) Inv Obj	(6) YTD % ret	(7) 4Wk % ret	(8) 1 Yr-R	3 Yr-R	5 Yr-R	(9) Max Init Chrg	(10) Exp Ratio
		Mutual Series								
35.82	+0.16	Beacn	GI	−0.3	+0.5	+24.8 E	+17.9 A	+19.2 A	0.00	0.75
15.24	+0.05	Discovery	SC	+0.5	+1.9	+28.7 B	NA	NS	0.00	0.99
29.68	+0.13	Qualfd	GI	−0.2	+0.4	+25.9 D	+18.4 A	+19.9 A	0.00	0.73

Sources and notes: *Wall Street Journal*, Jan. 12, 1996; the National Association of Securities Dealers provides the *Journal* with NAV numbers; performance and cost data come from Lipper Analytical Services Inc.

227

1. **Net Asset Value**: Value of one share of the fund, in this case $35.82. This figure is calculated by dividing the fund's net assets (assets minus liabilities) by the number of shares outstanding.

2. **Net Chg:** Net change, or the amount the NAV has increased or decreased from the previous day: 16 cents a share for Mutual Beacon. I wouldn't place much emphasis on this figure.

3. **Fund Company:** Fund company's or fund family's name, in this case the Mutual Series fund group.

4. **Fund Name:** Name of the specific fund within the family. The three listed here are Mutual Beacon, Mutual Discovery, and Mutual Qualified.

5. **Inv Obj:** The fund's investment objective; GI stands for growth-and-income and SC for small-company. This helps you compare the fund's performance with that of similar funds. The newspaper gives definitions for all 26 of the investment objective categories it uses.

6. **YTD % ret:** The fund's total return for the calendar year to date, in this example just the first 11 days of 1996.

7. **4Wk % ret:** The fund's total return for the most recent four weeks.

8. **1 Yr-R, 3 Yr-R, 5 Yr-R:** The fund's total return and rank (**R**) for the most recent one, three, and five years. The capital letters following the returns tell you whether the fund ranked among the top 20% of funds with the same investment objective for that period (A), the next 20% (B), and so on until the bottom 20% (E). The rankings for Mutual Beacon and Mutual Qualified—A for three and five years— show that while these funds weren't top gainers in the raging bull market of 1995, they have excellent long-term track records. Mutual Discovery's three-year return wasn't available at press time (hence the NA), and the fund hadn't existed long enough to have a five-year return (NS).

9. **Max Init Chrg:** The maximum initial sales charge or front-end load, if any. The Mutual Series funds do not have sales

loads, so the figure reads 0.00. Redemption and distribution charges (aka 12b-1 fees) are designated in footnotes. No footnotes appear here since the Mutual Series funds do not levy such fees.

10. **Exp ratio:** The fund's annual expense ratio, expressed as a percentage of the fund's assets. This figure shows you how much of the fund's return is eaten up by operating expenses and distribution and marketing charges, if any. Comparing this figure against that of funds with similar investment objectives can tell you how your funds' costs stack up against competitors'.

Making Use of Personal Finance Magazines

By focusing their attention more closely on investing, personal finance magazines can usually deliver fairly in-depth analyses of funds and recommend both investing strategies as well as specific funds. Of course, I have to admit to a certain bias in my opinions on this topic. For more than 10 years I have written and edited numerous mutual fund stories for **MONEY** magazine, where I am an associate editor. It's not surprising, therefore, that I believe personal finance magazines' coverage of funds is generally more practical than what you'll find in newspapers. It also shouldn't come as a shocker that I consider **MONEY** magazine's fund coverage to be the best around.

To my mind, virtually any way you look at it—sheer volume of coverage in **MONEY** magazine's monthly "Fund Watch" section and feature stories, depth of analysis, useful advice, and the presentation of this material in a way that makes it understandable and even enjoyable to read—**MONEY** magazine beats its competitors hands down. That said, I also think that several of

MONEY magazine's major competitors do a credible job. In fact, I believe that if you are a serious fund investor, you should read a variety of personal finance magazines at least occasionally. After all, if building a portfolio of funds with varying objectives and styles is important, wouldn't it follow that you're also better off sampling a diversity of fact, analysis, and opinion from a range of magazines and other sources?

Basically, personal finance magazines can help you with your fund investing by providing three things:

1. Statistical information and analysis. Regular readers of **MONEY** magazine's "Fund Watch" section, for example, will find listings of one-, three-, five-, and 10-year performance leaders among both stock and bond funds, as well as updates of the returns of the 10 largest stock and taxable bond funds. "Fund Watch" also ranks top performers by one-year returns in each of seven stock fund investment objective categories and six bond fund categories. In addition to providing the leaders' one-year returns, the listings also provide three-, five-, and 10-year returns (for funds that have them), as well as one-, three-, five-, and 10-year returns for each stock and bond fund category average. This is the type of information that can be useful in choosing funds as well as in monitoring performance. By perusing **MONEY** magazine's "Fund Watch" listings, for example, investors can not only tell what funds are leading the pack over a variety of time periods, they can also compare how their own funds are faring versus others with similar investment objectives. *Kiplinger's* "Mutual Fund Monitor" section also contains scads of performance data on funds, while *Worth's* one-page "Fund Laboratory" offers a modest amount of statistical information. *Smart Money* provides no regular section with fund performance data.

2. Feature stories that offer investing advice. All the magazines just mentioned regularly provide their readers with feature articles that can give fresh insights on investing or provide recommendations for investing in specific funds. Such stories can definitely provide useful tips to help you launch new investing strategies or reexamine techniques you're currently using. The fund recommendations in feature articles can also provide a good starting point for choosing funds for your own portfolio, whether you're adding new funds or looking for solid candidates to replace a losing fund you already own.

3. Special rankings packages that offer a wealth of comparative performance data. Most personal finance magazines—as well as many other publications, including **MONEY,** *Barron's, Business Week, Forbes, Fortune,* and *U.S. News & World Report*—run special fund rankings issues that provide a plethora of performance data on funds. Typically these issues appear in January or February and include the previous year's results, although some magazines, such as **MONEY,** also publish semiannual rankings that feature midyear results. Even if you don't regularly read personal finance magazines, you should probably spring for a copy of one or more of these rankings issues (or peruse one at the library), because the wealth of statistical information alone can go a long way toward helping you choose funds and keep track of the progress of funds you already own.

For example, **MONEY** magazine's February 1996 62-page mutual fund guide and rankings package contains comprehensive performance and risk data on 3,247 funds, including such information as each fund's investment objective, investing style, and risk level; one-, three-, five-, and 10-year total returns; percentile rankings for each of the past four calendar years; and an analysis of fund fees and expenses. The 36-page rankings section also provides the average total returns for 16 different fund investment objectives as well as for seven widely followed market indexes. Using this extravaganza of stats, fund investors can see how their funds have performed versus competitors as well as against appropriate stock and bond market benchmarks.

Keep in mind, though, that you can effectively put to work only so much advice, no matter how trenchant it is. Once you've assembled the funds that make up your portfolio, you don't want to keep adding new ones or replacing ones you own just because a new magazine article recommends "The Ten Greatest Funds That Ever Were And Ever Will Be." Indeed, if you acted on all the recommendations personal finance magazines make, you would be swimming in funds (not to mention paperwork). Remember, just because magazines have to come out with a new issue and new recommendations each month doesn't mean you have to act on their advice. Once you've decided where to invest your money, your main reason for reading these magazines should be more to monitor your holdings and replace the occasional laggard fund, not to turn yourself into a robo-investor ready to rearrange your portfolio at the whim of every personal finance writer.

Should You Subscribe to Fund Newsletters?

I don't think there's any doubt that some of the 80 or so newsletters that cover funds exclusively can give you access to detailed information about funds and the financial markets and provide recommendations about investing strategies or specific funds. But will the information you get from these publications really translate to better performance results? Even more to the point, how do you separate the ones that are worth the $80 to $200 a year such publications typically charge subscribers from the ones that you probably wouldn't read even if they were free?

My feeling is that if you really like reading about funds, such publications can be helpful. But I don't think you necessarily need them to be a better investor or that you should expect them to boost your returns dramatically. As to the issue of separating the good from the bad and the ugly, you have a few options. One is to judge the newsletters simply on the basis of their fund picking ability. The monthly *Hulbert Financial Digest*

($135 a year, $37.50 for a five-month trial subscription; 703-683-5905) calculates the return subscribers would have earned following the specific recommendations of some 160 financial newsletters (about half of which write primarily about funds) and then rates them over various time periods. By consulting a few issues of *Hulbert,* therefore, you can at least get an idea of how you would have fared following a newsletter's advice.

I would be wary, however, about using a newsletter's performance rating as the only gauge of its usefulness. A newsletter could generate high returns by advocating risky strategies that may be inappropriate for you. Similarly, some newsletters require that you pay almost fanatical attention to them so that you can move large portions of your portfolio from one fund to another. One specialized breed, known as market-timing newsletters, may require that you switch out of stock or bond funds and into money-market portfolios at a moment's notice. You've got to ask yourself, then, whether you really want to devote the time and effort some newsletters demand, in order for you to follow their advice.

What's more, some newsletters consist of little more than reams of charts and statistical tables that purport to explain some arcane investing theory or system. So while the editor's picks might be good (over some periods of time, at least), you might learn precious little about funds and investing. I think of such publications as the newsletter equivalent of a fad diet. You might lose a few pounds on the "All The Lettuce You Can Eat" diet, but you probably won't learn much about nutrition in the process. My view is that you should be reading a fund newsletter primarily for financial nutrition. You want to gain insight, knowledge, and an overall sense of how investing works, so that rather than mindlessly follow some investing guru's telephone hot-line advice, you can learn to make savvy investing decisions on your own.

I suggest, therefore, that before subscribing to any newsletter you see listed in this book or elsewhere, you call or write the publisher and ask for a few free back copies. By reading those, you can get an idea of how much work is required to follow the letter, whether the strategies it recommends seem plausible to you, and whether you like the overall quality and tone of the publication. Some publications also offer trial publications, so you can give them a test ride without paying the full yearly rate.

Below are seven publications that I have found useful over the years. I'm not suggesting these are the only ones I like or that you should sign up for them immediately. Rather, I just think they're as good a place as any to begin your search.

1. *No-Load Fund Analyst* ($225 a year, $55 for a three-month trial subscription; 800-776-9555). This monthly covers a relatively small number of no-load funds (about 100), but editors Ken Gregory and Craig Litman offer insightful and thorough analysis, not to mention outstanding quarterly reviews that include detailed write-ups on the funds they monitor. This publication demands some time and attention—but it's worth it.

2. *No-Load Fund Investor* ($99 a year for new subscribers, $119 for renewals, $59 for a six-month subscription; 800-252-2042). Editor Sheldon Jacobs's concise monthly updates on fund performance, managers' strategies, and the economic outlook keep his readers on top of what's happening in funds and the financial markets. The newsletter also recommends funds for three model portfolios designed for capital growth, income, or a combination of both and lists performance and risk data on a variety of fund categories, market indexes and some 794 funds.

3. *InvesTech Mutual Fund Advisor* ($160 a year, $99 for a seven-month 10-issue trial; prices include subscription to *InvesTech Market Analyst;* 406-862-7777). Published 18 times a year, this newsletter emphasizes technical indicators tracked by editor James Stack and can occasionally lead its readers to be overly defensive, as was the case in 1995 when Stack recommended a huge cash position. But the real value of this newsletter lies in the historical perspective it brings to investing and funds. Stack remembers all too well the "trees grow to the skies" mentality of the 1960s go-go era in funds (which was followed by the early 1970s crash) and frequently uses inanities of the past to teach lessons about potential excesses in today's markets.

4. *Morningstar Investor* ($79 a year; 800-735-0700). With a relatively low $79 price tag, this monthly should be a favorite of value investors. It's packed with news, performance stats, investing advice, fund profiles, and mini feature stories that tackle a wide range of investing issues. Overall, *Morningstar Investor* is a good cost-effective way for investors to keep up with funds and the financial markets.

5. *Moneyletter* ($88 a year, $49 for a six-month trial subscription; 800-433-1528). Published twice a month, this eight-page newsletter manages to offer something to fund novices as well as seasoned investors. Issues typically begin with an overview of current developments in the economy and financial markets and then move on to the latest fund news and practical investment advice. The "Fund Scorecard and Recommendations" section provides recent returns and buy, sell, or hold advice on domestic and foreign stock and bond funds and also offers a wealth of risk-related stats for the number junkies among us. Issues also highlight the top-yielding taxable and tax-exempt money-market funds and end with an insightful profile on a fund or fund family.

6. *Fidelity Insight* ($99 for new subscribers, $127 for renewals, $39 for four-month trial; 617-369-2500). If you invest mostly or solely with Fidelity, you might consider this monthly, which follows Fidelity portfolios exclusively. Edited by ex-Fidelity staffer Eric Kobren, *Fidelity Insight* offers commentary on Fidelity funds, provides monthly performance updates, and tracks the progress of four model porfolios made up exclusively of Fidelity funds. Kobren also edits *FundsNet Insight*, a monthly designed for people who own funds through one of the discount broker fund networks described in Chapter 12.

7. *The Independent Adviser for Vanguard Investors* ($89 for new subscribers, $99 for renewals; 800-777-5005). Investors who stick mostly to Vanguard funds might find this publication useful. Editor Daniel Wiener gives concise reports on what's happening in the financial markets and at Vanguard, updates readers on the performance of Vanguard funds, and provides four model porfolios (growth, conservative growth, income, and a growth index fund portfolio) consisting entirely of Vanguard funds.

For the Fund Aficionado: Fund Ratings Services

If you're a serious fund investor who wants to put real time and effort into analyzing funds, you should look into one of the fund ratings services. Indeed, even if you aren't a fund fanatic, I think you ought to consider consulting one of these services when you are first choosing funds, so you will at least have access to detailed comparative data when making your initial investing decisions.

The two services most accessible to individual investors are *Morningstar Mutual Funds* ($395 a year or $55 for a three-month trial subscription, and $145 a year or $45 for three months for a less comprehensive version that covers only 650 no-load funds; 800-735-0700) and the *Value Line Mutual Funds Survey* ($295 a year, $49 for a three-month trial subscription; 800-833-0046). Yes, they're pricey, so you probably shouldn't subscribe unless you'll use one regularly and expect to improve your investing results. On the other hand, one or both of these services are available at many public libraries, so you may not have to shell out any money to take advantage of the information and advice they offer.

Morningstar Mutual Funds is generally considered the more comprehensive of the two. Its one-page reports on more than 1,500 stock and bond funds contain an analyst's review of the fund plus a wealth of statistical information, including historical performance figures for a variety of periods, comparative performance data vs. indexes such as the Standard & Poor's 500, a risk analysis, a recent breakdown of the holdings in the fund's portfolio, a brief profile of the manager, information on the fund's fees and expenses, and an investment style box that shows you at a glance how the fund attempts to achieve its investment objective. (You can also buy Morningstar's one-page reports for individual funds at $5 apiece. For a look at a Morningstar report as well as some tips on how to use one, see pages 239–242.)

Value Line Mutual Funds Survey covers more funds—about 2,000—but doesn't provide quite the level of detail that Morningstar does. Nonetheless, Value Line too can provide you with virtually all the information you need to pick solid funds. Both services update their fund write-ups every 20 weeks. Subscribers also get updated performance information for all funds mailed to them every two weeks from Morningstar and once a month from Value Line.

For investors who prefer splicing and dicing data on their PC, Morningstar and Value Line also offer electronic versions of their service that give you access to the firms' databases of some 7,000 stock and bond funds. *Morningstar Ascent* ($195 a year with monthly updates, $95 with quarterly updates, $45 for one disk; CD-ROM or floppy disk, Windows only) allows you to screen for funds that meet specific criteria, say, ones that have beaten the average return for their investment objective and the S&P 500 over the past one, three, and five years. Morningstar also offers two more comprehensive versions of its database: *Principia for Mutual Funds* ($395 a year with monthly updates, $195 for quarterly updates; CD-ROM or floppy disk, Windows only) and Mutual Funds OnDisc ($795 a year for monthly updates, $495 for quarterly updates; CD-ROM), both of which include more detailed portfolio statistics than *Ascent*, such as the average weighted price-earnings ratios for a stock fund's holdings. You can also get a so-called "electronic binder" CD-ROM version of

Principia, which contains copies of the fund write-ups from the *Morningstar Mutual Funds* print service for $495 with quarterly updates and $795 for monthly updates.

Value Line also has a computerized rendition of its database called *Fund Analyzer* ($295 a year for disk or CD-ROM, $395 a year for a CD-ROM version that includes the Value Line's one-page fund analyses in the *Value Line Mutual Fund Survey;* Windows only). In addition to allowing you to screen for specific fund picks from a database of some 6,000 funds, *Fund Analyzer* let's you put together a portfolio of mutual funds and then track how that portfolio would have fared over various time periods. What's more, the program calculates risk statistics such as standard deviation not just for the individual funds, but for your custom portfolio as well, so you can see how the risk-reward ratio changes as you add or drop different funds. *Fund Analyzer* subscribers get monthly updates by mail, or they can get weekly updates to the database through Value Line's on-line service, which also gives investors access to Value Line's *Mutual Fund Advisor* newsletter.

There are two other less expensive fund software programs you might want to consider: Steele System's *Mutual Fund Expert—Personal* ($107 a year with quarterly updates, $221 for monthly updates; Windows or DOS; 800-237-8400, ext. 767), which lets you sift through a database of some 7,500 funds, including 1,500 money funds; and the Amerian Association of Individual Investors' *Quarterly Low-Load Mutual Fund Update* ($50 a year or $39 for AAII members; DOS and Macintosh; 800-428-2244), which allows you to screen and rank 1,000 or so funds using variables such as risk, return, and yield and is one of the few programs available to investors with Macs.

Don't Get Starry-Eyed

Unfortunately some investors turn to these services for the wrong reason—namely, to choose funds on the basis of the ratings Morningstar, Value Line, and others assign. Limit yourself to Morningstar five-star funds (one star is the lowest rating, five stars the highest) or funds rated number one by Value Line ("1" is the best rating, "5" the worst), the theory goes, and you will have a portfolio of top performers. Ah, if only stargazing could lead to terrific fund picks.

Fact is, these ratings do not—repeat, do not—predict future performance. They only show how a fund has fared in the past. What's more, because of differences in ratings formulas, a fund could get the highest ranking from one service and a mediocre grade from another. Generally the ranking systems tend to identify funds whose investing styles have recently been hot. When another style begins to outperform, then funds with that style will rise in ratings and the previously highly rated funds will fall. Indeed, Morningstar estimates that 40% of the 200 or so funds that have its top rating at any given time will slip to a lower rating within a year. So use the ratings services not so much for the fund ratings, but for the wealth of statistical information they provide.

How to Read a Morningstar Report

As this reproduction of a Morningstar report shows, Morningstar's fund analyses contain an impressive—some might say daunting—amount of information. Here is a 10-step program for reading the report so you can glean its most important parts:

Volume 27, Issue 1, February, 16, 1996. Reprinted with permission.

Twentieth Century Ultra Investors

	Ticker	Load	NAV	Yield	SEC Yield	Assets	Objective
	TWCUX	None	$26.11	0.0%	---	$14551.2 mil	Aggr. Growth

Twentieth Century Ultra Investors seeks capital growth.

The fund typically invests at least 90% of assets in equity securities selected for their appreciation potential. The majority of these securities are common stocks issued by companies that meet management's standards for earnings and revenue trends. The fund may purchase securities only of companies that have operated continuously for three or more years.

Historical Profile
Return High
Risk High
Rating ★★★★ Above Avg

Growth of $10,000
- Investment Value ($000) of Fund
- Investment Value ($000) S&P 500
▼ Manager Change
∇ Partial Manager Change

Investment Style History
Equity
Average Stock %

| | 99% | 99% | 99% | 97% | 94% | 93% | 92% | 97% |

Portfolio Manager(s)
James E. Stowers III. Since 11-81. BS'81 Arizona State U.
Christopher K. Boyd, CFA. Since 1-91. BS'81 U. of Kansas; MBA'86 Dartmouth C.
Derek V. Felske, CFA. Since 9-93. BA'80 Dartmouth C.; MBA'91 Wharton.

Performance 12-31-95

	1st Qtr	2nd Qtr	3rd Qtr	4th Qtr	Total
1991	40.75	-6.19	18.57	19.09	86.45
1992	-6.92	-11.03	2.65	19.13	1.27
1993	-0.11	14.03	10.25	-2.99	21.81
1994	-1.82	-8.29	5.14	1.81	-3.62
1995	4.61	15.19	15.56	-1.13	37.68

Trailing	Total Return %	+/- S&P 500	+/- Russ 2000	% Rank All Obj	Growth of $10,000
3 Mo	-1.13	-7.14	-3.29	93 64	9,887
6 Mo	14.25	-0.18	2.00	11 38	11,425
1 Yr	37.68	0.14	9.24	6 32	13,768
3 Yr Avg	17.36	2.04	2.90	7 30	16,164
5 Yr Avg	25.00	8.42	4.01	3 20	30,521
10 Yr Avg	19.81	4.93	8.49	2 3	60,929
15 Yr Avg	---	---	---	---	---

Most Similar Funds in MMF
Twentieth Century Vista Investors	Strong Fit
Alger Small Capitalization	Strong Fit
Scudder Development	Strong Fit

Tax Analysis
	Tax-Adj Return %	% Pretax Return
3 Yr Avg	16.46	94.8
5 Yr Avg	24.43	97.7
10 Yr Avg	17.83	90.0
Potential Capital Gain Exposure		33% of assets

Analysis by Peter Di Teresa 02-02-96

Twentieth Century Ultra Investors woke in 1995 to a booming growth market.

After posting stellar 86% returns in 1991, this fund drifted off in 1992, stirred briefly in 1993, and slumbered again in 1994. Its normally strong long-term returns slumped as a result, though its risk scores were still high. Many of the investors drawn to the fund by its successful earnings-acceleration strategy must have been stumped by its soporific performance.

The fund may have been too stuffed with new investments to get off the couch—1992 and 1993 were not good years for growth, and required deft maneuvering. As assets have grown, the managers have opted to take bigger positions rather than increase the size of the portfolio. Because each holding thus represents more of a company's total issuance stock liquidity is a greater concern, and the fund has taken on larger-cap holdings. Although the fund's aggressive strategy hasn't

changed, its median market cap is now one of the largest in its group. (The fund does still buy small- and mid-cap companies; the increase in market cap also reflects the success of once-smaller stocks.)

The fund needed some help waking up. It got just that in 1995, as its massive technology exposure (70% of stock assets) boosted it to top-quartile returns through September. The fund did suffer in the fourth quarter when tech corrected. Despite the portfolio's unusually high price risk, however, the fund's losses were mild and it finished 1995 in the top third of its group. (A sizable health-care stake gave it a helping hand.) Unlike many of its peers, the fund kept most of its tech (its services holdings include networking and software issues), because the managers still see strong earnings growth.

Although 1995 was no 1991, the fund did show that it could still run with a rally and earn returns consistent with its level of risk.

Address	4500 Main Street P.O. Box 419200	Minimum Purchase	$2500	Add: $50	IRA: $100
	Kansas City, MO 64141-6200	Min Auto Inv Plan	$50	Systematic Inv: $50	
Telephone	800-345-2021 / 816-531-5575	Date of Inception	11-02-81		
Advisor	Investors Research	**Expenses & Fees**			
Subadvisor	None	Sales Fees	No-load		
Distributor	Twentieth Century Investors	Management Fee	1.00%		
States Available	All	Actual Fees	Mgt: 1.00%	Dist: ---	
Report Grade	A	Expense Projections	3Yr: $32	5Yr: $55	10Yr: $122
Income Distrib	Annually	Annual Brokerage Cost	0.21%		

History
1984	1985	1986	1987	1988	1989	1990	1991	1992	1993	1994	12-95	
6.41	8.10	8.92	6.23	7.06	8.53	9.30	17.34	17.56	21.39	19.95	26.11	NAV
-19.45	26.37	10.26	6.69	13.32	36.94	9.36	86.45	1.27	21.81	-3.62	37.68	Total Return %
-25.71	-5.37	-8.42	1.43	-3.29	5.25	12.48	55.74	-6.35	11.75	-4.93	0.14	+/- S&P 500
-12.15	-4.69	4.58	15.46	-11.57	20.69	28.87	40.40	-17.14	2.91	-1.79	9.24	+/- Russell 2000
0.00	0.00	0.14	0.08	0.00	2.37	0.00	0.00	0.00	0.00	0.00	0.00	Income Return %
-19.45	26.37	10.12	6.61	13.32	34.57	9.36	86.45	1.27	21.81	-3.62	37.68	Capital Return %
97	42	84	17	36	6	7	1	88	15	51	6	Total Rtn %Rank All
71	66	55	18	47	17	7	2	76	36	56	32	Total Rtn %Rank Obj
0.00	0.00	0.01	0.01	0.00	0.20	0.00	0.00	0.00	0.00	0.00	0.00	Income $
0.26	0.00	0.00	3.26	0.00	0.95	0.03	0.00	0.00	0.00	0.65	1.30	Capital Gains $
1.01	1.01	1.01	1.00	1.00	1.00	1.00	1.00	1.00	1.00	1.00	1.00	Expense Ratio %
-0.30	0.10	0.00	-0.50	-0.30	2.21	-0.30	-0.50	-0.40	-0.60	-1.00	-0.30	Income Ratio %
93	100	99	137	140	132	141	42	59	53	78	87	Turnover Rate %
445.6	385.4	286.9	247.8	255.6	345.5	458.3	2939.7	5299.3	8353.2	9850.8	14551.2	Net Assets ($mil)

Risk Analysis
Time Period	Load-Adj Return %	Risk %Rank All	Morningstar Risk	Morningstar Risk-Adj Rating
1 Yr	37.68			
3 Yr	17.36	95	57	1.41 ★★★
5 Yr	25.00	97	88	2.20 1.61 ★★★★
10 Yr	19.81	97	88	2.63 1.47 ★★★★★
Average Historical Rating	(121 months)			3.2 ★s

*1=low, 100=high

Other Measures		Standard Index S&P 500	Best Fit Index Wil 4500
Standard Deviation	15.98	Alpha	0.9	-0.1
Mean	17.37	Beta	1.17	1.39
Sharpe Ratio	0.83	R-Squared	36	67

Portfolio Analysis 12-31-95

Share Chg (10-95) 000	Amount 000	Total Stocks: 134 Total Fixed-Income: 0	Value $000	%Net Assets
8750	12900	Sun Microsystems	589369	4.05
0	12400	3Com	578925	3.98
1458	7458	cisco Systems	557019	3.83
0	7850	Amgen	465603	3.20
4473	11223	Bay Networks	460836	3.17
0	6600	Pfizer	415800	2.86
1050	6250	Merck	410938	2.82
0	9000	Oracle	381375	2.62
1730	4400	Ascend Communications	357225	2.45
650	6150	Intel	349397	2.40
100	3550	Johnson & Johnson	303969	2.09
0	3450	US Robotics	303169	2.08
0	3000	IBM	275250	1.89
0	3500	Intuit	273438	1.88
0	6700	Applied Materials	263394	1.81
-500	2800	Microsoft	245875	1.69
1550	3850	Adobe Systems	239175	1.64
0	3550	Citicorp	238738	1.64
-250	6750	Dell Computer	234984	1.61
1004	7454	Informix	224098	1.54
2750	5500	America Online	205219	1.41
1500	3500	Schering-Plough	191625	1.32
0	2150	Cascade Communications	183019	1.26
0	2400	StrataCom	175800	1.21
2636	2636	MFS Microsystems	165409	1.14

Investment Style
Style Value Blend Growth
Value | | Stock Portfolio Avg | Rel S&P 500 | Rel Objective |
|---|---|---|---|
| Price/Earnings Ratio | 37.4 | 1.84 | 1.28 |
| Price/Book Ratio | 9.2 | 2.13 | 1.68 |
| 5 Yr Earnings Gr % | 31.1 | 3.09 | 1.26 |
| Return on Assets % | 15.4 | 1.89 | 1.39 |
| Debt % Total Cap | 15.2 | 0.55 | 0.62 |
| Med Mkt Cap ($mil) | 5714 | 0.57 | 2.73 |

Special Securities % of assets 10-31-95
Private/Illiquid Securities	0
Emerging-Markets Secs	Trace
Short Sales	0
Options/Futures/Warrants	Yes

Composition % of assets 12-31-95
Cash	2.9
Stocks	97.1
Bonds	0.0
Other	0.0

Index Allocation % of stocks
S&P 500	47.3
S&P Mid	16.5
US Sm Cap	33.0
Foreign	3.5

Sector Weightings
	% of Stocks	Rel S&P
Utilities	1.2	0.11
Energy	0.4	0.04
Financials	5.4	0.41
Industrial Cyclicals	1.1	0.06
Consumer Durables	0.1	0.03
Consumer Staples	1.8	0.16
Services	19.9	1.98
Retail	0.6	0.13
Health	22.7	2.19
Technology	46.8	5.65

M🌟RNINGSTAR Mutual Funds

1. Investment objective: This section gives you a brief description of the fund's investment objective and what kinds of securities it buys to achieve it. You should also look across the page to see which investment objective category Morningstar has assigned the fund to—in this case, aggressive growth.

2. Analyst's review: Here you get a Morningstar fund analyst's insights on how the fund has performed, what the manager is presently doing, any special risks or situations the fund faces, and, sometimes, a comment on the fund's future prospects.

3. Manager history: This section lets you know who is running the fund and how long the present management has been there. If management is new, you should be wary of putting much weight on long-term past performance.

4. Investment style: The nine-section style box tells you at a glance how the manager pursues the fund's investment objective. In this case the manager primarily buys large growth companies. By checking the historical style boxes at the top right-hand side of the page, you can see this fund has shifted from a small-growth to large-growth style over the years.

5. Index allocation: Here you see what percentage of the fund's holdings consist of stocks found in various market indexes. Some 47.3% of Twentieth Century Ultra Investors' stocks could be found in the S&P 500; that makes sense for a company investing in large growth stocks. But a small-company fund that has a large percentage of its portfolio in S&P 500 stocks should lead you to question whether the manager has switched strategies—as well as question whether you should stay in the fund.

6. Sector weightings: This section gives you a breakdown of the fund's holdings by industry sectors, allowing you to see whether the fund is taking on more risk by investing heavily in particular industries. Even though this fund had reduced its technology holdings from 70% to 46.8% of its portfolio, it is still making a huge bet on tech stocks.

7. Historical performance: In this area you'll find total return figures for a slew of periods as well as the fund's percentile ranking versus all funds and funds with the same investing objective. Note the substantial 11% drop in value in the second quarter of 1992. Take a look too at the boxes with horizontal bars just above this section and to the right. These bars show whether the fund's total return in a given calendar year placed it within the top, second, third, or fourth (and lowest) 25% of funds with similar objectives. This is a good indicator of whether the fund has been a consistent winner.

8. Calendar–year returns: Here you can scan the fund's returns for the year to date as well as for each of the past 11 calendar years (or the number of years since inception, whichever is shorter). Compare the annual returns to the annualized figures over longer years (section 7) to see how much the fund's returns each year have bounced around from the longer-term averages.

9. Risk analysis: This section gives you an idea of the fund's riskiness on a scale of 1 (lowest) to 100 (highest) compared with all funds as well as funds with the same objective. Morningstar uses a risk measure based on the number of months and the extent to which a fund has underperformed risk-free Treasury bills over the past three years. You will find a risk-adjusted rating that factors in risk as well as a fund's raw returns and, immediately below this section, other statistical measures that can help you better understand the interplay of risk and return.

10. Expenses and fees: A quick glance here tells you what sales commission, if any, you're paying for a fund as well as what ongoing annual expenses the fund charges. If you scan the expense ratio section of the annual performance history (just below section 8), you can see whether the expense ratio has gone up or down over the years.

Lost in Cyberspace: Funds on the Information Superhighway

If you prefer sorting through fund information on your computer, you're in luck. Every day, it seems, more fund data becomes available on-line, either through one of the established commercial services such as America Online, CompuServe, or Prodigy or on the exponentially expanding number of home pages popping up on the Internet. In fact, the sheer volume of info available on-line is growing so quickly that it's virtually impossible to keep track of it. That said, all I can do here is name a few places where you can get information today and then suggest that you surf the Net on your own to look for more. Here, then, is a brief rundown on what cyberspace is serving up for fund investors:

• **Commercial on-line services:** The three major on-line services—America Online, CompuServe, and Prodigy—are fine if you want general information about funds or you would like to read recent personal finance magazine stories or chat with other investors about funds. But they're not the ideal place to go for the kind of comprehensive information you probably want when you are trying to figure out which funds to buy. Why? Because even though all three of the services have fund databases that provide statistical information and allow you to screen for funds that meet specific performance criteria, none offers the quality of information or screening ability you'll find in the diskette and CD-ROM fund databases mentioned earlier.

The best of the lot is the "Fund Watch" section in the *MONEY Personal Finance Center* on CompuServe, which lets you roam through a database of nearly 5,000 funds and choose portfolios based on a limited number of largely performance-related criteria. Log on to America Online and you can tap into a *Morningstar Mutual Funds* database of more than 6,500 funds, but you have virtually no ability to screen for funds using criteria such as returns for various periods or risk levels. Prodigy's *Mutual Fund Analyst* offers access to statistical information on more than 6,000 funds and offers updated lists of top-performing funds for several time periods. But it too has limited screening power and costs an extra $14.95 a month on top of Prodigy's regular monthly rate.

Several fund companies have also opened cyberoffices on the on-line services, providing information about their funds, brochures on investing, and, in some cases, allowing investors to order prospectuses or even download them. For example, you can find Twentieth Century and Dreyfus on CompuServe; Fidelity, Dreyfus, and Scudder on Prodigy; and Vanguard and T. Rowe Price on America Online. The three on-line services also have portfolio update software that allows you to track the value of your fund portfolio on-line. Of the three, America Online's update service, which you can find under its "Quotes and Portfolios" menu, is the easiest to use.

Finally, all three services provide an array of business and personal finance magazines that investors can browse through in search of recent articles on funds and investing, not to mention several investing forums if you want to put questions to or just shoot the breeze with other investors.

• **Web sites of funds and fund organizations:** A growing number of fund groups also have their own home pages on the World Wide Web. Investors who tap into Fidelity's, T. Rowe Price's, or Vanguard's on-line sites can get information on specific funds, gather news and general advice about fund and retirement investing, and download fund prospectuses and information kits. (Their URLs, or Internet addresses, are http://www.fid-inv.com, http://www.troweprice.com and http://www.vanguard.com) Vanguard has even presented a six-week introductory fund investing course—Vanguard Online University—which included assigned reading materials, on-line discussion groups on investing topics hosted by a different guest expert each week, and, of course, a final exam. Vanguard also plans to offer on-line courses on retirement planning and an advanced fund investing course. And in early 1996 Calvert (http://www.calvertgroup.com) became the first fund family to allow its shareholders to check their fund balances and get other account information on-line.

More than 50 other fund groups, including such well-known families as Gabelli, Twentieth Century, and Scudder, have home pages that you can reach through the site of a company called NETworth (http://www.networth.galt.com). NETworth also gives investors access to a database of more than 6,800 funds and allows for limited screening to find fund picks that meet specific criteria. The 100% No-Load Mutual Fund Council, a trade organization of funds that do not levy sales fees, also has a site within NETworth, which offers profiles of no-load funds from some 35 fund families.

• **Other sites for fund investors:** There are scads of other sites scattered across the Internet, all dishing out information of varying quality about funds and other investments. If you'd like to check out current yields on bond and money funds, for example, you can log on to the home page of IBC/Donoghue (http://www.donoghue.com), a company that publishes several newsletters on bond and money funds for institutional investors. The *MONEY Personal Finance Center* Web site (http://pathfinder. com/money) provides quotes on stocks, funds, and indexes, as well as new feature stories on funds and investing each week. Log on to the *Wall Street Journal* "Money and Investing Update" site after midnight (http://update.wsj.com) and you can get a peek at what news stories will be on the paper's front page the next day. One way to scout out potentially helpful sites is to go to a service called Yahoo (http://www.yahoo.com), which acts as a sort of wired telephone directory of Web sites. Type into Yahoo's search menu a keyword like "mutual funds" and it will generate a list of sites ranging from fund company home pages to investing newsletters to fund investor chat groups that hold on-line discussions or allow you to post investing tips or questions.

Before you get all wired up about surfing the Net for fund help, however, I'd like to leave you with one caveat. While there is plenty of useful information in cyberspace, there's also an incredible amount of self-serving blather, blatant promotionalism, advertising masquerading as advice, blowhards making like fund savants, and generally unfiltered malarkey. So for now, at least, unless it comes from an organization you know and trust, take the info you see on the Web with a healthy dose of skepticism. Otherwise the seemingly sage advice you're downloading could come back to megabyte you.

CHAPTER 14

Fund Lingo: Investment Terms You Should Know

As if making investment decisions isn't confusing enough, mutual fund companies, stockbrokers, financial planners, and a host of other investment advisers often make things even murkier by slipping into their own private language. Call it Wall Street–ese: an argot of jargon and technical terms that is indecipherable to people weaned on standard English. What follows are brief definitions of many common (and some uncommon) terms you may run across in the course of investing in mutual funds.

AGGRESSIVE GROWTH FUND: a fund that shoots for maximum capital appreciation, often by investing in shares of companies whose revenues and profits are growing at a rapid rate. These funds usually trade shares frequently, and many invest in stock market indexes and options. Some may also engage in risky strategies such as borrowing money to buy securities or selling short, a technique that allows investors to profit on falling stock prices by borrowing securities, selling them, and then (if things work out) replacing them at a cheaper price. These funds should come with seat belts because they offer a rollicking ride.

ANNUAL AND SEMIANNUAL REPORT: reports that a fund sends to shareholders, discussing recent performance and listing all the securities in the fund's portfolio as of the end of the period. These reports include a letter to shareholders written by one of the fund's head honchos, who usually takes credit for the fund's performance when it shines and, when the fund hasn't done so well, describes how the fund manager nonetheless struggled valiantly against all odds.

ASSET ALLOCATION: fancy name for not putting all your eggs in one basket. For fund investors, asset allocation is the process of divvying up investment holdings among stock, bond, and money-market funds. Though it may seem counterintuitive, the proportion in which you own stock, bonds, and money funds has a far greater impact on your returns than the individual funds you choose.

ASSET-ALLOCATION FUND: a fund that diversifies its holdings among stocks, bonds, and cash equivalents such as Treasury bills and short-term corporate IOUs called commercial paper. Some asset-allocation funds hold their stocks-bonds-cash mix relatively constant; others shift it in response to changing market conditions. Some asset-allocation funds also hold shares of gold-mining companies or real estate–related stocks as a hedge against inflation.

AUTOMATIC INVESTING PLAN: also known as **systematic investing,** this is a program many funds offer that allows investors to direct a fixed amount of money regularly (usually monthly) from their bank accounts or paychecks into a fund. By using such a plan you are essentially dollar-cost averaging into the fund, which is an excellent way to invest and build wealth.

AVERAGE MATURITY: the number of years, on average, before the bonds in a bond fund portfolio will be repaid. Since the calculation to arrive at average maturity gives greater weight to the fund's larger holdings, this figure is often referred to as **average weighted maturity**. In general, the longer a bond fund's average maturity, the more its value will increase (or decrease) when interest rates drop (or rise).

BACK-END LOAD: a sales charge levied by some load funds when you withdraw money. Also known as **deferred contingent sales charges,** back-end loads usually start at 5% or 6% if you withdraw money within a year of buying the fund and then decline by a percentage point or so each year until they disappear.

BALANCED FUND: a fund that generally keeps 50% to 60% of its assets in stocks and the rest in bonds, although the manager may have wide latitude to change that mix. Because of the interest payments of the bonds and other interest-earning securities in their portfolios, balanced funds typically have the highest yields of all stock funds and tend to hold up better than other stock funds when the market falls. Since their gains come from a combination of dividends, interest payments, and capital gains, balanced funds, along with growth-and-income and equity-income funds, are often referred to as **total return funds**.

BETA: a statistical gauge of risk that measures how much a fund's value fluctuates relative to a standard benchmark, usually the Standard & Poor's 500 stock index in the case of stocks and stock funds. By definition the S&P 500's beta equals 1. Thus a fund with a beta of 1.1 would be expected to return 10% more than the S&P 500 when stock prices are rising and fall 10% more when stock prices drop. Drawback to beta: it tells you how a fund rises or falls relative only to a particular benchmark. So a fund could have a low beta but still be quite volatile. Gold funds, for example, are among the most volatile of funds, yet they have low betas because they tend to move up or down with gold prices rather than with stock prices.

BOND FUND: a fund that invests in bonds or other debt securities.

CAPITAL GAIN (OR LOSS): profit (or loss) that results when the price of a security rises above (or falls below) its purchase price. If the security is sold, then the capital gain (or loss) is realized; if the security is still being held, the gain (or loss) is unrealized. If the security has been held more than a year, the gain (or loss) is long-term; otherwise it is short-term.

CAPITAL-GAINS DISTRIBUTION: a payment the fund makes to shareholders from the capital gains a fund realizes when it sells securities for more than it paid for them. Capital gains are generally paid out once at the end of the year.

CASH EQUIVALENTS: short-term debt securities such as Treasury bills, money funds, and, to a lesser extent, bond funds with maturities of two years or less. Such investments are referred to as cash equivalents (or even simply cash) for two reasons: They are highly liquid (that is, they can be sold quickly) and their short maturities keep their value stable even if interest rates blip up.

CONVERTIBLE BOND FUND: a fund that invests in bonds that can be converted to underlying shares of stock in the issuing company.

CORPORATE BOND FUND: a fund that invests in bonds and other debt securities issued by corporations.

CREDIT RISK: the possibility that a bond fund will drop in value because issuers of bonds in the portfolio fail to make timely interest payments or repay the principal of their bonds. To evaluate that risk, ask the bond fund representative for the average credit rating of a fund's portfolio based on the ratings systems used by Standard & Poor's or Moody's Investors Service.

DERIVATIVE: an investment whose value is derived from some other asset, index, interest rate, or other benchmark. Although derivatives can be highly risky—witness how certain types of derivatives derailed several supposedly safe short-term government bond funds and Orange County's investment pool in 1994—many derivatives are also used as hedging devices to lower risk.

DISTRIBUTION YIELD: also known as **distribution rate,** this way of expressing the income a fund pays out can be manipulated to mislead investors by returning their own capital to them. For a more accurate idea of how much income a fund is generating, ask for the fund's 30-day or SEC yield.

DIVERSIFIED FUND: a fund that spreads its holdings among securities of many different companies or, in the case of bonds, different issuers. A nondiversifed fund, conversely, concentrates its holdings among a relative handful of companies, while a sector fund limits itself to the securities of a single industry.

DIVIDEND DISTRIBUTION: a payment the fund makes to shareholders from interest payments the fund receives from bonds or dividends paid by the fund's stocks. Shareholders can elect to receive the dividends in cash or have them reinvested in additional shares of the fund.

DOLLAR-COST AVERAGING: the technique of investing the same dollar amount at regular intervals, say, monthly. This method of investing works especially well with no-load mutual funds since you can regularly deposit small amounts of cash without having to pay sales commissions. Contrary to popular misconception, dollar-cost averaging doesn't assure you'll get the highest returns. It can reduce risk, however, and the discipline of regular investing regardless of how the market is faring can prevent you from investing most of your money when stock or bond prices are rising and euphoria reigns (and the market may

251

be vulnerable to a downturn) or pulling out your money after prices have crashed (which often is the time when you find the best bargains).

DURATION: a measure of a bond or bond fund's sensitivity to interest rate fluctuations that takes into account maturity, the possibility of early redemptions, and interest payments. As with average maturity, the higher a fund's duration, the more its value will increase when interest rates fall and drop when rates rise. A fund with a duration of 10 would lose 10% of its value if interest rates rose by one percentage point, 20% if rates increased by two percentage points. The fund would gain the same amounts were rates to fall.

EQUITY-INCOME FUND: a fund that invests in a mix of bonds and dividend-paying stocks. Equity-income funds are similar to growth-and-income funds, except that they are more likely to hold bonds and they tend to focus more on stocks that pay higher-than-average dividends. Equity-income funds generally have higher dividend yields than growth-and-income funds and stock funds overall, a characteristic that helps them hold up better than most equity funds when the market sours. Like balanced and growth-and-income funds, equity-income funds are also known as **total return funds** because their returns usually consist of a combination of capital gains, dividends, and interest payments.

EXPENSE RATIO: a fund's total annual expenses expressed as a percentage of average net assets. This figure, as well as other information about the fund's expenses, is included in the fund's prospectus and also available in many magazines and fund-rating firms' publications. Compare your fund's expense ratio with that of competitors to see whether you're overpaying for performance.

FRONT-END LOAD: a sales charge levied by some funds at the time of purchase.

GINNIE MAE FUND: a fund that invests in mortgage-backed securities issued by the Government National Mortgage Association (GNMA). Such funds typically also hold mortgage-backed securities issued by other government-related organizations such as the Federal National Mortgage Association (Fannie Mae or FNMA). These funds react to interest rate movements much like bond funds, with one important exception—investors have less of an opportunity to earn capital gains when interest rates drop. Reason: Homeowners refinance (and pay off their old high-rate mortgage in the process) when rates fall, thus eliminating high interest rate mortgages from the fund's portfolio.

GLOBAL FUND: as its name implies, a fund that can invest anywhere around the globe. Thus, unlike international or foreign funds, global funds will often hold U.S. securities.

GOVERNMENT BOND FUND: a fund that invests in U.S. government securities. Those securities may be direct obligations of the U.S. Treasury, such as Treasury notes and bonds, or they may be securities issued by government agencies or government-sponsored agencies, such as the mortgage-backed securities known as Ginnie Maes, which are issued by the Government National Mortgage Association. A fund can call itself a government bond as long as it invests at least 65% of its assets in government securities.

GROWTH-AND-INCOME FUND: a fund that holds a combination of dividend-paying stocks and securities that pay current interest, such as various types of bonds and preferred stock. Some growth-and-income funds take a more aggressive stance than others by tilting their mix toward fast-growing stocks and away from bonds and dividend-paying shares. Because their gains result from capital gains, dividends, and, sometimes, interest payments, growth-and-income funds are often called **total return funds,** as are balanced and equity-income funds.

GROWTH FUND: a fund that aims for capital growth, often by buying shares of fast-growing companies, although growth funds may also focus on shares of companies whose assets are undervalued; these funds may invest in companies of virtually any size, but they generally concentrate their holdings in medium to large companies, which makes them somewhat less volatile than their aggressive growth counterparts; generally, growth fund returns mirror those of the overall stock market. These funds are typically recommended as core holdings for investors looking for long-term capital growth.

GROWTH INVESTING: see **investing style.**

HIGH-YIELD FUND: fund-industry euphemism for junk bond fund.

INDEX FUND: a fund designed to track the performance of a standard market benchmark such as the Standard & Poor's 500 stock index. A successful index fund is one whose return tracks its index very closely.

INTEREST RATE RISK: the chance that a fund's value will fall in response to rising interest rates. Two ways to gauge the extent of that risk are to look at the fund's duration or at its average maturity.

INTERMEDIATE-TERM BOND FUND: a bond fund with an average maturity of four to 10 years.

INTERNATIONAL FUND: a fund that invests in securities issued outside the United States, as opposed to a global fund, which invests in U.S. and foreign securities.

INVESTING STYLE: the manner in which a fund pursues gains. Growth investors home in on companies with rapidly growing profits, while value investors look for companies whose assets are selling at a discount to their true value; some managers use a blend of growth and value styles. Managers may also focus on small, medium, or large companies; thus a manager's investing style could be described as small-company value, large-company growth, medium-company blend, etc.

INVESTMENT ADVISORY FEE: see **management fee.**

JUNK BOND FUND: a fund that invests in corporate bonds that have received below investment-grade ratings from ratings services such as Standard & Poor's and Moody's Investors Service. Junk bond funds are also euphemistically known as **high-yield funds,** and, indeed, their yields are higher than those of most other bond funds—as are the risks they carry.

LOAD: a sales charge, typically 3% to 5.75% of the amount invested, that you pay when buying a fund through a broker, financial planner, or other salesperson. A portion of the load compensates the salesperson. Some funds that sell their shares directly to the public also carry loads, but their charges usually range from 1% to 3%.

LOAD FUND: a fund that imposes either a front- or back-end sales charge. Funds with a sales charge of 3% or less are often referred to as **low-load funds**.

LONG-TERM BOND FUND: a bond fund with an average maturity of 10 or more years.

MANAGEMENT FEE: the fee a fund pays to the fund's investment adviser to choose and monitor securities for the fund. This fee, expressed as a percentage of the fund's average net assets, is disclosed in the prospectus.

MARKET TIMING: the practice of putting all or most of one's money into stocks or stock funds when it appears stock prices are headed up and, when it seems stocks are about to fall, selling one's stock investments and plowing the proceeds into money funds or other secure investments. Nice idea, if only someone could really predict the path of stock prices in the near future.

MONEY-MARKET FUND: a type of mutual fund that invests in very short-term debt securities, such as Treasury bills and corporate IOUs known as commercial paper. The Securities and Exchange Commission requires that money funds maintain an average maturity of no more than 90 days, a rule that reduces the chances of a money fund posting a loss if interest rates spike upward. Money funds attempt to maintain a constant $1 price per share or net asset value, although neither the funds themselves nor any government entity guarantees that the price won't slip below $1.

MUNICIPAL BOND FUND: a fund that invests in tax-exempt securities issued by states, cities, and other local governments as well as agencies of states and local governments. With rare exceptions all income from muni bonds is free of federal tax. Single-state muni funds invest in the securities of one state, thereby providing income free of federal and state taxes if you are a resident of the state issuing those securities.

MUTUAL FUND: a portfolio of investments in which individuals may own shares. Technically a mutual fund is an investment company that pools money from a variety of investors and uses it to buy securities such as stocks, bonds, or money-market instruments such as Treasury bills or corporate IOUs known as commercial paper.

NATIONAL ASSOCIATION OF SECURITIES DEALERS: an industry organization that oversees mutual fund marketing as well as the sales practices of brokers and others who sell securities. If you have complaints about the way a fund or other investment was marketed to you, contact the NASD at 800-289-9999.

NET ASSET VALUE: the value of a share of a mutual fund. Net asset value, or NAV, is calculated each business day by the fund by taking all the fund's assets, subtracting any liabilities (such as interest the fund owes if it has borrowed money), and then dividing the result by the number of fund shares outstanding.

NO-LOAD: a fund that investors typically buy directly from the fund company without paying a sales charge. In order to legally use the term no-load, the fund should also not impose annual marketing or distribution charges (also known as **12b-1 fees**) of 0.25% or more.

NORTH AMERICAN SECURITIES ADMINISTRATORS ASSOCATION (NASAA): organization of state securities regulators. If you have complaints about a mutual fund or other investment, call NASAA at 202-737-0900 and ask for the name and number of the securities regulator in your state. NASAA can also help you check a broker's or financial planner's background to see if he or she has been disciplined for ethical or legal actions or has any such complaints pending.

PORTFOLIO: term used to describe a group of securities or a group of funds. Ideally the securities or funds within a portfolio should be chosen carefully to achieve some goal, such as long-term growth of capital or a combination of capital growth and current income. Alas, many investors' portfolios are mere grab bags of whichever funds caught their fancy at one time or another.

PORTFOLIO TURNOVER: a measure of how frequently a fund buys and sells securities. A fund with an annual turnover rate of 100% essentially replaces its entire portfolio throughout the course of a year, while a fund with a 50% turnover rate replaces half its holdings. The average turnover rate for U.S. diversified stock funds is roughly 75%.

PROSPECTUS: a legal document or booklet that funds must provide to investors that contains information required by the Securities and Exchange Commission, including the fund's investment objectives, data on fees and expenses, a description of the services offered by the fund and its policies on redemptions and additional investments, and a discussion of the risks investors face when investing in the fund. Prospectuses are notorious for being written by and for lawyers; hence they are typically boring, replete with jargon and fractured English, and generally guaranteed to induce a coma-like state. Nonetheless investors should read at least key portions of the prospectus that describe the fund's investment objectives, fees, and risks. Several fund companies are working to improve their prospectuses. Let's hope they hurry.

REDEMPTION FEE: a charge, usually 0.25% to 1.00%, imposed on withdrawals from a fund. Unlike a back-end load, which is a sales charge, redemption fees usually are paid to the fund. Redemption fees are used as a way to discourage investors from jumping in and out of a fund frequently and creating trading and administrative costs that drag down shareholders' returns.

RUSSELL 2,000 INDEX: an index of the stocks of 2,000 small U.S. companies that is often used as a benchmark to follow the performance of small-company stocks and small-company funds.

SECTOR FUND: a fund that restricts its holdings to the securities of companies in a particular industry, such as technology, banking, or precious metals. The theory behind such funds is that investors can tell in advance which sectors will be hot, which not. Nice theory, anyway.

SECURITIES AND EXCHANGE COMMISSION (SEC): federal agency charged with assuring that mutual funds as well as investment advisers, brokers, and other investment professionals comply with federal securities laws and, generally, treat investors fairly. Investors who have a complaint about a mutual fund or other investments should contact the SEC's Office of Investor Education and Protection at 202-942-7040.

SHORT-TERM BOND FUND: a bond fund with an average maturity of two to four years.

SMALL-COMPANY FUND: a fund that primarily buys shares of small companies, typically those with a total stock market value (or **market capitalization,** as it's usually called) of less than $1 billion and often $500 million or less.

STANDARD & POOR'S 500 STOCK INDEX: an index composed of 500 stocks of large U.S. companies in a variety of industries. The S&P 500 is generally considered a good benchmark for gauging returns for the U.S. stock market overall.

STANDARD DEVIATION: a statistical barometer of risk that measures how widely a fund's monthly returns fluctuate around its average return for a given period, usually three or more years. The higher a fund's standard deviation, the more volatile—and more risky—the fund is.

STATEMENT OF ADDITIONAL INFORMATION (SAI): also known as Part B of the prospectus, this document contains detailed information on the fund's investment adviser, fees paid to the adviser and the fund's directors, the firms the fund uses to buy and sell securities, and other topics. Funds will provide the SAI, free of charge—but only if you request it.

STOCK FUND: a fund that invests exclusively or mostly in stocks of companies. Since stocks are also referred to as **equities,** stock funds are also sometimes called **equity funds**.

SYSTEMATIC WITHDRAWAL PLAN: a program offered by many funds in which shareholders receive payments from their fund at regular intervals, generally monthly. You can usually stipulate that the payment be a fixed dollar amount or a percentage of your account's assets.

TAXABLE EQUIVALENT YIELD: a figure that allows you to compare a muni bond or bond fund's tax-free yield to that of a taxable bond or bond fund. To calculate a muni fund's taxable equivalent yield, divide the tax-free yield by one minus your tax rate. (See pages 270–272 in the appendix for examples.)

TAX-FREE FUND: another name for a municipal bond fund.

TOTAL RETURN: a comprehensive measure of performance that reflects a fund's gains or losses from all sources—namely, any dividends and capital gains the fund has distributed to shareholders, plus any increase or decrease in the price of the fund's shares.

TOTAL RETURN FUND: a fund that offers a combination of capital growth and current income by investing in a combination of dividend-paying stocks and bonds; another name for balanced, equity-income, and growth-and-income funds.

TREASURY SECURITIES: securities issued by the U.S. Treasury, including Treasury bills (maturity of one year or less), notes (maturity of two to 10 years), and bonds (maturities of 10 to 30 years). From the standpoint of risk of losing your principal, these are considered the safest investments.

TURNOVER: see **portfolio turnover**.

12B-1 FEE: an annual charge, typically 0.25% to 1.00% of the fund's assets, levied against fund assets to pay for the cost of marketing and distributing (in other words, selling) the fund. A portion of the 12b-1 fee typically goes to the financial planner or broker who sold the fund. A real no-load fund will not have a 12b-1 fee, although a fund can still call itself a no-load and pay brokers what is called a **service fee** (for allegedly providing ongoing service after selling the fund) as long as that fee is less than 0.25%. This fee gets its catchy name from the Securities and Exchange Commission rule that allows such fees.

VALUE INVESTING: see **investing style.**

VOLATILITY: a standard gauge for measuring risk in a fund. The more volatile a fund is—that is, the more its returns bounce up or down—the more risky it is considered to be. Beta and standard deviation are two risk measures based on volatility. Volatility isn't necessarily bad if an investment produces gains that are large enough to compensate for the bumpy ride.

YIELD: a measure of the amount of income a fund generates annually as a percentage of the fund's latest share price. The best gauge for a bond fund's yield is its 30-day or SEC yield, a figure that eliminates some of the tricks funds resort to to pump up their yields. Money-market funds, on the other hand, often quote seven-day compound yields. While yield is useful for getting an idea of how much income a money-market, bond, and some types of stock funds can throw off, for a more comprehensive view of performance you should also look at a fund's total return.

ZERO-COUPON BOND FUND: a fund that invests in zero-coupon bonds. Zero-coupon bonds pay no current interest. Instead they are sold at a large discount to their face value and are repaid at face value when they mature. When interest rates rise or fall, the price of zeros fluctuates much more than that of interest-paying bonds with similar maturities. As a result, zero-coupon bond funds, especially those that invest in long-term zeros, are among the most volatile of bond funds.

APPENDIX

TABLE 1: FOURTEEN FUNDS FOR CASH-POOR INVESTORS

The 14 stock funds below, all of which have strong track records, offer automatic investing plans that require initial investments of $50 to $500 and subsequent investments of just $50 or $100. And not a single one levies a sales charge.

Fund	Type	Style	Minimum Investment for Automatic Investing Plan:		Telephone (800)
			Initial	Subsequent	
Babson Value	G&I	Md/Val	$100	$100	422-2766
Baron Asset	Agg	Sm/Gro	500	50	992-2766
Harbor Capital Appreciation	Gro	Lg/Gro	500	100	422-1050
Heartland Value	Agg	Sm/Val	50	50	432-7856
Invesco Total Return	AA	Lg/Val	50	50	525-8085
Janus	Gro	Lg/Gro	500	100	525-8983
Janus Worldwide	Intl	Lg/Gro	500	100	525-8983
Neuberger & Berman Guardian	G&I	Lg/Val	50	50	877-9700
Strong Schafer Value	Gro	Md/Val	500	100	368-1030
Strong Opportunity	Gro	Md/Bl	50	50	368-1030
T. Rowe Price Equity-Income	Eq Inc	Lg/Bl	50	50	638-5660
T. Rowe Price International Stock	Intl	Lg/Bl	50	50	638-5660
T. Rowe Price Small Cap Value	Agg	Sm/Val	50	50	638-5660
T. Rowe Price Spectrum Growth	Gro	Lg/Gro	50	50	638-5660

Source: MONEY magazine, April 1995.

Notes: Stock types: **AA**—asset allocation; **Agg**—aggressive growth; **Eq Inc**—equity-income; **G&I**—growth-and-income; **Gro**—growth; **Intl**—international.

Stock investing styles: **Gro**—Buys stocks of companies with increasing earnings; **Val**—buys stocks that are inexpensive relative to their earnings or assets; **Bl**—Buys stocks with a blend of growth and value characteristics; **Lg**—Buys stocks with total market values of more than $5 billion; **Md**—Buys stocks with total market values between $1 billion and $5 billion; **Sm**—Buys stocks with total market values of under $1 billion.

TABLE 2:
THE 20 LARGEST NO- AND LOW-LOAD
FUND FAMILIES

Fund Family	Total Assets (in billions)	Number of Stock Funds	Number of Bond Funds	Telephone (800)
Fidelity Group	$240.0	86[1]	54	544-8888
Vanguard Group	146.3	42	31	662-7447
T. Rowe Price	42.3	30	28	638-5660
Twentieth Century	31.0	11	9	345-2021
Dreyfus Group	26.9	33	33	645-6561
Janus Group	22.8	9	4	525-8983
Scudder Funds	18.1	14	18	225-2470
PIMCo Funds[2]	14.2	3	14	426-0107
Mutual Series	13.0	4	0	553-3014
USAA Group	12.0	11	10	382-8722
AARP Funds	11.6	3	3	322-2282
Invesco Funds	11.4	29	9	525-8085
Neuberger & Berman	9.4	13	8	877-9700
Strong Funds	8.4	9	10	368-1030
MAS Funds	7.6	10	12	354-8185
Benham Group	6.1	6	21	331-8331
Warburg Pincus Funds	5.6	15	6	257-5614
Sanford Bernstein Funds[3]	5.5	1	9	212-756-4097
DFA Investment Dimensions	5.3	17	4	310-395-8005
Harbor Funds	5.0	5	2	422-1050

Source: Morningstar.

Notes: Assets as of 9/30/95; No- and low-load funds are those with maximum sales charges no greater than 3%. [1]Includes Fidelity Destiny funds, whose loads are greater than 3% [2]Some funds have minimums as high as $1 million, although minimums may be lower if you buy through a discount broker network or financial planner [3]Minimum initial purchase of $25,000 required.

Taxing Questions:
How to Calculate Gains and Losses
When You Sell Fund Shares

Root canal without anesthesia aside, one of the great pleasures in life is trying to figure out your taxable gain—or loss—when you sell fund shares. Funny thing is, in many cases you can wind up either in the black or the red, depending on the calculation method you choose. Following are brief descriptions of the four IRS-approved methods for figuring your gain or loss on shares you've sold. Needless to say, I can't give you all the ins and outs of each of these techniques, nor can I cover every possible scenario under which you might want to choose one or the other. (I don't want to bore you to death, and besides, this is an investment book, not a tax tome.) So if you are unloading a large number of shares that can have a significant effect on your tax bill, you might want to consult a tax adviser. One caveat: Whichever of the following four methods you use, be sure to adjust your gain or loss to reflect the appropriate sales load or redemption fees, if any, from your gain. So, for example, you would add back any front-end load you paid on shares that you're selling, which would reduce your taxable gain (or increase your loss). If you forget to do this, you will be paying tax not just on your gain, but on the sales commission as well.

• **First-in-first-out (FIFO):** Unless you say otherwise, the IRS will assume that the shares you sold were the oldest ones you owned—that is, the first ones you bought—and expect you to pay tax on any profit you realize from those shares. The advantage to the FIFO method is simplicity. To figure the gain on the sale of, say, 100 fund shares, you deduct from the proceeds of the sale the cost of the first 100 shares you acquired, including any you bought with reinvested dividends or capital gains. But there are two major disdvantages to this method. First, unless the value

APPENDIX

of your fund has been falling since you bought it, chances are good that this approach will produce the highest gain and the biggest tax. Second, you have no flexibility in determining the size of your gain or loss.

• **Specific identification:** Under this method you identify exactly which shares you want to sell, which in turn gives you the best shot at minimizing your tax bill. If you pick shares that cost you more than the per-share price you got upon selling, then you would have a loss that can offset profits you have made on different funds or other investments. Alternatively, if you already have losses on other investments, you could select fund shares that would produce a capital gain. Depending on how long you've been investing in the fund and the variety of prices at which you've bought shares, you might even be able to control the tax rate you pay on any gain. By choosing shares that you've held more than a year, you would pay tax at the capital-gains rate, which, depending on your income, can be lower than the ordinary income tax rates on short-term capital gains (any profits resulting from selling fund shares held a year or less). On the other hand, if you can drive down your taxable gain far enough by selling the shares you bought within the past year, you might wind up with a lower tax bill even at the higher ordinary income tax rates. That's the beauty of the specific ID method: it gives you lots of choices.

But the documentation requirements are ugly. At the very least, the IRS demands that you specify to the fund at the time of sale precisely which shares must be sold. You should do that in writing, giving the dates of purchase and the price you paid for the shares you now wish to sell. Even doing that may not satisfy the IRS. The confirmation statements most fund companies send out after sales do not detail which fund shares were sold. At this point it's still unclear whether the IRS considers these fund company statements adequate proof that the proper shares were sold. (It's also unclear whether the IRS would challenge you if you sent in the proper documentation but the fund company didn't hold up its end with a similarly detailed confirmation statement.) If you plan to use the specific ID method, consider first talking to a tax adviser who is familiar with the IRS's policies on fund taxation.

• **Single-category average:** Under this method you take the cost of all the shares you have in the fund, including those you acquired through reinvested dividends and capital gains, and divide that figure by the number of shares you own. This gives you your average cost per share. You then deduct that average cost from the sales price per share and multiply the result times the number of shares you are selling. The result will be your gain or loss. If the value of your fund has generally increased since you've begun investing, this technique will likely produce a lower taxable gain than the FIFO method. But, like FIFO, the average cost procedure gives you no flexibility in minimizing your tax bill. What's more, once you choose this method, you are stuck with it for that account. Investors who chose FIFO or specific ID, however, can later switch to the average cost method, although once they do that they too must then stick with it.

• **Double-category average:** With this method you calculate two average costs: one for all the shares you have owned for more than a year and another for shares you've held a year or less. You then decide whether the shares you sold came from the long-term share group or the short-term share group, making your decision on the basis of the tax you would pay, based on the size of the respective gains for each group as well as the difference between the tax rates on long- and short-term capital gains. This method gives you more wiggle room than the single-category average, but not as much leeway as specific ID. As with the single-category average, if you choose this method, you must continue to use it for that account.

TABLE 3:
TWO DOZEN MONEY-MARKET FUNDS
THAT BEAT THE BANK

The 24 funds in the table below—all of which are part of a no- or low-load fund family—don't necessarily tout the highest yields at any given moment, and by no means are they the only funds worthy of investors' cash. But their size (assets greater than $1 billion) as well as their record for keeping expenses relatively low and returns relatively high make them excellent choices for anyone looking for a money fund. If you do most of your stock or bond fund investing with a particular fund family, however, for the sake of convenience you may want to invest in that family's money fund, even if it's not listed below.

	Minimum Initial Investment	Yield[1]	Minimum Check Amount[2]	Charge Per Check	Telephone (800)
TAXABLE FUNDS—GENERAL-PURPOSE					
Strong Money Market	$1,000	5.2%	$500	None	368-1030
Dreyfus Basic MMF[3]	25,000	5.2%	1,000	$2	782-6620
Vanguard MMR/Prime Portfolio	3,000	5.2%	250	None	851-4999
USAA Money Market	3,000	5.1%	250	None[4]	382-8722
Fidelity Spartan Money Market	20,000	5.1%	1,000	$2	544-8888
Fidelity Cash Reserves	2,500	5.1%	500	None	544-8888
Fidelity Daily Income Trust	5,000	5.0%	None	$1[5]	544-8888
Benham Prime Money Market	1,000	5.0%	100	None	331-8331
T. Rowe Price Prime Reserve	2,500	4.8%	500	None	638-5660
Twentieth Century Cash Reserve	1,000	4.9%	500	None	345-2021
U.S. GOVERNMENT MONEY FUNDS					
Dreyfus Basic U.S. Government MMF[3]	$25,000	5.2%	$1,000	$2	782-6620
Vanguard MMR/Federal Portfolio	3,000	5.1%	250	None	851-4999
Fidelity U.S. Government Reserves	2,500	5.1%	500	None	544-8888
Vanguard Admiral/U.S. Treasury	50,000	5.2%	250	None	851-4999

	Minimum Initial Investment	Yield[1]	Minimum Check Amount[2]	Charge Per Check	Telephone (800)
Vanguard MMR/U.S. Treasury Portfolio	$3,000	5.0%	$250	None	851-4999
Capital Preservation Fund	1,000	4.7%	100	None	331-8331
Fidelity Spartan U.S. Treasury	20,000	4.9%	1,000	$2	544-8888
TAX-EXEMPT MONEY FUNDS					
Strong Municipal MMF	$2,500	3.5%	$500	None	368-1030
Calvert Tax-Free Reserves	2,000	3.2%	250	None	368-2748
Dreyfus Basic Muni	25,000	3.2%	1,000	$2	782-6620
Vanguard Muni Bond MM Portfolio	3,000	3.3%	250	None	851-4999
USAA Tax-Exempt MMF	3,000	3.3%	250	None[4]	382-8722
Fidelity Spartan Municipal MF	25,000	3.3%	1,000	$2	544-8888
Fidelity Tax-Exempt Money Market Trust	5,000	3.0%	None	None	544-8888

Source: IBC/Donoghue, Inc.

Notes: [1]Seven-day compound annual yield as of April 16, 1996 [2]All the funds in this table allow you to write an unlimited number of checks [3]Dreyfus also has a line of money funds that pays a lower yield but has a lower minimum initial investment ($2,500), lower check minimum ($500), and no charge per check. [4]Onetime $5 fee to set up check-writing feature. [5]For checks under $500.

TABLES 4 AND 5:
HOW TO TELL IF YOU WILL EARN MORE
IN A TAX-EXEMPT OR TAXABLE BOND FUND

The following two tables demonstrate how much a taxable bond fund would have to yield in order to deliver the same income after taxes as a tax-exempt fund. The first table applies to national muni bond funds because it takes only federal taxes into account.

APPENDIX

The second table explains how to figure in state and local income taxes when calculating the taxable equivalent yield of a single-state muni fund.

TABLE 4

Tax-Exempt Yield	Taxable Equivalent Yield in the . . .				
	15% Federal Tax Bracket[1]	28% Federal Tax Bracket[2]	31% Federal Tax Bracket[3]	36% Federal Tax Bracket[4]	39.6% Federal Tax Bracket[5]
3%	3.5%	4.2%	4.3%	4.7%	5.0%
4%	4.7%	5.6%	5.8%	6.3%	6.6%
5%	5.9%	6.9%	7.2%	7.8%	8.3%
6%	7.1%	8.3%	8.7%	9.4%	9.9%
7%	8.2%	9.7%	10.1%	10.9%	11.6%
8%	9.4%	11.1%	11.6%	12.5%	13.2%
9%	10.6%	12.5%	13.0%	14.1%	14.9%

Notes: 1996 taxable income of [1]$24,000 or less for single taxpayers, $40,100 or less for married couples filing jointly [2]more than $24,000 but not over $58,150 for singles, $40,100/$96,900 for married couples [3]more than $58,150 but not over $121,300 for singles, $96,900/$147,700 for married couples [4]more than $121,300 but not over $263,750 for singles, $147,700/$263,750 for married couples [5]more than $263,750 for singles and married couples.

TABLE 5:
FIGURING TAXABLE EQUIVALENT YIELDS
FOR SINGLE-STATE FUNDS

Follow these five steps to calculate the taxable equivalent yield for a single-state muni fund. This example shows that a single-state fund yielding 5% would have a taxable equivalent of 7.5%, assuming state income taxes of 4.4%, city taxes of 3%, and federal taxes at the 28% marginal rate.

1. Total your state and (if any) city tax rates, expressed as a decimal.	0.03 (local tax rate) plus 0.044 (state tax rate) equals 0.074
2. Multiply the result by 1 minus your federal tax rate (1 minus 0.28).	0.074 times 0.72 equals 0.0533
3. Add the result to your federal tax rate.	0.0533 plus 0.28 equals 0.3333
4. Subtract the sum from 1.	1 minus 0.3333 equals 0.6667
5. Divide the single-state tax-free fund's yield, expressed as a decimal, by the result in step 4.	0.05 divided by 0.6667 equals 7.5%.

Result: In this example, a 5% yield free of state and local taxes equals a 7.5% taxable yield.

TABLE 6:
STOCK AND BOND MUTUAL FUNDS THAT ARE
WORTH A LOOK . . . AND MAYBE YOUR MONEY

Do not—repeat, not—go out and buy the stock and bond funds listed below purely on my say-so. Why? Because I don't believe investors should blindly follow anyone's advice, mine included. Furthermore, it's also possible that the manager responsible for the outsize performance that got the fund on this list may have switched to another fund—or the same manager could have switched investing styles recently. So rather than thinking of the following funds as no-brainer buys, think of them as examples of solid-performing funds you might consider for investment—after you've applied the standards I discuss throughout this book and, in particular, in Chapter 9. Better yet, you should do your own independent analysis and then compare your own list of candidates with these. Above all, I caution you against simply running your finger down the total return columns and picking out the funds with the biggest gains. Remember, you want to own a variety of funds with different objectives and investing styles, not just a group of funds that had stellar returns over a specific period of time. Before you invest in these or any other funds, make sure you also check out their risk levels. Seeing what kinds of setbacks they've had during lousy markets, for example, is a good way of determining whether you really have the stomach to own them.

Finally, in no way should you consider these the "best" funds or the only ones worthy of consideration. Indeed, many terrific funds did not make this list for any number of reasons. In some cases good funds missed the cut because they barely fell short of a single performance criteria. What's more, there is also a subjective element to this list. For example, whenever possible I favored no-loads over loads (especially in the case of bond funds) and low-expense funds over ones with high expenses. I also strongly urge you to consider index funds. A few are included in the roundup below, but you'll find a more complete list in Chapter 11. The funds below are ranked by five-year returns within their group. For more on how I compiled this group of funds, see the notes at the bottom of the table.

% Annualized total return for

LARGE-CAP STOCK FUNDS	Type	Investing Style	One Year[1]	Three Years[1]	Five Years[1]	% Maximum Sales Charge	Expense Ratio	Minimum Initial Investment	Telephone (800)
Harbor Capital Appreciation	Gro	Lg/Gro	30.8	18.6	18.1	None	0.75	$2,000	422-1050
Davis NY Venture A	Gro	Lg/Bl	33.8	15.6	18.1	4.75	0.90	1,000	279-0279
Babson Value	G&I	Lg/Val	29.0	19.4	17.8	None	0.98	1,000	422-2766
Clipper	Gro	Lg/Val	36.4	16.8	17.7	None	1.11	5,000	776-5033
Kemper-Dreman High Return A	G&I	Lg/Val	41.7	16.9	17.2	5.75	1.25	1,000	621-1048
20th Century Ultra Investors	Agg	Lg/Gro	33.9	18.1	17.1	None	1.00	2,500	345-2021
Neuberger & Berman Guardian	G&I	Lg/Bl	24.6	14.6	16.5	None	0.80	1,000	877-9700
Dodge & Cox Stock	G&I	Lg/Val	29.3	17.9	16.0	None	0.60	2,500	621-3979
T. Rowe Price Equity-Income	Eq Inc	Lg/Val	29.4	16.5	15.9	None	0.88	2,500	638-5660
Hotchkis & Wiley Equity-Inc	Eq Inc	Lg/Val	29.0	14.6	15.7	None	1.00	5,000	346-7301
Fidelity Disciplined Equity	Gro	Lg/Bl	26.0	14.4	15.5	None	0.93	2,500	544-8888
Vanguard Quantitative	G&I	Lg/Val	31.8	15.3	14.7	None	0.47	3,000	662-7447
T. Rowe Price Growth & Inc	G&I	Lg/Bl	28.7	13.0	14.5	None	0.84	2,500	638-5660
Vanguard Equity-Income	Eq Inc	Lg/Val	29.1	14.1	14.0	None	0.45	3,000	662-7447
Dodge & Cox Balanced	Bal	Lg/Val	22.3	13.6	13.7	None	0.58	2,500	621-3979
Dreyfus Appreciation	Gro	Lg/Gro	34.6	16.4	13.7	None	0.96	2,500	645-6561
Vanguard U.S. Growth	Gro	Lg/Gro	35.4	16.0	13.7	None	0.44	3,000	662-7447
Babson Growth	Gro	Lg/Bl	26.2	13.3	12.2	None	0.85	500	422-2766

% Annualized total return for

SMALL/MIDCAP STOCK	Type	Investing Style	One Year[1]	Three Years[1]	Five Years[1]	% Maximum Sales Charge	Expense Ratio	Minimum Initial Investment	Telephone (800)
John Hancock Special Equities A	SC	Sm/Gro	45.1	24.1	27.8	5.00	1.62	$1,000	225-5291
SunAmerica Small Co Grth A	SC	Sm/Gro	40.6	20.9	21.8	5.75	1.57	500	858-8850
Baron Asset	SC	Sm/Gro	40.7	24.7	21.6	None	1.40	2,000	992-2766
Delaware Trend A	Agg	Sm/Gro	33.9	16.2	21.2	4.75	1.36	250	523-4640
Fidelity Low-Priced Stock	SC	Sm/Val	28.0	16.8	19.9	3.00	1.11	2,500	544-8888
Warburg Pincus Emerg Gr Comm	SC	Sm/Gro	43.1	20.4	19.7	None	1.26	2,500	257-5614
Managers Special Equity	SC	Sm/Gro	36.9	15.8	18.7	None	1.44	2,000	835-3879
Franklin Balance Sheet Invmt	SC	Sm/Val	22.8	17.4	18.6	1.50	1.17	2,500	342-5236
Mutual Shares	G&I	Med/Val	28.9	17.6	18.3	None	0.72	5,000	553-3014
Mutual Beacon	G&I	Med/Val	28.0	17.4	18.2	None	0.75	5,000	553-3014
T. Rowe Price Small-Cap Val	SC	Sm/Val	29.4	15.3	18.1	None	0.98	2,500	638-5660
Strong Schafer Value	Gro	Med/Val	28.4	15.5	17.7	None	1.28	2,000	368-1030
Fairmont	SC	Sm/Bl	33.7	17.5	16.7	None	1.74	1,000	262-9936
Crabbe Huson Equity	Gro	Med/Val	18.5	14.9	16.6	None	1.40	2,000	541-9732
Dreyfus New Leaders	SC	Sm/Bl	29.5	15.0	16.4	None	1.19	2,500	645-6561
Wasatch Growth	Gro	Sm/Bl	39.1	21.1	15.4	None	1.50	2,000	345-7460

% Annualized total return for

INTERNATIONAL STOCK	Type	Investing Style	One Year[1]	Three Years[1]	Five Years[1]	% Maximum Sales Charge	Expense Ratio	Minimum Initial Investment	Telephone (800)
GAM International	Intl	Md/Bl	5.1	21.1	18.1	5.00	1.57	$10,000	426-4685
Managers Intl Equity	Intl	Lg/Bl	20.0	16.4	13.3	None	1.58	2,000	835-3879
USAA International	Intl	Md/Bl	22.3	15.3	12.7	None	1.17	3,000	382-8722
Warburg Pincus Intl Eq Comm	Intl	Lg/Val	20.1	16.0	12.5	None	1.39	2,500	257-5614
T. Rowe Price Intl Stock	Intl	Lg/Bl	19.0	15.1	11.3	None	0.91	2,500	638-5660
Babson-Stewart Ivory Intl	Intl	Md/Gro	18.0	13.7	11.2	None	1.30	2,500	422-2766
Vanguard Intl Growth	Intl	Lg/Bl	21.8	17.9	10.6	None	0.58	3,000	662-7447
IAI International	Intl	Lg/Val	12.7	12.6	10.4	None	1.72	5,000	945-3863
Scudder International	Intl	Lg/Bl	19.3	12.8	9.4	None	1.19	1,000	225-2470

U.S. GOVERNMENT BOND	Type	Investing Style	% Annualized total return for			% Maximum Sales Charge	Expense Ratio	Minimum Initial Investment	Telephone (800)
			One Year[1]	Three Years[1]	Five Years[1]				
Strong Govt. Securities	Gov	Int/Hi	11.0	6.5	9.8	None	0.90	$1,000	368-1030
Vanguard F/I GNMA	MBS	Int/Hi	10.7	5.9	8.1	None	0.29	3,000	662-7447
Fidelity Mortgage Securities	MBS	Int/Hi	11.7	7.5	8.1	None	0.77	2,500	544-8888
Warburg Pincus Intrm Mat. Gov	Gov	Int/Hi	9.7	5.1	7.8	None	0.60	2,500	257-5614
T. Rowe Price GNMA	MBS	Int/Hi	9.7	5.6	7.6	None	0.76	2,500	638-5660
Dreyfus Short-Interm Govt	Gov	Sh/Hi	8.5	5.0	7.4	None	0.66	2,500	645-6561
Sit U.S. Government Secs	Gov	Sh/Hi	8.9	6.0	7.3	None	0.80	2,000	332-5580
Dreyfus 100% U.S. Treas. Sh Term	Gov	Sh/Hi	7.5	4.8	7.2	None	0.65	2,500	645-6561
Vanguard F/I Short-Term Fed	Gov	Sh/Hi	8.4	4.9	6.9	None	0.27	3,000	662-7447
Asset Mgmt Short U.S. Govt. Secs	Gov	Sh/Hi	7.5	4.7	6.6	None	0.49	10,000	527-3713

INVESTMENT-GRADE CORPORATE

INVESTMENT-GRADE CORPORATE	Type	Investing Style	% Annualized total return for			% Maximum Sales Charge	Expense Ratio	Minimum Initial Investment	Telephone (800)
			One Year[1]	Three Years[1]	Five Years[1]				
SteinRoe Income	IGC	Int/Med	12.1	6.8	9.7	None	0.82	$2,500	338-2550
Columbia Fixed-Income Securities	IGC	Int/Hi	11.2	5.9	8.9	None	0.65	1,000	547-1707
Vanguard Bond Index Total Bond Market	IGC	Int/Hi	10.6	5.9	8.3	None	0.18	3,000	662-7447
Vista Bond	IGC	Int/Hi	10.5	5.8	8.2	None	0.31	2,500	648-4782
Strong Short-term Bond	IGC	Sh/Med	10.0	5.2	7.5	None	0.90	1,000	368-1030
Vanguard F/I Short-Term Corp.	IGC	Sh/Hi	8.5	5.4	7.4	None	0.27	3,000	662-7447
Wasatch Income	IGC	Sh/Hi	7.5	5.2	6.7	None	1.00	2,000	551-1700

HIGH-YIELD CORPORATE— i.e., JUNK BOND FUNDS

HIGH-YIELD CORPORATE— i.e., JUNK BOND FUNDS	Type	Investing Style	% Annualized total return for			% Maximum Sales Charge	Expense Ratio	Minimum Initial Investment	Telephone (800)
			One Year[1]	Three Years[1]	Five Years[1]				
Fidelity Spartan High-Income	HYC	Int/Lo	17.9	12.7	17.2	None	0.80	10,000	544-8888
Colonial High-Yield Secs A	HYC	Int/Lo	14.9	10.4	16.8	4.75	1.23	1,000	248-2828
Fidelity Capital & Income	HYC	Int/Lo	12.7	9.3	16.6	None	0.96	2,500	544-8888
Federated High-Income Bond A	HYC	Int/Lo	15.2	9.5	16.0	4.50	1.21	$500	235-4669
Aim High Yield A	HYC	Int/Lo	13.8	9.4	15.5	4.75	1.00	500	347-1919
Federated High-Yield	HYC	Int/Lo	15.1	9.0	14.9	None	0.85	25,000	245-5040
Kemper High-Yield A	HYC	Int/Lo	15.6	10.6	14.9	4.50	0.90	1,000	621-1048

278

% Annualized total return for

NATIONAL MUNICIPAL BOND	Type	Investing Style	One Year[1]	Three Years[1]	Five Years[1]	% Maximum Sales Charge	Expense Ratio	Minimum Initial Investment	Telephone (800)
Vanguard Muni High-Yield	Muni	L/Med	7.8	6.2	8.9	None	0.21	$3,000	662-7447
Scudder High-Yield Tax-Free	Muni	L/Med	7.8	5.2	8.4	None	0.80	1,000	225-2470
T. Rowe Price Tax-Fr Hi-Yld	Muni	L/Med	8.4	6.2	8.4	None	0.79	2,500	638-5560
Fidelity Spartan Muni Income	Muni	L/Hi	8.9	5.7	8.1	None	0.55	10,000	544-8888
T. Rowe Price Tax-Fr Income	Muni	L/Hi	7.6	5.6	8.1	None	0.59	2,500	638-5560
Vanguard Muni Intermed-Term	Muni	Int/Hi	7.4	6.0	8.0	None	0.21	3,000	662-7447
Scudder Medium-Term Tax-Free	Muni	Int/Hi	8.0	5.6	7.8	None	0.63	1,000	225-2470
Fidelity Aggressive Muni	Muni	L/Med	6.8	5.1	7.7	None	0.64	2,500	544-8888
Strong Municipal Bond	Muni	L/Med	2.5	3.6	7.6	None	0.80	2,500	368-1030
Fidelity Limited-Term Muni	Muni	Int/Hi	7.8	5.6	7.5	None	0.57	2,500	544-8888
USAA Tax-Exempt Interm-Term	Muni	Int/Med	8.0	5.7	7.5	None	0.40	3,000	382-8722
Dreyfus Intermediate Muni	Muni	Int/Hi	6.9	5.4	7.4	None	0.73	2,500	645-6561

% Annualized total return for

WORLD BOND	Type	Investing Style	One Year[1]	Three Years[1]	Five Years[1]	% Maximum Sales Charge	Expense Ratio	Minimum Initial Investment	Telephone (800)
T. Rowe Price Intl Bond	WI	Int/Hi	5.4	9.4	11.5	None	0.98	$2,500	638-5660
IDS Global Bond A	WI	L/Hi	10.5	7.7	10.6	5.00	1.25	2,000	328-8300
Capital World Bond	WI	Int/Hi	11.6	9.4	9.6	4.75	1.12	1,000	421-4120
Warburg Pincus Global FixInc	WI	Int/Med	16	9.6	9.1	None	0.95	2,500	257-5614
Scudder International Bond	WI	Int/Hi	6.7	2.3	7.8	None	1.30	1,000	225-2470
Federated Intl Income A	WI	Int/Hi	7.7	11.6	—	4.50	1.30	500	245-5040

Source: Morningstar, Inc.

Notes: [1]Returns to April 1, 1996; **Stock types: Agg**—aggressive growth; **Bal**—balanced; **Eq Inc**—equity income; **G&I**—growth and income; **Gro**—growth; **Intl**—international; **SC**—small company. **Stock investing styles: Gro**—Buys stocks of companies with increasing earnings; **Val**—buys stocks that are inexpensive relative to their earnings or assets; **Bl**—Buys stocks with a blend of growth and value characteristics; **Lg**—Buys stocks with total market values of more than $5 billion; **Md**—Buys stocks with total market values between $1 billion and $5 billion; **Sm**—Buys stocks with total market values of under $1 billion. **Bond fund types: Gov**—U.S. Government bond; **HYC**—high-yield corporate; **IGC**—investment-grade corporate; **MBS**—mortgage-backed securities; **Muni**—municipal bond; **WI**—world income. **Bond fund investing styles: Hi**—High quality: buys bonds rated AA or better; **Med**—Medium quality: buys bonds rated BBB or better; **Lo**—Low quality: buys bonds rated BB or lower; **L**—Long term: buys bonds with maturities over 10 years; **Int**—intermediate term: buys bonds with maturities between four and 10 years; **Sh**—short-term: buys bonds with maturities under four years.

Criteria: To make this list, these funds had to go through a rigorous screening process. They all outperformed funds with similar investing styles for the one, three, and five years to January 1, 1996. In the case of the stock funds, they also displayed consistent year-to-year performance relative to funds with similar objectives. Furthermore, the funds for the most part had Morningstar return scores that exceeded or were very close to their Morningstar risk scores. This doesn't mean these funds can't be risky (they can be, especially the ones that have a growth investing style); rather, it suggests that investors were amply rewarded for the risks the fund manager took. In cases where it was impossible to find enough funds with higher return risk scores, I opted for funds that displayed below-average risk scores. Although I did not weed out load funds entirely, I gave the nod to no-loads whenever possible. Similarly, I eliminated some—but not all—funds that had high expense ratios. I did not automatically exclude funds with 12b-1 fees, although I did jettison some funds for having especially high 12b-1s. In short, this was an attempt to arrive at a group of decent funds worth a look—not an attempt to come up with a definite list of the all-time greatest funds.

INDEX

INDEX

INDEX

INDEX